The Story of Hebrew

LIBRARY OF JEWISH IDEAS
Cosponsored by the Tikvah Fund

The series presents engaging and authoritative treatments of core
Jewish concepts in a form appealing to general readers who are curious
about Jewish treatments of key areas of human thought and experience.

The Story of Hebrew

LEWIS GLINERT

Princeton University Press

Princeton and Oxford

Copyright © 2017 by Princeton University Press

Published by Princeton University Press, 41 William Street,

Princeton, New Jersey 08540

In the United Kingdom: Princeton University Press, 6 Oxford Street,

Woodstock, Oxfordshire OX20 1TR

press.princeton.edu

Jacket calligraphy by Michel d'Anastasio; jacket design by Faceout Studio

Library of Congress Cataloging-in-Publication Data

Names: Glinert, Lewis, author.

Title: The story of Hebrew / Lewis Glinert.

Description: Princeton; Oxford: Princeton University Press, [2016] | Series: Library
of Jewish ideas | Includes bibliographical references and index. | "This book tells two
stories: first, how Hebrew has been used in Jewish life, from the Israelites to the
ancient Rabbis and across 2,000 years of nurture, abandonment, and renewal,
eventually given up by many for dead but improbably rescued to become the
everyday language of modern Israel. Second, it tells the story of how Jews—and
Christians—have perceived Hebrew, and invested it with a symbolic power far
beyond normal language"—ECIP introduction.

Identifiers: LCCN 2016022084 | ISBN 9780691153292 (hardcover : alk. paper)

Subjects: LCSH: Hebrew language—History. | Hebrew language—Revival. | Hebrew
language—Usage.

Classification: LCC PJ4545 .G55 2016 | DDC 492.4/09—dc23

    LC record available at https://lccn.loc.gov/2016022084

British Library Cataloging-in-Publication Data is available

Publication of this book has been aided by the Tikvah Fund

This book has been composed in Gentium

Printed on acid-free paper. ∞

Printed in the United States of America

10 9 8 7 6 5 4 3 2 1

For Joan

Contents

Figures

The Story of Hebrew

Introduction

This book tells two stories: first, how Hebrew has been used in Jewish life, from the Israelites to the ancient Rabbis and across two thousand years of nurture, abandonment, and renewal, eventually given up by many for dead but improbably rescued to become the everyday language of modern Israel. Second, it tells the story of how Jews—and Christians—have conceived of Hebrew, and invested it with a symbolic power far beyond normal language.

As befits any stirring and suspenseful tale, we will follow it as it unfolded. But this book is more than an exciting story and certainly more than an exercise in historical linguistics. It will examine the history of Hebrew using ethnographic, sociolinguistic, and philosophical approaches. What purpose did Hebrew serve? How has it figured in the popular and learned imagination? How did Hebrew figure into Jews' sense of identity, and how did that relationship change with the advent of Zionism? What kept Hebrew from dying out completely, and what made its near-impossible revival possible? And what can its remarkable story teach about the workings of human language in general?

In short, this is not so much a book about what Hebrew words mean as about what the Hebrew language has meant to the people who have possessed it. To explore this topic, we will examine what they wrote about Hebrew and the various ways in which they used it. We will also look beyond the words and grammatical structures to communication styles and to the "para-language" of scripts, fonts, spellings, formats. In many cultures, people see script and spelling as inseparable from the language; in others, writing is in itself sacred. No account of language can ignore the pull of para-language.

Jews have done a great deal of thinking about Hebrew—more, perhaps, than most peoples have thought about their language—and for a good reason. For much of their history, Hebrew was not a mother tongue to be spoken naturally. Rather, Jews kept it alive by raising their young men to study and ponder Hebrew texts. This was true for a period of some two thousand years, stretching from the close of the biblical era down to the early twentieth century and the restoration of spoken Hebrew.

But how did Hebrew mean so much to them and how could Jews keep it alive so well that, after two millennia, it could be restored almost overnight? The restoration of Hebrew, first as a mother tongue and then as an all-purpose language of a modern Jewish state, was an act without precedent in linguistic and sociopolitical history. I seek to explain this revival in those terms, but also by exploring the ideas, emotions, and sensibilities that made it possible.

The engine of Jewish existence for those two millennia was the study of the Torah, Judaism's sacred texts: Bible, Midrash, Talmud, and the teachings springing from them. In the words of Psalm 119:97, "How dearly I love Thy Torah; I speak about it all day long." Jews intensively studied the wording of these texts for every conceivable nuance. The loss of their Temple, their liberty, and then their homeland in the first centuries of the Common Era imperiled but ultimately strengthened knowledge of the Torah and the Hebrew language as a core component of Jewish identity.

Jews, of course, were not the only people who believed the Hebrew Bible to be sacred. Not surprisingly, at various times, significant numbers of Christians became interested in the language of their Old Testament. As we shall see in chapters 6 and 7, the High Middle Ages brought a succession of intellectual upheavals and religious crises to Catholic Europe that formed a potent brew of curiosity, envy, and dark suspicion of the Jews' command of Hebrew and of the biblical text.

Two religious goals dominated Christian thinking about the Hebrew language: spiritual renewal and the conversion of the Jews. With the Renaissance, the Reformation, and the Counter-Reformation, this interest became intense, and intense conflict also ensued. The focus varied wildly: Kabbalah-mania, Talmud-phobia, vernacular Bible study, millennialism, rabbinic political thought, Puritan dreams of a New Israel. Religion aside, many minds in the Christian Renaissance also found philosophical and political significance in the Hebrew language and its literature.

By early modern times, Christian enthusiasm for Hebrew had achieved its goals or changed tack. For Jews, however, the Hebrew narrative went on and soon took extraordinary turns: not as the language of religion but as the language of national identity.

Almost throughout their history, Jews have taken for granted that they are a people as well as a religion. This national consciousness, rooted in biblical memory, held firm across the centuries of Diaspora and provided a cogent and inspirational rationale for modern Zionism. The Hebrew language and its literature have been critical elements in this national identity, often as a counterforce to rival cultures and languages—Greek in the ancient world, Arabic in the Middle Ages, European vernaculars in the modern era, and now global English. Pride in the force and grace of the language underpinned the secular Hebrew literature of the medieval Diaspora and the modern revival as much as religious commitment has underpinned Hebrew's sacred literature.

Even in secular Israeli and Western circles, where Jewishness is proclaimed to be a matter of culture rather than religion, the Jewish ethnic heritage is loudly celebrated. But Hebrew had to defeat fierce competition from within in order to become the language of secular Jewish culture. In the nineteenth and twentieth centuries, a variety of modern political and social movements seized on Yiddish as a preferred national Jewish language, sometimes with catastrophic intent for Hebrew and its users. But Hebrew has emerged victorious, while Yiddish, though not dead, has receded to the margins.

Modern secular culture—and above all literature—prizes creativity, which is the third rail supplying the current of Jewish Hebraism. Whether religious or national in spirit, or both, creativity has driven the Hebrew language and its literature to ever-new vistas and forms. It has had both classical and romantic inclinations: esteem for clarity and adherence to strict biblical models, and a penchant for enigma and innovation. There have been ferocious battles and cruel aspersions. But never, it seems, have Hebrew artists been content merely to pick over the ancient scriptures. Medieval liturgical poems, the worldly poetry of the medieval Spanish and Italian "golden age," ḥasidic tales, and twentieth- and twenty-first-century Israeli fiction are just four products of this creative force.

Scientific and technical writing could also be creative. With little access to Latin or Greek, the Jews of medieval Christian Europe who could read Arabic scientific texts tailored a variety of Hebrew styles and terminologies to produce their own technical-scientific literature for training generations of Jewish doctors and academics—an endeavor that also boosted these scholars' sense of pride in their faith and their language.

Even in the centuries between ancient and modern "normality," there was (and still is) much about the Hebrew of the Diaspora that characterizes a living language rather than a dead one. And then there is the mundane. Nowhere, perhaps, has Diaspora Hebrew felt so much part and parcel of Jewish life as in the centuries of business jottings or personal letters often couched in the holy tongue, sometimes intermingled with the vernacular.

Diaspora Hebrew has also tenaciously survived the enormous changes brought by modernity. Even among the non-Orthodox, it is common for children to learn to chant at the very least a few verses in Hebrew for their bar or bat mitzvah, even if these children will probably never know enough Hebrew to understand a text or order a soda. Yet Diaspora Jewish parents continue to have their children invest months in this "ordeal by language." And the vast majority of Diaspora synagogues incorporate at least some Hebrew into the prayer service. Especially in our generally monolingual society, this is a tribute to the strength of commitment to the Hebrew language.

For Diaspora Jews, then, perhaps as much as for Israeli Jews, Hebrew is a key element of Jewish identity. Social and personal identity are intricate concepts and much debated, and Jewish identity has always had its own particular tangles. How did preexilic biblical Hebrews define themselves? And what of modern secular Jews, whose sense of Jewish identity is often strong, even if it is divested of what was long the core of Jewishness. Perhaps the biggest twist in Jewish identity was the early Zionist formulation of a novel Hebrew identity to replace a Jewish one. This formulation now itself seems antiquated, but it has left in its wake a new notion of Israeliness, spanning a gamut of identities (many of them new, not all of them Jewish) for millions of Israeli Jews.

Should Hebrew, then, be considered a Jewish language? This question has obsessed some modern ideologues. For entirely different reasons, it unsettled Christian Hebraists from Jerome down to the Renaissance. Ultimately, it is a matter of definition, but, as we will see, the broad facts are clear: from late antiquity to the nineteenth century, Jewish sacred texts were allusively present in much of the Hebrew being read or written. Israeli Hebrew, however, has since evolved a spoken and written style that, though rooted linguistically in the sacred texts, has become independent of them.

And what of Hebrew's theological implications? "The holy tongue" was long a synonym for Hebrew, and not just among Jews. Why, in what sense, and for whom was it holy? A widespread misconception (telling in itself) has it that ultra-Orthodox Jews refuse to speak Hebrew because it is sacred. Even more prevalent is the misconception that Hebrew in the Diaspora was used *exclusively* for prayer and study. It is true that ultra-Orthodox Jews believe Hebrew to be holy, as did pre-Zionist diasporic Jews. But there was and is little consensus about what this sanctity entails. The greatest of medieval Jewish thinkers were deeply divided on the question. Hebrew (or perhaps the biblical text) has been hailed as divine language, esoteric tool, demonic weapon, and the acme of linguistic purity.

As for modern Hebrew, its origins lie not with Zionism but with the Jewish Enlightenment of the late eighteenth and early nineteenth centuries. And its adoption by Zionism was by no means predetermined. Indeed, the so-called language wars threatened to tear the early Zionist movement apart.

Continuity over the millennia and rebirth from the dead have become bewitching (if seemingly incompatible) tropes for Hebrew. In every age, a conservative Hebrew spirit has wrestled with one of innovation and experimentation, and in present-day Israel it still does. But continuity does not imply sameness. Throughout this book, we will keep seeing the same pieces on the board, but they will be moving around ad infinitum.

If there is a language that has been and continues to be identified as Hebrew, it is not just for linguistic reasons. Powerful ideas are at work. Underpinning them is the Jewish belief that Hebrew is a key to their traditions and a warranty for the Jewish future.

1

"Let There Be Hebrew"

Hebrew as the Hebrew Bible Saw It

Where did Hebrew come from? For the best part of three millennia, the answer has regularly been sought in the Bible itself:

> In the beginning God created the heaven and the earth. And the earth was without form, and void; and darkness was upon the face of the deep. And the Spirit of God moved upon the face of the waters. And God said, Let there be light: and there was light.

These famous words, verses 1–3 of Genesis 1 as rendered in the 1611 King James Version, speak of God speaking. They might thus be construed as describing the creation of the Hebrew language.

Or again, they might not. The Hebrew Bible (the *Tanakh*, as Jews traditionally call it) is studiously silent about Hebrew. In fact, the entire twenty-four books provide what amount to just three mentions of the Hebrew language by name, if indeed *yehudit* (the language of Judea) and *sefat Kena'an* (the language of Canaan) actually denote Hebrew. As for the two names that Jews have historically most often used for Hebrew, *ivrit* and *leshon ha-kodesh* (the holy tongue), neither appears in the Bible. The language in which the Hebrew Bible was written and, one might assume, the language used by the Israelites since the birth of the Hebrew nation in Egyptian slavery, just seems to be there, humming in the background.

So are we meant to assume that Jacob and his sons spoke Hebrew? Going back further, what about Abraham? Noah? Adam? The text contains some hints about these questions, but it is by no means clear what to make of them. Take, for instance, this passage from Genesis 2, which comes after God has created Adam and placed him in the Garden:

> Then the Lord God said, "It is not good that the man should be alone; I will make him a helper fit for him." So out of the ground the Lord God formed every beast of the field and every bird of the air, and brought them to the man to see what he would call them; and whatever the man called every living creature, that was its name. The man gave names to all cattle, and to the birds of the air, and to every beast of the field; but for the man there was not found a helper fit for him. (Genesis 2:18–20)

Genesis here is making a major statement about language and society. What that statement is remains the subject of endless debate, but this much seems clear: Adam is not presented with words for the various animals; he devises them himself, whether arbitrarily or logically. But in what language? The Bible does not appear to say. But then comes Adam's promised "helper," and this:

> She shall be called woman (*ishah*) because she was taken out of man (*ish*). (Genesis 2:23)

Not only does Adam coin the word for woman, he also assigns the woman a name:

> And Adam called his wife's name Eve (*Ḥava*) because she was the mother of all living (*ḥay*). (Genesis 3:20)

By these linguistic associations, which work for Hebrew but by no means for other languages, Genesis is subtly implying that Adam spoke Hebrew. And similar linguistic associations are offered to explain the names of his sons Cain and Seth. So, too, for Noah:

> and he called his name Noah, saying, "Out of the ground which the Lord has cursed, this one shall bring us relief (*yenaḥamenu*) from our work and from the toil of our hands." (Genesis 5:29)

These are but a few examples. The Bible explains the naming of scores of persons and places, overtly or implicitly, by Hebrew word association.

True, much later on, the biblical prophets also liked to take advantage of the way the names of foreign places and potentates resonate in Hebrew. But they are clearly engaging in literary wordplay. Genesis, by contrast, seems to want us to imagine Adam, Noah, and certain other figures speaking Hebrew. Indeed, at one juncture, when Jacob, ancestor of Israel, and Laban the Aramean are staking a geographical boundary between their respective spheres of influence, Jacob assigns the boundary cairn a Hebrew name, while Laban assigns it a name that is clearly the Aramaic equivalent.

The first explicit reference to language in the Bible is in the Tower of Babel story. Before the tower, we're told, "the whole earth was of one language, and of one speech." But after:

> Therefore is the name of it called Babel; because the Lord did there confound (*balal*) the language of all the earth: and from thence did the Lord scatter them abroad upon the face of all the earth. (Genesis 11:9)

What was the "one language"? Presumably, if Adam spoke Hebrew, that would be the answer. Some have suggested that this Hebrew, or whatever it was, could instead have been just a shared lingua franca rather than a universal mother tongue—a kind of antediluvian Esperanto. But that is not the obvious sense. What the book of Genesis seems to be telling us, implicitly and explicitly, is that in the beginning, humanity spoke Hebrew.

Digging below the Surface

What language, then, does God speak? We read that God creates light by verbal fiat:

> And God said, "Let there be light." And there was light.

Ten times, in fact, God "speaks" in order to create (although some things He simply creates without speaking). In the Middle Ages, Moses Maimonides and other rationalist Jewish philosophers held that all instances of divine speech in the Bible should be understood metaphorically. Mystics, on the other hand, took this passage to mean that, by these speech acts, God was creating or deploying Hebrew itself, rather than waiting for a human being to do so. And this reading is not far from the plain sense of the text.

A closer look at the opening verse of Genesis gives reason to believe that Hebrew is being accorded primordial status. The first three words are *bereshit bara elohim*, usually translated "In the beginning God created" or, if we follow the word order of the Hebrew, "In-the-beginning, created God." The first two words begin with the same string of three letters, *bet resh alef*. What this might mean is altogether beyond the plain meaning of the words. At the very least, the Bible seems to be signaling something through the phonetic or graphic *resonances* between these first two words. Perhaps, then, the Hebrew letters or strings of letters *throughout* the Bible convey a level of significance (a "semiotic," to use linguistic terminology) quite separate from the plain sense of the words these letters form.

Of course, many talented authors, writing in many languages, have relied on meaningful resonance. But Hebrew's intrinsic features made it especially reverberant in a way that European languages are not. Almost the entire Hebrew word stock consists of groups of related words (what linguists call "clusters"), constructed on a skeleton of consonants (the "root") that vaguely conveys a meaning; through the insertion of specific vowels and the addition of prefixes and suffixes, real words, with specific meanings, are generated.

The closest thing to this in English would be a consonant skeleton like *b-n-d*, which yields the word cluster *bind, bound, band, bond, binder, bondage,* and the like. So, for instance, in biblical Hebrew, the root *sh-m-r* yielded: *shamar* (to guard, wait), *nishmar* (to take care, to be on guard), *mishmar* (detention), and *mishmeret* (vigil). Similarly, *sh-l-m* yielded *shalam* (to reach completion), *shilem* (to pay or to compensate), *hishlim* (to make peace), *shalem* (intact), *shalom* (peace), *shalmon* (bribe), and so forth. The Hebrew ear was always attuned to picking out these underlying patterns, and from them the authors of the Bible could create resonances on a grand scale. Every episode echoes to them; every name is pregnant with possibilities.

To return to an example used above: after the birth of Noah (Noaḥ), a corrupted mankind declares that "this one [Noah] shall bring us relief (*yenaḥamenu*) . . . from the toil of our hands," but "the Lord was sorry (*vayinaḥem*) that He had made man," and decides, "I will blot out (*emḥeh*) man." However, "Noah found favor (*ḥen*) in the eyes of the Lord." These verses play on the two possible meanings of *n-ḥ-m* (relief or regret), the similarity between *n-ḥ-m* and *n-ḥ*, the similarity between these and *m-ḥ* (bear in mind that *n* and *m* are similar sounds), and the mirror image between *n-ḥ* and *ḥ-n*.

Poetry and Prose in the Bible

As noted above, resonances and wordplay are among the basic tools of poets, and biblical poetry is replete with them. But the just-cited example of Noah confirms that they pervade biblical prose as well. And here, as Shemaryahu Talmon has observed, is one of the most striking distinctions between the Bible and the national and religious literatures of surrounding peoples:[1] the Bible tells the history of Israel almost entirely in prose, deliberately turning its back on the epic poetry with which the cities of Ugarit, Ur, and every other Near Eastern cultic center recounted their cosmic beliefs. I would add that in so doing, the biblical authors injected a little of the stylistic flavor of everyday speech, and everyday transactions, into the elevated style of their sacred message. The biblical narrative is suffused with dialogue; what people say (and do) far overshadows how they look or even what the author says about them. Far from reinforcing the usual barriers between literate priesthood and presumably less literate people, biblical prose breaks them down.

Two other features of biblical style must have further sharpened its linguistic consciousness. First, the poetry is rich in metaphor. This is typically not the breathtaking or enigmatic sort of metaphor so common in modern poetry, but what Adele Berlin has called the "expressive permutations"[2] of mundane, naturalistic comparisons with trees, animals, the skies, and so forth—thus the book of Psalms likens a righteous man to "a tree planted by the rivers of water" and the ungodly to "chaff which the wind driveth away"—as well as more elaborately constructed metaphorical "conceits" depicting, for example, wisdom and folly as two women of contrasting reputations.

Second, perhaps the most pervasive and familiar feature of biblical poetry (and often prose) is augmentation, or what is sometimes called parallelism: organizing verses into two matching or contrasting halves through syntax, semantics, meter, or some combination of these:

To every thing there is a season, and a time to every purpose
under the heaven.

(Ecclesiastes 3:1)

Sometimes, such verses read like "thought rhymes" or simple par-
allels, but often the parallel says (in James Kugel's words), "and
what's more . . ."[3] And regularly, the parallel turns on delicate nuance and an attentive ear:

How can I curse whom God has not cursed?
How can I denounce whom the Lord has not denounced?

(Numbers 23:8)

Or:

Saul killed his thousands,
And David his ten thousands.

(1 Samuel 18:7)

Those for whom the Bible was the major (or the sole) written
text could not help developing a sensitivity to such subtleties, and
the resultant linguistic acuity became an ever-present feature of
Hebrew culture in Israel and later in the Diaspora.

Biblical Hebrew is also stunningly flexible. Narrative, prophecy,
law, proverbs, philosophy, elegy, romance—the biblical canon en-
compasses all of these genres and more. Here are some brief sam-
ples of its stylistic breadth:

And Caleb the son of Hezron begat children of Azubah his wife,
and of Jerioth; her sons are these: Jesher, and Shobab, and Ardon.
(1 Chronicles 2:18)

And if a man borrow aught of his neighbor, and it be hurt, or die,
the owner thereof being not with it, he shall surely make it good.
(Exodus 22:14)

And I looked, and, behold, a whirlwind came out of the north, a great cloud, and a fire infolding itself, and a brightness was about it, and out of the midst thereof as the color of amber, out of the midst of the fire. Also out of the midst thereof came the likeness of four living creatures. And this was their appearance: they had the likeness of a man. (Ezekiel 1:4–5)

He that observeth the wind shall not sow; and he that regardeth the clouds shall not reap. (Ecclesiastes 11:4)

How long wilt thou forget me, O Lord? For ever? How long wilt thou hide thy face from me? (Psalms 13:1)

Behold, thou art fair, my love; behold, thou art fair; thou hast doves' eyes within thy locks: thy hair is as a flock of goats, that appear from Mount Gilead. (Song of Songs 4:1)

Running through it all is a spiritual thread that binds Israel's past, present, and future into divinely ordained duty and destiny. And this leads us to a perennial question.

Human Language? Or Divine Code?

Much of the Bible is explicitly presented as the word of God. One might then expect its texts to contain their fair share of mystery, as indeed they sometimes do. One might even expect wording that strains the bounds of human language. But that is generally not the case: the majority of the Bible is in a coherent and comprehensible Hebrew, regardless of subject matter. Yes, there are exceptions: in Job, and in many of the Psalms, the vocabulary is unusual, the syntax dense, the verb forms often intentionally ambiguous. But generations of interpreters have taken it for granted that there is also a plain sense even to such highly charged Hebrew.

Still, beyond the sounds and letters, did the biblical authors engage in hidden code? In Jeremiah 25 we find a mystifying reference to the "King of Sheshach." This is the only mention of such a kingdom in the Bible, and the name does not resemble any found in ancient inscriptions or texts. If, however, we apply the so-called *atbash* cipher—whereby the first letter of the Hebrew alphabet (*aleph*) is replaced with the last (*tav*), the second with the penultimate, and so forth—Sheshach becomes *Bavel*, or Babylon. In the context of the verse, it makes perfect sense that Jeremiah would speak of the king of Babylon here, and one can even imagine that he coded his speech to avoid angering the wrong people.

The earliest reference we have to the *atbash* cipher is hundreds of years later, in the Talmud, but the possibility that it was used deliberately in Jeremiah is, at the very least, seductive. Nevertheless, if not the sole example of code in the Bible, it is one of the very, very few. The biblical authors are not reticent about saying what they mean.

And what of numerology (*gimatria* or *gematria*), an interpretive tool later favored by many rabbis that assigns the letter *alef* the value 1, *bet* 2, and so on? Did the biblical authors knowingly employ a system whereby the reader could deduce hidden meanings by computing the numerical values of words? For instance, some rabbis noted that the phrase *safa aḥat* (one language) in the Babel story has the same numerical value as *leshon ha-kodesh* (holy tongue). Yet, once again, nothing so strange has been found in the Bible as to compel us to think that the biblical authors had numerology on their minds.

A Life outside the Bible

We have postponed two basic questions: What *was* the Hebrew Bible itself in the biblical age, and when was it composed?

The Hebrew Bible as we know it finished taking shape in the land of Israel in the second century CE, when the rabbinic sages decided for posterity which books should be deemed Jewish scripture and which not. They called this canon of twenty-four holy books the *Tanakh*. Christians often call it the Old Testament. A religiously more neutral term is the Hebrew or Jewish Bible.

How most of the twenty-four books of the Hebrew Bible took shape—and when—is largely a matter of speculation. The earliest parts date back to the second millennium BCE, the latest to the first centuries after the exile to Babylon in 586 BCE—a time span approaching one thousand years. Just a single fragmentary biblical text has been unearthed by archaeologists from the biblical era itself: the Priestly Blessing from the book of Numbers, etched on two silver amulets dated to the seventh century BCE, the age of the Judean monarchy.

Although no full-length nonbiblical works in Hebrew have been found from this period, either, archaeologists have uncovered hundreds of short inscriptions stretching back to the tenth century BCE. These are official letters, cultic formulas, seals, jar labels, business receipts, petitions, and so forth, all written in a very biblical Hebrew:

> Two months: (fruit) picking
> Two months: sowing
> Two months: late sowing
> One month: flax harvest
> One month: barley harvest
> One month: final (?) harvest
> Two months: pruning (vines)
> One month: summer fruit
> *Gezer Calendar*

FIGURE 1. Israelite fieldwork: The Gezer Calendar (10th century BCE).

In the tenth year. From Sag [locality]. Owner: Gadyo. A jar of fine oil.

Samaria ostracon

May God cause my lord to hear tidings of peace and of good. . . . Who is your servant, a dog, that you sent your servant the [unclear]? Your servant has also returned the letters to my lord. May God cause you to see the harvest successfully, this very day. . . .

From Lachish Letter 5

All my brethren will witness on my behalf, they who reap with me in the hot sun, my brethren will witness on my behalf: Verily, I am free of guilt. Restore my garment. And I will pay the governor in full. [. . .]

From the Hashaviahu inscription

It all amounts to very little by comparison with the wealth of documents and literature from ancient Egypt, Syria, or Mesopotamia. An ancient Israelite archive has yet to be found, and may never be.

As for what the writing on our existing fragments looks like, every preexilic Hebrew inscription yet discovered is in an angular Old Hebrew script (sometimes dubbed "paleo-Hebrew script"), which looks entirely different from the familiar square and cursive scripts that have been used by Jews for the last two millennia. (More on this in the next chapter.) Although the Bible makes enigmatic reference to the Ten Commandments as "the writing of God," nothing in the Bible even hints at the nature of the Hebrew script in use then—or at its having any special significance.

Our main witness to ancient Hebrew is, therefore, the Bible itself—but here is another problem. The oldest manuscripts of the standard Hebrew Bible are relatively recent: the Aleppo Codex (tenth century CE) and the Leningrad Codex (1008 CE). By "standard Hebrew Bible," I mean the text traditionally used by Jews. Thanks to the Dead Sea Scrolls and several ancient translations, we can go back another one thousand to twelve hundred years, but this would still be two or three centuries after the last events described in the Bible—and these versions vary unpredictably from the standard Jewish text in wording, spelling, and sometimes entire passages. On the other hand, some of the Dead Sea Scrolls vouch for the antiquity of the standard Jewish text.

Who spoke Hebrew? Throughout the region that now comprises Israel, Lebanon, Syria, and Jordan (that is, ancient Phoenicia, Moab, Ammon, Aram, and Canaan), scholars have found inscriptions that are similar or very similar to the Hebrew of the Bible—and in the same script. (The paleo-Hebrew script was used as far afield as Syria, and was also the basis for the Greek and, indirectly, Latin and Cyrillic alphabets as well.) Scholars long insisted that Hebrew was simply one of many Canaanite dialects, albeit the only one that happened to survive into the Common Era. More recent evidence would group it more closely with Aramaic. People may well have called it

Canaanite, just as the Promised Land was known to Abraham and Joshua as the land of Canaan.

But there is no doubt that, at some point, Israelites began to *feel* they were speaking a distinctive ethnic tongue. What language Abraham had spoken before he arrived in Canaan seems not to have mattered. The Sumerian or Aramaic of his earlier life? A Hebrew all his own? The question would be much debated by medieval Jewish and Christian commentators, but on this topic the Bible itself maintains a discreet silence.

Behind the scenes, however, a tradition-minded scribal culture was at work writing the Bible in a quite homogeneous style and copying it—which makes it possible to speak of biblical Hebrew as one consistent language, with just minor changes in its final phase. For most of its history, moreover, that language is relatively free of foreign influences; even the account in Genesis and Exodus of Israel in Egypt has fairly few Egyptian linguistic touches.

What dialects there were, what spoken Hebrew was really like, and how much literacy existed, we will probably never know—although some of the famous Lachish Letters from the early sixth century BCE were clearly written by Judean soldiers rather than by scribes. In the entire Bible there is only one reference to dialectal variation: this is the famous passage in which one warring tribe (the Gileadites) identifies another (the Ephraimites) by the latter's inability to pronounce the *sh* sound in the word *shibboleth* (watercourse), pronouncing it instead like an *s—sibboleth*.

Many other differences there surely were. Ephraim, Gad, and the other northern and eastern tribes of Israel, chronically detached from the southern tribes, most likely evolved their own varieties of spoken Hebrew, even if we have no evidence of it. These differences would have been reinforced when the country split into two rival monarchies after the death of Solomon, with the kingdom of Israel in the north frequently in political and religious conflict with Judea in the south. Some evidence of these differences shows through in the biblical works apparently composed in the north, among them the story of Gideon and some of the Psalms that today make up the Hallel prayer, but scribal schools maintained strict and almost uniform standards. These standards for literary Hebrew continued to hold down to the end of the Israelite era and for centuries afterward—testimony to the prestige of literary Hebrew and the literature written in it.

The End?

A fateful series of invasions displaced Hebrew from its comfortable niche. In 722 BCE, the Assyrians put an end to the northern kingdom of Israel, deporting its inhabitants and replacing them with deportees from other conquered nations. Many surviving Israelites fled south to Judea, but Judea in turn was ravaged in 597 and 586 BCE by Babylonian armies. Jerusalem was destroyed, and the Judean elite was exiled to Mesopotamia or fled to Egypt, leaving the peasantry behind. What happened to Hebrew after this exile is the subject of our next chapter.

2

Jerusalem, Athens, and Rome

Introduction

In 538 BCE the conquering Persian monarch, Cyrus, decreed that the Jews could reestablish themselves in Judea. Many thousands returned. The exile to Babylon had marked the end of the Israelite era and the end of an era for Hebrew. But the millennium that followed (approximately 500 BCE to 500 CE) produced a fresh start: a new Judaism grounded in devotion to the Torah, and a new Hebrew. The shape of the Jewish world was also quite new: a far-flung and religiously diverse Diaspora revolved around a spiritual center in the land of Israel whose fortunes perilously waxed and waned with geopolitical realities and its own internal religious conflicts. In many parts of the Diaspora, Hebrew was soon forgotten. In the land of Israel it was zealously preserved in Judea, vanishing from colloquial use only when Rome's armies crushed the last Judean uprising in the second century CE.

But at the very same time, in a remarkable textual act of spiritual resistance, the Rabbis chose Hebrew as the medium in which to preserve the Midrash and Mishnah, their vast oral interpretations of the Torah—and approved a suite of Hebrew prayers for Jews to memorize wherever they might find an abode. Out of this grew a great corpus of Hebrew literature, embodying the religion and culture of the Jews down to modern times.

Conventional histories often divide the millennium from 500 BCE to 500 CE into two: the Second Temple period (to 70 CE) and the Roman-Byzantine period, which ended with the Arab conquest (638 CE). In the Second Temple period, the Jewish presence in Judea, Galilee, and Transjordan grew and thrived, despite severe harassment by neighboring and invading regimes. The Maccabean uprising starting in 167 BCE even produced a century of Jewish self-rule. But internecine Jewish strife and harsh Roman occupation culminated in the ravaging of Jerusalem and Judea in 70 CE, and again in 135 CE, and the decimation of the Jewish population. In the ensuing five centuries, the Roman-Byzantine regime, abetted by an ascendant Church, steadily wore down a shrinking if still substantial Jewish population in the region Rome and the Church renamed Palestine.

Despite the momentous political and social changes that separate 500 BCE and 500 CE, from a linguistic perspective it makes sense to see this era as one whole. For Jews everywhere, both in the Diaspora and in the land of Israel, Hebrew found itself in unremitting competition with other languages and cultures—above all, the political power of Greek, Latin, and Aramaic (the last-named being the lingua franca of Middle Eastern business and administration until the Arab conquest in the seventh century CE). In many locales, these cultures supplanted Hebrew entirely through a complex process—demographic, political, and social-spiritual, along with a bitter dose of Greco-Roman military and cultural imperialism. One long-term result was the demise of native spoken Hebrew in the first and second centuries CE. But sometimes, paradoxically, the rival cultures served as irritants that drove the Jewish and Hebrew spirit to extraordinary new heights.

"Little" languages and cultures are not inevitably devoured—at least not where they have a densely settled homeland, a proud heritage, and the means by which to instill dedication to that heritage in younger generations. This was the case in the tiny territory of Judea. In the centuries following the Babylonian conquest, Judea would become the cradle of a reborn Jewish nation, a newly revitalized form of Hebrew, and a great Hebrew literary canon that would define Judaism as we know it today. There, even after the ravages of Rome, Jews continued to live a religious life centered on the study and endless interpretation of their holy texts—the Bible and later the Mishnah, the *midrashim*, and liturgy. Such study required a profound understanding of the Hebrew language, which some clearly possessed and which many more aspired to achieve. This era would continue in force down to the fourth century CE and beyond.

Scattered minorities, by contrast, soon find themselves at cultural and linguistic risk. Many, probably most, Jews lived in the Diaspora—in Babylonia-Persia, Egypt, and throughout the length and breadth of the Roman Empire. We know little about these diasporas, but it appears that in most of them, with the remarkable exception of Babylonia, Hebrew knowledge all but vanished. And yet, by the time Jewish life in the Holy Land became unsustainable after the Arab conquest, various locations in the Diaspora would become important centers of Jewish culture and religion. And then, improbably, the Diaspora would again make Hebrew great.

The Jewish Bible Takes Shape, Quietly

The greatest legacy of this era was the Jewish Bible, the world's most influential body of literature—written almost entirely in Hebrew. Of course, the contents of the Bible largely date back to the Israelite era, as we have seen in the previous chapter. But in many ways the Bible as we know it today is a product of the "postbiblical" era. For a long time, the textual content of the Bible varied widely, particularly for ideological or pedagogic purposes—witness the Greek versions and the Dead Sea Scrolls—and the very question of which books were in the canon and which were out wasn't settled conclusively by the Rabbis until the second century CE. But even after the canon was closed, standardizing the actual text proved to be an extraordinary challenge that would take centuries to complete. A system for transcribing the pronunciations of Hebrew would not be fully developed until after the seventh and eighth centuries.

I've referred here to the "Jewish" rather than the "Hebrew" Bible for the (slightly pedantic) reason that two books, Daniel and Ezra, have come down to us partly in Aramaic, more specifically the imperial Aramaic of the Babylonian court. They date from the early centuries after the exile to Babylon, as do several other biblical books, including Esther, Zechariah, and Malachi; the latter, however, are written entirely in Hebrew: striking evidence for a revival of literary and spoken Hebrew following the return to Zion.

Why some sections of Daniel's visions and Ezra's historical records were set down in Aramaic is obscure, but at all events the later editors of the Bible appear to have greatly valued Aramaic and chose not to "upgrade" these sections into Hebrew. As we will see, Jewish respect, indeed reverence, for Aramaic would continue, and deepen, in the centuries to come.

The New Script

The Jews who chose to return from exile in Babylonia had virtually forgotten how to write in the old Hebrew script of their grandparents. Instead, they employed the imperial script used for writing Aramaic, the official language of administration and business in the Babylonian and Persian Empires. The script had twenty-two letters, corresponding one-to-one with the old twenty-two-letter Hebrew script.

By the second century BCE, this Aramaic script—the Talmud dubs it *ktav ashuri*, or "Assyrian script"—had itself become the distinctive Jewish script, and it is what we today know as the Hebrew alphabet. Bible scrolls were eventually deemed sacred *only* in this Assyrian script. The Talmud attributes the switch to Ezra the scribe, who played a key role in the canonization of Hebrew scriptures starting around 450 BCE. How quickly the new script superseded the old, and why, Jewish sources do not say.

It is quite possible that, although many of the returning exiles resolved to use Hebrew as a language, the *script* did not much matter to them. Either way, in Aramaic or Hebrew, the sacred texts would be preserved. (The exiles also brought back several other Babylonian cultural practices that would become part and parcel of Judaism, including the names for the lunar months.)

Religious politics might well also have had a hand. The new script may have been a means for Jews to distinguish themselves from a persistent foe, the Samaritans, who inhabited the central mountains and claimed descent from the preexilic Israelites—although the biblical book of Kings and Assyrian records describe them as pagans shipped in by the invading Assyrians back in the eighth century BCE after the mass deportation of the northern tribes (the so-called Ten Lost Tribes). The Samaritans, as they called themselves, had constructed a distinct Israelite identity—and a grand temple of their own on Gerizim, their holy mountain. The returnees shunned them, and they were deemed quasi-Jews or even Gentiles for centuries.

Despite (or because of) Ezra's reforms, the Samaritans one-upped the Jews in holiness. Besides maintaining the Holy Tongue (as they called it) in composing their prayers, they also cleaved to the Old Hebrew script for other sacred purposes; in fact, down to modern times they have used it for writing their Torah scrolls. The Jews, too, would use the Old Hebrew script on occasion—but, as we will see, this would soon become a political or religious "statement" of a different sort.

In many ways, the centuries stretching from 530 BCE to the Roman conquest (63 BCE) seem like "Dark Ages": apart from the last biblical works, little Jewish writing from those times has survived, and most of it has come down to us not in Hebrew but in Greek or Aramaic compositions preserved by the Church. But this was not the end of Hebrew composition. A magnificent rabbinic Hebrew literature would eventually put down roots and blossom even as the Roman occupation intensified.

The Bible and Popular Biblical Literacy

It is hard to imagine what would have become of the Bible without Ezra. This charismatic scholar-priest led a new wave of Jewish returnees from Babylonia around 458 BCE, authorized by the empire to administer Jewish religious and judicial life. Once in Judea (according to the book that bears his name), Ezra orchestrated a religious revival and strove to bring the Torah to the masses.

The day when Bible study became pivotal to Jewish life, in central Jerusalem before the assembled populace, is depicted in the book of Nehemiah (originally a continuation of the book of Ezra):

> And they asked Ezra the scribe to bring the book of the teaching
> of Moses which the Lord had given to Israel. . . . And he read from
> it facing the square before the Water Gate from early morning
> until midday, in the presence of the men and the women and
> those who could understand. . . . And they gave the sense and interpreted the text. (Nehemiah 8:1–8)

Ezra's grand project bore fruit. In place of prophecy and sacred sites, mainstream Second Temple Judaism, according to the later testimony of the talmudic rabbis, came to revere the biblical scrolls, the scholars who expounded them, the synagogue, and the house of study.

Not that biblical literacy could have come easy. To read from the Bible meant reading aloud from a consonantal text that included only occasional vowel markings and no punctuation, and was couched in a Hebrew often quite unlike what people spoke or wrote. Indeed, many Jews were no longer competent in Hebrew; and even among those whom the Babylonians had left alone, the influx of new populations had mixed all manner of Aramaic, Nabatean, and Greek into many people's speech. The Bible itself recalls the shock and fury of the statesman Nehemiah upon encountering the hybrid tongues spoken in the port of Ashdod, by now a very Phoenician city:

> Half of their children spoke the language of Ashdod, and they could not speak the language of Judea but spoke the language of various peoples. And I contended with them and cursed them and beat some of them and pulled out their hair; and I made them take an oath in the name of God, saying, "You shall not give your daughters to their sons, or take their daughters for your sons or for yourselves. Did not King Solomon of Israel sin on account of such women?" (Nehemiah 12:24–26)

And yet, despite its rocky start at the beginning of the Second Temple period, Hebrew education seems to have thrived. It wasn't just the realm of scholars or scribes. Fathers tutored sons, and sages their disciples. Study groups seem to have abounded, combining prodigious literacy with oral erudition. "Find yourself a teacher," urges an early adage, "and acquire a study partner. Eat with him, drink with him, read Scripture with him, and study with him" (Avot d'Rabbi Natan). A network of synagogues can be traced back to at least as early as the first century CE, combining Sabbath morning worship and scriptural teaching and a religious school for the young. The Ashkenazi word for synagogue, *shul*, is an echo of this. The Talmud also speaks of the *bet midrash*, where some adults could devote their day to study.

The knowledge of scripture—and the prodigious memorization of its intricate everyday applications—came to run deep and wide, to judge by the many humble folk who acquired the status of sage. The Talmud is full of anecdotes about the learning of *tinokot shel bet rabban* (rabbinic schoolchildren). "Bible when you're five, Mishnah when you're ten," taught one sage—"and not a moment before," taught another, "but then you can stuff them like an ox."

"Should any one of us," declared the historian Josephus in a spirited defense of Judaism against its Greek detractors, "be asked about our laws, he would more easily recount them all than supply his own name" ("Against Apion," book 2:19). He was no doubt thinking chiefly of boys and men, although the Talmud mentions Beruriah and Yalta as distinguished female scholars.

One didn't need to *speak* Hebrew to achieve this—intensive study of texts, which were widely copied, could yield extraordinary results, as is still found in very traditional Diaspora schools today. In later centuries, the Talmud records, it was common practice in the land of Israel and Babylonia for no fewer than seven men to be invited to recite, unaided, from the Torah scroll when it was read in the synagogue.

Nor was Hebrew just frozen in the past. Legal documents were often composed in the language. An erudite biblical style (albeit colored with Aramaic) was cultivated for literature.

And there was also a simple vernacular Hebrew, the everyday language of many Jews in the land of Israel whose families had never been sent into exile. Barely a trace of it is found in the Bible, not surprisingly; ancient vernaculars have generally left little trace. But tantalizing clues to a Hebrew vernacular do exist. Caves near the Dead Sea have yielded papyrus correspondence, some of it in a very everyday Hebrew, from Bar-Kokhba's revolt against Rome circa 133 CE, containing traditional pronunciations still alive today, particularly as recited by Yemenite Jews: thus *lakh, likh* (to you: masc., fem.) rather than *lekha, lakh*. Language and spellings in some Dead Sea Scrolls are also pointers to unbiblical pronouns like *anu* (we), *atema* (you), and lose or confuse guttural consonants. On a much grander scale, we have the Mishnah and Midrash, first- and second-century CE rabbinic compilations of practices and Bible interpretations couched in a simple grammar and syntax quite unlike the Bible's and oozing with the vocabulary of everyday city and country life—unmistakable signs of a lively colloquial tongue. We will come back to all of this shortly.

While the Second Temple stood, however, vernacular Hebrew commanded little prestige. The authors of Ezra and other postexilic religious works—examples include the Wisdom of Ben Sira, the book of Jubilees (both second century BCE), and the book of Esther—strove to re-create a biblical style, albeit colored by vernacular Hebrew. Or else they simply wrote in Aramaic. Megillat Taʿanit, the rabbinic listing of minor feast days, is a case in point.

Despite the Jewish restoration in the land of Israel, well-heeled Judeans, prizing their personal and political connections with the Gentile gentry, would have known and maybe even preferred Aramaic, the prestige language of the entire region. Indeed, until the Arab invasions in the seventh century CE, Aramaic would be the main language of most Jews in the Middle East, including most of the land of Israel outside of tiny Judea.

Hellenization: A Bridge to Nowhere?

But then came Greek. Alexander the Great arrived and conquered the Holy Land in 333 BCE. He would be generally remembered as a benevolent ruler, but his most important legacy came to be hated by many. That legacy was Hellenism: the aggressive planting of Greek values, gymnasia, urban architecture, and schools, as well as Greek-speaking settlers, wherever he went. The goals of Hellenism were vigorously (and sometimes thuggishly) pursued by Alexander's successor regimes in the Middle East, the Syrian Seleucids and the Egyptian Ptolemies, under whose rule so many Jews lived. Hebrew stood to be a major loser.

Thanks in part to the story of Ḥanukkah and the Maccabees (of which more anon), Jews often remember Hellenism as either a destructive force or a bridge to nowhere. The great Jewish community of Alexandria is said to have hellenized itself out of existence. But in reality, the nature of Hellenism varied widely, as did its cultural and spiritual impact on Jewish life; even the Talmud bears witness to this.

In Egypt, Greece, Syria, and Asia Minor, the huge Diaspora communities rapidly hellenized—linguistically, socially, and culturally. The shift shows in given names. Around 300 BCE, most Egyptian Jews had Hebrew names. Fifty years on, their names were mostly Greek, though monotheistic rather than pagan—as in Theodotos, Theodoros, Dorothea (all variations on "gift of God").

These several million Jews—considerably outnumbering those in the land of Israel—were a mixed multitude: scholars, merchants, migrants from Judea, and large numbers of local proselytes. They did not use Greek exclusively; many were equally at home in Aramaic and some in Hebrew, to judge from the numerous papyri and ostraca (pieces of engraved pottery) discovered in those languages.

They were synagogue-goers and Sabbath-observers; they regarded the land of Israel as their real homeland and its kings as their kings; and they made regular donations to the Jerusalem Temple. Their synagogue services were probably conducted in a mixture of Hebrew, Aramaic, and Greek. Until the discovery of the Dead Sea Scrolls, and later the even more ancient fragment with the Priestly Blessing mentioned in chapter 1, the oldest known copy of a biblical text was a Jewish-Egyptian papyrus with the Hebrew *Shema* and Ten Commandments (dating to ca. 150 BCE). A Jewish religious literature in Greek also flourished, culminating in the writings of the philosopher Philo of Alexandria (ca. 25 BCE–ca. 50 CE), who appears to have known little if any Hebrew. Like most hellenized Jews, he would have known his Tanakh in Greek.

The greatest symbol of Jewish hellenization was the Greek translation of the Tanakh known as the Septuagint. Few translations have ever enjoyed such extremes of fortune. Intended by the Egyptian-Hellenist King Ptolemy (third century BCE) as a bureaucratic rendering of the Torah for an archive of his subjects' laws and customs, it would eventually be immensely popular. Some rabbis (and many churchmen) considered it divinely inspired. A legend appears in the Talmud that Ptolemy took seventy-two scholars and locked them in separate rooms so that each would produce his own independent translation—and, lo and behold, all translated it almost identically. The point of this legend is that it was quite possible to capture the spirit of the Hebrew Torah in as alien and un-Semitic a tongue as Greek.

The entire Bible was eventually translated. But far from observing the proprieties of literary Greek, the translators boldly hebraized. Thus where the Tanakh renders "every man" as *ish ish* (literally, man man), they offered a very un-Greek *anthropos anthropos*. Pagan resonances were also zealously avoided: thus *prophetes* rather than *mantis*. In sum, this was a veritable Hebrew-Greek semantics, which the early Church would inherit and make its own.

There were in fact several Jewish-Greek translations. Many congregations heard the weekly portions of the Torah in Greek, or at least with a running Greek translation. The second-century sage Shimon ben Gamliel taught that "the only language [other than Hebrew] that is permitted us for Torah scrolls is Greek" (Talmud Megillah 8b). His view was approved, and the Talmud finds evidence in the Torah itself: when Noah blessed his sons Japhet and Shem, he prayed that the words of Japhet (i.e., Greece) should be heard in the tents (i.e., synagogues) of Shem (i.e., Israel).

Could this grand Greek-Jewish culture have lasted? Maybe. But times changed. Most important, early Christianity made a pact with Hellenism. When Constantine embraced Christianity in 313 CE and moved his capital to the Greek-speaking eastern part of the Roman Empire, Hellenist Christians gained the upper hand. The Jews, in response, turned back to their Hebrew roots. As for the great Jewish community of Alexandria, historians no longer believe that its disappearance was due to assimilation; rather, it never survived the bloody Jewish uprisings in the second century CE across the Roman Empire. The Septuagint did survive, but not among the Jews; it was adopted as the official biblical text by the Greek Orthodox Church. A bitter rabbinic teaching would declare that "when the Septuagint was translated, three days of darkness enveloped the world" (Megillat Ta'anit).

The Judean Hebrew Resistance

In Judea itself, the battle between Judaism and Hellenism—and thus between Hebrew and Greek—began shortly after Alexander's death in 323 BCE with Judea in the grip of his general Ptolemy, whose physical image was already flaunted on his first coinage for Judea.

Here the issues were clearer, and the stakes much higher. Slowly but surely, the Jewish ruling class was drawn to Greek language and city culture, to the cult of the gymnasium, and to Homer—and strife flared. The Gentile cities that the Greeks set up around the country were a particular irritant. Tensions came to a head with an attempt by the Syrian-Greek regime to paganize the Jewish population forcibly. A guerrilla uprising ensued (167 BCE), led by the priestly Hasmonean family (the "Maccabees"), and foreign armies were triumphantly expelled.

But the Jewish state that emerged under the Hasmonean dynasty still wobbled, and at times lurched, between Jewish and Hellenistic identities. You can spot this duality in the mix of Hebrew and Greek in the names of Hasmonean rulers (Yoḥanan, Hyrkanos, Yannai, Alexander) and in the mix of Jewish and pagan ethics in their statecraft.

At this point, we see Hebrew clearly being marshaled in the name of the Jewish nationalist cause. Heroic narratives like the first book of Maccabees and Judith were composed in Hebrew. But the second book of Maccabees, a stirring Jewish tale of repression and liberation, was composed in Greek a mere generation after the events it describes; that book recounts the martyrdom of Hannah and her seven sons, ordered to consume swine's flesh. Before dying, each makes a defiant speech in *hē patrios phōnē* (the ancestral tongue). Last to be killed is Hannah, whose final moments are described thus:

> Though she saw her seven sons perish in a single day, she bore it with good courage because of her hope in the Lord. She spurred each one of them in the language of their fathers. Noble in spirit, she steeled her woman's feelings with the courage of a man.

FIGURE 2. Coin minted in 68 CE during the Jewish uprising against Rome. The inscription reads, "*shekel Yisrael/Yerushalayim hakedosha*" (shekel of Israel/Holy Jerusalem)

Similarly, the obsolescent preexilic script was mobilized to the cause. Coins, the supreme token of Jewish independence, bore the Hasmonean rulers' names in this script—evoking biblical glory days. *Yehohanan ha-Kohen ha-Gadol ve-Hever ha-Yehudim* (John the High Priest and the Judean Council), read the first coins. (On the other side, ironically, his descendants stamp their names in Greek.) Two centuries on, the preexilic script would transmit its last message on the coins of the first and second revolts against Rome (67–70 and 132–135 CE, respectively): *herut Tsion* (freedom of Zion) and *le-herut Yerushalayim* (for the freedom of Jerusalem).

For everyday language choice, however, people then as now put practical benefits before ideology and belief. Increasingly, ordinary Jews in Judea used Aramaic, while the upper classes and big city-dwellers adopted Greek. Everyday Hebrew was now in a steady decline.

In the first–second centuries BCE we see the emergence of the Sages (*hakhamim*), a new religious-scholarly elite who seem to have overlapped with various interrelated groups known as *hasidim* (pious ones), *perushim* (Pharisees), scribes, and (eventually) the Rabbis. Prior to the destruction of the Temple in 70 CE, very little is known about these groups, about the relationships among them, or about their linguistic preferences. We do know, however, that the Sages were linguistic revolutionaries. Their legal and moral teachings employed a simple, even folksy style, more like vernacular Hebrew than the Hebrew of the Bible, full of lists of everyday things, easily memorized blocks, snappy anecdotes. Indeed, the syntax, tenses, and verb and noun patterns were in many ways quite unlike those of Genesis or Chronicles.

This was in stark contrast to the pseudobiblical style of First Maccabees or other noncanonized works. Where a biblical word was outdated, even one closely bound up with religious practice, the Sages did not hesitate to abandon it; thus *tefillin* replaced *totafot* (phylacteries) and *ḥag* (literally, feast) supplanted *ḥag ha-Sukkot* (the Feast of Tabernacles). For prayers, they used what most likely seemed to them a more formal style, often mixing biblical diction (as in *asher kidshanu*, "Who sanctified us") and postbiblical diction (*ner shel shabbat*, "light of Sabbath," rather than *or shabbat*).

Linguistic upheaval is often related to social upheaval, and so it was here: the Sages were at the forefront of a grassroots rebellion, facilitated by the Maccabean revolt, against the power of the landed priestly aristocracy. The Sages' religious values and practices were based on oral and popular tradition as well as on the written Torah. To preserve the spirit of the Law, a sage like Hillel could creatively interpret the letter of the Law. Once, when Passover Eve fell on a Sabbath, he even appealed to popular memory to decide how it should be observed.

The new grassroots Hebrew that the Sages were now employing was almost certainly a reflection of this social-religious philosophy. This Hebrew was eventually enshrined in the Mishnah, the great religious code of Judaism compiled in the first–second centuries.

Hence the conventional academic name for this, Mishnaic Hebrew. The Sages simply dubbed it *leshon ha-kodesh* (the Holy Tongue)—or referred to it as *leshon ḥakhamim* (the language of the Sages) when they wished to distinguish it from biblical Hebrew.

Surprisingly, the Sages, committed though they were to preserving Hebrew despite the growing competition from Greek and Aramaic, were not purists. They made considerable use of Greek culture, logic, and science while shunning Greek philosophy and of course paganism. At least one thousand Greek words relating to government, commerce, war, law, and everyday life are found in the Talmud and Midrash: words like *kategor* (prosecutor, cf. category), *pinkas* (writing pad), *polmos* (conflict, cf. polemic), *karon* (carriage), *pundak* (tavern), *kruv* (cabbage), and even that most revered of institutions, the *Sanhedrin* (the rabbinic high council). Latin also wormed its way in via Greek, especially for matters military, although in matters cultural the luster of Athens continued to outshine Rome.

Not everyone was on the same page. In the two centuries bracketing the start of the Common Era, deep in the Judean desert, most famously at Qumran, there lived messianic sectarian groups who were hostile to the Romans, the Sages, and almost everyone else. Preparing for a return to a pure biblical age, they depicted it in their writings, which have miraculously survived as the Dead Sea Scrolls. Many of their hymns, apocalypses, codes of conduct, and scriptural commentaries were largely in a quasi-biblical Hebrew style far "purer" than that of the Rabbis. Greek words were taboo. They zealously studied the Bible in Hebrew rather than Greek or Aramaic.

A dozen or so leather scrolls containing biblical texts have even been discovered in the forgotten preexilic script. The Dead Sea sectarians likely acquired them from the more mainstream, Jerusalem-based Sadducee sect that similarly revered the old script. But lan-

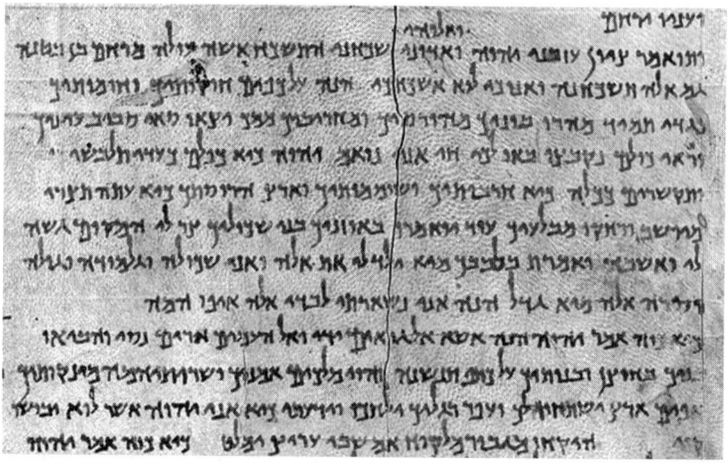

FIGURE 3. From the Great Isaiah Scroll (1st century BCE), discovered near the Dead Sea; Isaiah 49:14–25.

guage is an unruly force to be reckoned with: even these saintly sectarians were unable to resist the inroads of the colloquial. Meanwhile, some of the Dead Sea Scrolls had a quite different agenda. In the celebrated Isaiah Scroll, the prophet's grammar and spelling have been vulgarized for a broad readership; even the prophet's name Isaiah has been written *Yeshaya*, not *Yeshayahu* as in the Bible.

And then there's one scroll written not on papyrus but on a tightly wound sheet of metal, the mysterious Copper Scroll:

In the memorial in the third layer of stone 100 gold ingots.
In the large cistern [. . .] facing the top entrance 900 talents.
Under the Absalom Monument on the west side dig 12 cubits 80 talents

And so on. A guide to buried Temple treasures? Funds squirreled away from the Romans? Mystical fantasy? Scholars can't agree, but unlike any of the other scrolls it is written in an everyday idiom—as if to ensure that the right people found the money.

These sectarians, with their linguistic purism, were one more reason for the Rabbis to couch their own teachings in a Hebrew closer
to the masses. The sects would perish in the great revolt against
Rome, leaving rabbinic Judaism—and a new Jewish sect called Christians who would soon break with Judaism and with Hebrew.

Mother-Tongue Hebrew Goes Under
(for Two Thousand Years)

In the year 67 CE, the Jews of Judea and Galilee rose up against
Rome. Judea was decimated, Jerusalem and the Temple destroyed.
Sixty years later, when the Jews revolted again, the Romans re-
sponded with even greater savagery; little was left of Judea, and
Emperor Hadrian declared Jerusalem *judenrein*.

The last Judean speakers of Hebrew were among the million sold
into slavery or seeking refuge northward in Galilee or eastward beyond the Jordan. The number of Hebrew speakers is unknown, but
probably in the tens of thousands. By any sociolinguistic yardstick,
the prospects of native Hebrew's survival were now minimal. Scattered among non-Hebrew-speaking populations, the refugees would
have felt their spoken Hebrew atrophying—and their children must
have preferred to speak other tongues.

A poignant echo of Hebrew's last heartbeats is a set of military
and administrative letters, discovered in the Judean desert, that
were written around 133 by the fabled leader of the second revolt,
Shimon Ben-Koseba (a.k.a. Bar-Kokhba). Five of the letters are in an
angry Hebrew, studded with such colloquialisms as *lo* for *ein* (akin to
substituting *aren't* for *are not*) and *ta-* for *et ha* (to denote the direct
object of a sentence), weirdly anticipating the colloquialisms of today's Israel. They suggest that the writers still used Hebrew as a
spoken language, since languages that exist only in writing don't
have vernacular forms. An example:

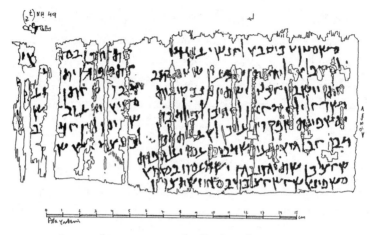

FIGURE 4. "From Shimon Ben-Koseba [leader of uprising against Rome, ca. 132 CE] to the men of Ein Gedi. . . . You sit and consume the goods of your Jewish brethren but show no concern for them . . ."

> From Shimon Ben Koseba to Joshua Ben Galgola, shalom.
> I invoke the heavens that I will have your feet clapped in irons like I did to Ben Aflul

But here is an apparent mystery: the Talmud and Midrash make no mention of any efforts to keep spoken Hebrew alive. Why not? Was it not a proud symbol of Jewish identity, emblazoned on Judea's last coins? Was it not chosen by the sages of the time to be the sole language of their prayers and collected teachings? Indeed, Judah the Patriarch, hereditary leader of the nation and redactor-in-chief of the Mishnah, lamented, "Who needs Aramaic in the land of Israel? Either Hebrew or Greek!" (As a friend of the emperor and the officially recognized Jewish leader, Rabbi Judah well knew the value of Greek.) And yet spoken Hebrew seems to have vanished with little fuss and no obituary.

The explanation is probably this: in those times, unlike today, an everyday spoken language commanded minimal respect. What counted was whether a nation possessed a cultivated written language and a literary culture (read or memorized) to match. So it hardly mattered whether Jews continued to speak *mundane* Hebrew with their wives and children as long as Hebrew could go on functioning in Jewish sacred literature (oral and written) and people continued to understand and transmit it—which they did, if imperfectly. It was all rather different from how language "death" or decline is normally conceived by sociologists of language.

A talmudic anecdote about the last gasps of spoken Hebrew makes this very point. Around the year 200 CE, in the Galilee, a group of Rabbi Judah's disciples came to ask him the meaning of two seemingly obscure words in the Mishnah, *serugin* and *halaglogot*. Uncertain who should go first, they were trickling in slowly until his maidservant chided them, "Please don't enter *serugin* [a few at a time]." Then along came a disciple with an armful of herbs, and she admonished him for littering her clean floor with *halaglogot* (purslane).

Was the Talmud having a dig at scholars for not being as well versed in Hebrew as an illiterate domestic? Maybe. More likely, it wished to emphasize Rabbi Judah's devotion to Hebrew as a spoken language: the great rabbi insisted that only Hebrew be spoken in his house, while other rabbis were content to let it live on as a purely literary idiom. According to the Talmud, spoken Hebrew died with him. (Historical linguistics can't confirm the specifics of this claim, but the evidence does suggest that it is chronologically plausible.)

The anecdote also serves to underscore the tenuous condition of Judaism. The scattered purslane is a metaphor for Hebrew's sorry state. With the collapse of Judea, maintaining spoken Hebrew may well have seemed a lost cause. If Rabbi Judah's servant woman had children, they would have spoken Aramaic.

Leshon ha-kodesh: The Holy Tongue

And yet. Amid the flames, the Sages planned for the future. They refocused Judaism entirely on Torah and its study, without (for the time being) a Temple, a king, or an army. To guarantee its survival, this new Judaism had to be meticulously ratified and codified. Thanks to a series of relatively benevolent Roman emperors, life for Jews in the Holy Land regained a semblance of normality. But who could foresee what new calamities and dispersions might lie ahead? So the Sages began to create a written record of their teachings and practices. Collected in the land of Israel in the second and third centuries CE, that record included a voluminous code of religious practice (the Mishnah) and several anthologies of interpretation on the Torah (known as the Midrash). The Sages also outlined an extensive liturgy.

Designed to be taught, recited, and studied by memory, the teachings found in these texts were known as the "Oral Torah," as distinct from the "Written Torah," meaning the Bible. Written copies were strictly for archiving. And, remarkably, all of these texts were written in Hebrew—the trademark rabbinic or Mishnaic Hebrew described earlier in this chapter.

No record survives of these monumental decisions about Hebrew; all we have are the classic texts themselves. And so we can only surmise the intentions of Rabbi Judah and his colleagues. But it is likely that they engaged in a shrewd linguistic calculus: if these texts were set down in Hebrew and duly imbibed, pondered, and memorized, the language could and would survive. Through the perpetuation of the vast workaday terminology (see further below) of the Oral Law in Hebrew, there was a prospect that the language could be kept, as it were, refrigerated until it might be restored to life. It was an extraordinary act of linguistic faith, and it would bear lasting fruit.

Hebrew was now, in the second and third centuries CE, above all else the language of the Bible and reciting or composing prayers and rabbinic texts. It had few other uses. For any Jew, it surely felt like a holy tongue. Outside the religious realm, most Jewish writing (correspondence, administrative documents, and the like) in the Roman-Byzantine period was in Aramaic, Greek, or other local languages.

However, this wasn't quite a zero-sum game for Hebrew and Aramaic. Aramaic was gaining an increasing role in Torah study, especially for translation and debate (see below). It was also used in marriage contracts and writs of divorce, documents "at the core of Judaism," as Meir Bar-Ilan has put it.[1]

Here and there, the Sages left us with fleeting glimpses of a philosophy of the holy tongue. The Midrash states, for instance, that "just as the Torah was given in the Holy Tongue, so too the universe was created with the Holy Tongue" (Genesis Rabbah). In some sense, then, Hebrew—or was it some special form of Hebrew?—transcends the physical world. But given that Hebrew is a *human* language, how could it be transcendent? And in what sense were the sun and seas and animals created by means of Hebrew? The Midrash does not say.

Something of Hebrew's power could, the Sages believed, be unlocked by special individuals through the combination, separation, and recombination of letters. The Talmud laconically relates that the biblical Bezalel, who designed the holy Tabernacle in the wilderness as related in Exodus, accomplished his task by "combining the letters with which heaven and earth were created." And muddled manuscripts survive of a mysterious work named *Sefer Yetsirah*

(The book of formation), which describes the world and every soul as driven by the twenty-two Hebrew letters combined with the ten divine attributes (*sefirot*), yielding a thirty-two-path interface:

> Twenty-two letters: He engraved them, He hewed them, He weighed them and permuted and combined them, and He thereby created the soul of every person and the soul of all speech which will be formed in the future.

Possibly as old as the second or third century, *Sefer Yetsirah* is never mentioned in the Talmud or the midrashim (perhaps because it was considered too esoteric), but would become hugely influential in the Middle Ages.

Paradoxically, there was another secret about which there was no secret: the ineffable Hebrew name of God. Formed with the four letters *yud, hey, vav, hey* (hence the Greek term *Tetragrammaton*), written hundreds of times in scripture, by rabbinic decree it could not be uttered except in the priestly invocations within the Temple. Elsewhere, it was pronounced by another divine name, *Adonay*, and memory of its original pronunciation vanished. The Rabbis connected it with the Hebrew word for existence and the divine attribute of mercy, but also told of Moses slaying an Egyptian taskmaster by uttering it aloud. They called it the "special" name, the "unique" name, or simply *Hashem* (the Name), pointing to the unknowable divine essence. From early school days, one learned not to read it by its letters: a daily brush with the Hebrew transcendental. Not surprisingly, however, it also fed a magical occult.

Could the holy tongue itself be profaned? As it ceased to be a language of everyday life, did its mundane use become taboo? Could one use it in places like the privy or bathhouse, where quoting the Torah was impermissible? The Talmud is quite clear: one of the Sages was heard in the bathhouse calling in Hebrew, *haviu neter, haviu masrek!* (bring the soap, bring a comb!), proving that the holy tongue could be used for such purposes. But in later times, debate would ensue as to whether even workaday Hebrew embodied some intrinsic sanctity.

By what means, then, was this massive body of written texts and oral traditions to be understood? Translations were an obvious aid, and the Sages indeed authorized Aramaic and Greek renderings of the Bible. Rabbi Ami of Tiberias (third century CE) declared it a duty to "review the entire weekly Torah portion in tandem with the community, twice in Hebrew and once in an approved Aramaic translation" (Babylonian Talmud, Berachot 8a), and this opinion was enshrined in practice. Some rabbis accorded these translations (known as *targumim*) virtually the same authority as the Oral Law itself. Two *targumim*, traditionally known as Onkelos and Yonatan, would figure prominently in Torah study in the Diaspora.

Another technique, which seems quite modern, was to teach the Bible in the Bible's own language. A midrashic interpretation of a verse in Deuteronomy appeals to parents to speak in Hebrew to their children when teaching them Torah:

> "And you shall teach them to your children to speak about them":
> When a child begins to talk, his father should speak with him in
> the holy tongue and teach him Torah.

We do not know how widespread this practice actually was.

However, none of this could guarantee that every verse of the Bible would receive a plain-sense interpretation. Many words and constructions had become obsolete. Many others lent themselves to multiple construals. And these problems grew only worse with the passage of time. In later centuries, as Jews moved from country to country in Europe and elsewhere and traded one vernacular for another, the old translations lost their value, leading to efforts to make new ones or to supplement older commentaries with more up-to-date ones. Translating the semantic and syntactic nuances of Hebrew was never easy. Producing European-language glosses for Middle Eastern plant life or forbidden bird species would prove to be all but impossible.

Midrash: Transcending the Plain Sense

The Rabbis saw far more meaning in the Bible than the plain sense; in fact, they saw multiple layers of meaning. Probing the subtlest nuances of biblical language and its frequent incongruities, they might take a word superliterally—or they might hear phonetic echoes of other words or look for hints and clues elsewhere within the immediate context, or through comparison with messages elsewhere in Tanakh, or by applying established rules of logic and inference. Still other layers of meaning were unpacked with the help of cryptographic techniques outside the normal realm of language, some of which we visited in the previous chapter: numerology (*gematria*), counting letters, ciphers like the *atbash* system, and interpreting a word as an acrostic of other words.

The general term for these rabbinic interpretations of the Bible is midrash. The Talmud itself is full of examples, and the Rabbis produced several complete collections starting in the fifth century and down to the tenth. To most Jews today, the most familiar piece of midrash is perhaps the "Four Sons" of the Passover Haggadah, which mixes and matches biblical versions of the commandment to tell your children about the Exodus in order to create four paradigmatic types of son, each of whom asks (or doesn't ask) about the Exodus in his own way and receives an appropriate response.

Midrash can be rather mystifying to modern readers and is best illustrated with examples. Here is a midrashic exegesis of the fourth commandment, concerning rest on the Sabbath:

Six days shalt thou labor and do **all thy work** (Exodus 20:9):

But can one do *all* one's work in six days? Rather, it means: "Desist from work [on the Sabbath] *as if* all your work were done." An alternative interpretation: "Don't even *think* about work." (Mekhilta)

Here the Rabbis saw the word *all* as unnecessary, but refused to accept it as idiomatic or stylistic—or accidental. Rather, they saw it as hinting at some additional lesson about the meaning of the Sabbath.

And there was legal midrash, applying inferences on a huge scale so that the brief biblical text could support a functional legal system. For example:

"If a man opens a pit or digs a pit and does not cover it, and an ox or donkey falls into it" (Exodus 21:33)

"And does not cover it": if he does not cover it adequately. (Mekhilta)

As "and does not cover it" is self-evident (how else would the ox fall in!), the Rabbis inferred that there is no liability if the pit is *adequately* covered—the man need not fill it in before leaving it. Alternatively, they added, it must be guarded by a *paid* guard.

Often, the Rabbis added strokes, or even whole episodes, to biblical narratives. Take, for instance, their comments on the verse "And [Pharaoh] harnessed his chariot" (Exodus 14:6):

Single-handedly! Normally, others bring the gear and harness the king's chariot, but the villainous Pharaoh did it himself; and seeing this, his nobles all harnessed their own chariots single-handedly. (Mekhilta)

A reader interested in the plain sense would assume that "he harnessed his chariot" was shorthand for "he ordered his men to harness his chariot." The Rabbis, however, basing their exegesis on a superliteral reading, draw a moral lesson: even the evil have something to teach the virtuous—in this case, single-mindedness, for few are as single-minded as the evil genius.

One axiom (Mishnah Avot 5:26) sums it up: "Turn it and turn it, for everything is in it"—wisdom, worldly knowledge, present woes, things to come. Nary a passage exists where the Rabbis fail to seize upon some subtlety of language or context as an exegetical opportunity, or opportunities. Take the figure of Noah: a saint—or something less? The text states: "Noah was a righteous man in his generations" (Genesis 6:9), which seems unequivocal enough. The midrash thinks otherwise:

> What is the sense of "in his generations"? Some read it as a compliment and some as a critique. Surely it was a critique: he was "righteous in his generations," but he would not have been considered righteous had he lived in more righteous times. Like a coin of silver amid 100 coins of copper: won't the silver coin seem splendid? (Midrash Rabba)

Then this midrash slides, without interruption, into a dissenting opinion:

> Surely it was a compliment: like a girl who, placed in the "bad girls" slave market, preserves her virtue; if placed in the "good girls" slave market, would she not be even more virtuous?

To what extent are people a product of their times? To what extent do perceptions matter morally? Midrash shoots from every angle.

In some ways, the midrashic mode of understanding the Bible can be seen as having its roots in the Bible itself, with its infinitely intriguing wordplay and names heavy with significance. In the holy tongue, it seems, there had always been more than met the eye. But as a body of literature, midrash was a specifically rabbinic project. Zest and playfulness leap off the page; indeed, much midrash was performed aloud by Aramaic-speaking synagogue preachers and then written down in Hebrew or, in later times, Aramaic.

But whatever its historical provenance may have been, midrash was to exercise a lasting effect on the way Jews see Hebrew, and language in general. It enriched the interpretation of Hebrew (even dry, legal Hebrew) for centuries to come. Every word, every unusual turn of phrase, seemed to promise an additional and unsuspected level of meaning. A well-known example:

> And the Egyptians worked the Israelites with rigor (be-farekh). (Exodus 1:13)

> Rabbi Eleazar says: be-farekh—with a gentle mouth (be-feh rakh)

> Rabbi Shemuel bar Nahmeni says: crushingly (bi-frikha)
>> Exodus Rabba 1, Talmud Sotah 11b

Imaginatively splitting the Hebrew word into two, Rabbi Eleazar is suggesting that the Egyptian state was able to entice more Israelites into slave labor by offering sweeteners.

One and the same word, used in two very different locations, could hint at a connection between disparate passages. When Moses was born, his home was filled with spiritual light:

> And she [Moses's mother] saw that he was good. (Exodus 2:2)

> The house filled with light. Here, it is written "And she saw that he was good (ki tov hu)" and there [Genesis 1:4] "And God saw that the light was good (ki tov)."

In later centuries, kabbalists, Hasidim, poets, and jesters would feel entitled to find connections between the most disparate-seeming passages and thereby uncover new and deeper meanings in Holy Writ.

Mishnah: A Hebrew Bricolage of Ancient Life

Midrash had its complement in the Mishnah, the prime code of rabbinic law, organized by topic, whose origins and development were discussed earlier in this chapter.

Much of the Mishnah consists of examples that drill down and define. An example from prayer: when reciting the daily prayers, one has to face Jerusalem, as Daniel did in the Bible. But what if one couldn't?

> If you are riding a donkey, you should dismount [to pray]. But if dismounting is impossible, you should turn your face [toward Jerusalem]. And if that, too, is impossible, you should focus your mind toward the Holy of Holies.

As with midrash, the underlying message is clear, if unarticulated: physical focus is desirable. Ultimately, though, mental focus is better than no focus.

Another passage, explaining which kinds of wicks may be used for illuminating the home on the Sabbath:

> What may and may not be used to kindle the lamp? One may not use cedar-bast, uncombed flax, floss-silk, willow fiber, nettle fiber, water weeds, pitch, liquid wax, cottonseed oil, defiled oil due to be burned, sheep tails, or tallow.

This passage, abstruse though it may sound, is actually a simple slice of life—a mirror to the FAQs that rabbis had to keep in their heads. It is also familiar in Hebrew to many Jews today because of its inclusion in the traditional Sabbath evening service. But its abstruseness to us highlights the Mishnah's contribution to the preservation of the Hebrew language. By recording these and thousands of other words for everyday items and practices, religious and legal terminology, and figures of speech, the Mishnah created a rich lexical heritage that could be passed on to future generations and that Hebrew poetry and prose would draw upon long after Hebrew had ceased to be a spoken language.

The Mishnah's style also deserves consideration. Its simplicity and economy would be emulated by generations of rabbinic authors. And despite its generally prosaic content, its language possesses a sort of poetic rhythm—a boon for memorization.

As long as Hebrew was spoken, however sparsely, the Sages kept the Oral Torah going entirely in that language. It is not a coincidence that Judah the Patriarch, remembered as one of the last committed Hebrew speakers, was the man responsible for compiling the Mishnah, the definitive work of postbiblical Hebrew.

Prayer: Fixed or Spontaneous?

The third great genre organized by the Rabbis and their precursors was prayer, both private and public. Many prayers simply existed as concepts or outlines; the individual would choose his own words (and language) to fit a fixed template. Certain prayers—like the *Amidah*, which forms the heart of the service, and specific benedictions—were set pieces, but to be memorized if possible. Those who had not memorized them would instead listen to the prayer leader and respond "amen." Although by the late first century few Jews could understand the Hebrew word for word, almost all of the standardized prayers were in Hebrew.

Why Hebrew? The Mishnah, after all, stressed sincerity and spontaneity of worship; after the demise of the Temple and its hereditary priesthood, might not local communities have wished to empower themselves to worship in the Aramaic or Greek vernacular? (A few in fact did so.) Furthermore, aside from fixed prayers, ordinary people were taught the importance of speaking to God whenever they needed to, unrehearsed, in their own words. Indeed, some eighty religious poems are known in the local Aramaic, perhaps of the fourth–fifth centuries, many of them laments and eulogies to be chanted by women. Nevertheless, it seems that Hebrew prayer gradually became the norm. The use of Aramaic for private prayer attracted some fierce condemnation in the Talmud. And perhaps people wanted to preserve an echo of the Hebrew prayers offered in the now-destroyed Temple. Perhaps they felt the pull of the holy language and biblical traditions, and the echoes of how David and Moses addressed God. In public worship (and even in private), there is much more to feeling than spontaneity. And even if they couldn't always follow all the Hebrew, they probably understood the gist, particularly if they spoke Aramaic.

Perhaps the most remarkable yet most familiar of these Hebrew forms of prayer were *berakhot* (blessings). An example, said before eating bread (in deference to Jewish practice, I have hyphenated the Hebrew name of God):

Barukh atah Ado-nay elo-heynu melekh ha'olam, hamotsi lehem min ha'arets.

Blessed are You, Lord, our God, king of the universe, who brings forth bread from the ground.

Ten words in the Hebrew, symbolically paralleling the ten ordinances governing production of bread (such as tithes and gleaning). But these simple words also affirm that bread ultimately depends not on technology but on God "producing bread from the ground."

Another, very different example:

Barukh atah Ado-nay elo-heynu melekh ha'olam, meshaneh habriyot.

Blessed are You, Lord, our God, king of the universe, who diversified His creatures.

This benediction was incumbent on anyone seeing an unusual-looking person or animal. Rather than pointing and taunting, one is to thank and praise God for the variety of His world.

Blessing-prayers also offered a way to address a transcendent and incorporeal God not as "Master" or "His Holiness," but, remarkably, as *atah* (You)—as if He were a family member or friend. Many benedictions begin with these same words, modulating between second and third person, a mark of the intimacy, alternating with awe, with which God is approached in the Bible itself. Centuries later, this usage of *atah* would be the point of departure for Martin Buber's theological treatise *I and Thou*.

The individual was also granted a limited taste of Hebrew's deeper powers. Psalms and other biblical passages, which of course could be found in writing, were also included in the liturgy. The Talmud promises the afterlife to all who recite Psalm 145 (popularly known as *Ashrei*) three times a day. Each verse begins with a successive letter of the Hebrew alphabet, as if to emphasize the connection between prayer and literacy.

Although mantric praise of God was discouraged in the Talmud ("Are your praises of your Maker complete?" a rabbi asked with heavy sarcasm), a few hymns built mantra-like around the Hebrew alphabet have been incorporated into common Jewish worship and home rituals, though few who sing them are conscious of the fact. One of them is the familiar Passover hymn *Adir Hu*, which in part may well originate in mystical texts that Meir Bar-Ilan dates to the fourth or fifth century. Such texts describe the mystical ascents by sages and prophets through *heykhalot* (palaces) to the divine throne, often amid angelic hymns praising God's attributes in alphabetic acrostics:

melekh ahuv hu, melekh barukh hu, melekh ge'eh hu, melekh dagul hu . . .

A beloved king is He; a blessed king is He; a proud king is He; a supreme king is He . . .

The effect would be something like:

An adored king is He; a blessed king is He; a cosmic king is He; a dominant King is He . . .

Some texts went even further. *Shiur Qomah*, believed to have evolved in early rabbinic times, uses meaningless (and un-Hebrew-sounding) letter combinations in place of recognizable words in order to emphasize that God transcends language—that "He is far, far above all blessings or hymns," as the Kaddish prayer puts it.

Adding spice (and mystique) to the Hebrew flavor of the prayers, fourth- and fifth-century synagogues began to insert original liturgical poems (*piyyutim*, from the Greek word for poem) rather than sequences of biblical verses. Eager to find new means of bringing Torah teachings to the masses, poet-scholars known as *paytanim* would recast biblical and midrashic narratives into poetry for the cantor to chant in the synagogue while the congregants followed from scrolls. As the service was much more fluid in those days, particularly in the land of Israel, synagogues would "commission" poetic variations on a theme, frequently intended for holidays or special Sabbaths, and it was often up to the cantor to select which he would use; some cantors also wrote their own.

We know several *paytanim* by name—among them, Yannai, Yose ben Yose, Eleazar Kallir (or Killir), Saadiah—but few as persons. They were prolific; Yannai composed some two thousand piyyutim. Many are still in common use today, including parts of the *Kedushah* (originally an elaboration on each paragraph of the Amidah), *Nishmat, Yismah moshe, Tikanta shabbat,* and, in the High Holy Day liturgy, *U-netaneh tokef* and *Seder Avodah;* indeed, they are a defining feature of Jewish prayer.

Initially, theme and form were simple—typically, unrhymed lines of four pairs of words, with mantra-like repetitions accentuating subtle variations, often running the gamut of the alphabet. Gradually, the poets were tempted to produce extravagant flights of verbal fancy, building new words from old in ways even native speakers would have been unlikely to attempt. Sixth- and seventh-century *piyyutim* were made up almost entirely of erudite allusions to midrashic learning and biblical phrases, teeming with obscure or invented words and constructions, and rhymes and acrostics galore—and congregations evidently loved them. The artistic effect, Yosef Yahalom has observed,[2] was quintessentially detail oriented, evoking the two-dimensional "jeweled style" of contemporary Byzantine imagery and the "structured repetition" so prized by medieval rhetoric.

Could the average worshipper fathom it all? Probably not. (Most modern Israelis can't, either.) Nonetheless, as spoken Hebrew became a thing of the distant past, Jews accepted that the prayers would be recited for feeling rather than sense, and developed a zest for the chanted sound. *Paytanim* continued to ply their art in medieval Italy, Germany, and Byzantium. Ashkenazi holiday and fast-day services are still replete with arcane *piyyutim*, which were even more abundant a century ago. No one today would dream of writing religious poetry in this abstruse mode, but hearing it recited gives many worshippers pure pleasure. They would hardly agree with the put-down by Mendele, father of modern Hebrew satirical prose: "This is the only sort of language Jews like, the sort the mind can't stomach. They don't understand it, so it must be deep" (*Sefer HaKabtzanim*).

What inspired the virtuoso *paytanim*? For some, as in the case of some modernist poets, it may have been variation and enigma for its own sake (in which Byzantine poets also indulged). But they were also motivated by a pride in the Hebrew language that bordered on infatuation, and were resolved to display its full potential. The Bible, for the *paytanim*, was just a sacred snapshot of what Hebrew could generate. So if the book of Jonah had a verb *nirdam* (to slumber) and Psalms a noun like *kedem* (front), a *paytan* could create a new noun, *redem* (slumber), combining the putative three-consonant root of the first with the vowels of the second. And since occasionally a feminine word like *shirah* (song or poem) had a masculine counterpart like *shir* (song or poetry), they felt free to invent masculine counterparts for any feminine noun when it suited their metrical purposes or rhyme schemes: for instance, *shoshan* for *shoshanah* (rose).

Expanding the Hebrew lexicon was an act of creativity in itself. After all, if the sages of the Mishnah had felt free to use Hebrew roots never seen in scripture, why shouldn't poets take a word like *ahalay* (if only) or *basis* (base) and conjure up verbs like *ihel* (to wish) and *bises* (to establish) with roots never seen before? This was a golden age; never again, as Aharon Mirsky has observed,[3] would Hebrew poets command such riches.

A New Hebrew Hybrid: The Talmud

In the centuries after that encounter of Rabbi Judah's students with his maid, Hebrew was in some senses dead but in others very much alive. The academies of Torah that dotted Judea, the Galilee, and Babylonia buzzed bilingually with two vast new projects. One was the Talmud, an interpretation of the Mishnah with an eye on a consensus of practice (*halakhah*); the other was the Aggadah, a new, narrative-oriented type of midrashic interpretation of the Bible. The first project produced the Jerusalem and Babylonian Talmuds (completed in the late fourth and late sixth centuries, respectively); the second yielded Midrash Rabba and similar works (dating from the fifth century to the ninth).

Studying these texts is like consuming a linguistic layer cake. In the oldest layers of the Talmud, a rabbi can be found musing philosophically or stating a legal dictum in the Hebrew of the Mishnah—and not just using stock phrases and legal jargon but employing a language bubbling with verbal creativity. At the same time, one also encounters the Aramaic vernacular, usually in cases where the Rabbis are engaged in more involved analysis or when the editors enliven things with an anecdote. Later rabbis will be described (in Aramaic) quoting earlier rabbis' opinions in Hebrew. And then there are the upper layers, in which later talmudic scholars add their own opinions in a vernacular variety of Aramaic seasoned with stock Hebrew phrases. As for the topping—critique and comment by the editors of the Talmud—that is pure Aramaic.

It was this split-function ("diglossic") Hebrew-Aramaic hybrid that centuries of students and rabbis would imbibe and follow in their own writings. And though it combined two languages, it was regarded as one linguistic package: a special form of *leshon ha-kodesh* (the Holy Tongue). The proportion of Hebrew or Aramaic might vary, but who was counting? This would become *the* language of talmudic and halakhic discourse up to and including modern times.

From Jerusalem to Diaspora

So far, we have trained our focus on the land of Israel. But by 600 CE, the spiritual center of gravity had moved to the East and West—to the Roman, the Byzantine, and especially the Babylonian Diasporas. It was the Babylonian Talmud that would reign supreme. And the Arab invasions would eventually spread Arabic across the Middle East, displacing Hebrew's sister and surrogate, Aramaic. It would all distance the Jewish people still further from their Hebrew roots.

But, as occurs so often in Jewish history, there would also be pushback—this time in the form of the Masoretes, small teams of scholars in the Galilee and Babylon dedicated to preserving the text of the Tanakh. Between the sixth and ninth centuries, as we will see in the next chapter, they succeeded in the vast task of standardizing its reading and spelling. And then, in the ninth century, we will meet a controversial new Jewish sect, the Karaites. Virtually forgotten today, the Karaites fashioned yet another new approach to the Tanakh and a new dawn for Hebrew literary and linguistic achievement.

3

Saving the Bible and Its Hebrew

Introduction

The millennium stretching, rather neatly, from the seventh to the seventeenth century saw the emergence of a rich diasporic Hebrew identity and culture—concentrated in three or four centers, but still tied to the land of Israel. It was an extraordinarily varied culture: sacred and mundane, artistic and scientific, oriented both to the past and to heady new ventures.

In the preceding chapter we watched the Hebrew culture of late antiquity unfold along two broad lines, quite separate but seemingly complementary. In one direction lay the Hebrew of the Bible, a great textual heritage frozen in time, though open to widely different understandings. In the other lay the Hebrew of the rabbis and *paytanim* (liturgical poets), an ever-growing body of literature evolving a religious aesthetic that was dynamic, unpredictable, linguistically and imaginatively creative, and above all religiously erudite—what might be called a rabbinic aesthetic.

However, between the years 800 and 1000, this comfortable cultural system began to come apart. Babylonia, gradually ceasing to be the center of Diaspora culture and rabbinic learning, was overtaken and eventually displaced by European and North African Jewish communities. It was during this time that the cores of what would later become Sephardi and Ashkenazi Jewry emerged, although there were still many other major groupings as well.

This chapter discusses the period 600–900—between the closing of the Talmud and the efflorescence of talmudic scholarship in Europe. It is traditionally known to European historians as the Dark Ages. (Jewish historians use the obscure title "the geonic period.") But, for Jews, there was nothing dark about this era; and so, in order to emphasize the continuity with what would come next, we shall use the term "early medieval."

While the big story of the talmudic period involved the preservation of the oral Torah, the big story of the early medieval period involved the preservation of the written Torah. This era also saw the Arab conquest of the Middle East, which exposed Jews to a host of new ideas that would have a lasting effect on Hebrew.

The Masorah: Preserving the Biblical Sound

What it took to teach or study Hebrew's holy writings in the year 700 is hard to comprehend today. Biblical texts, copied by scribes, were strings of consonants, with the letters *yod* (*y*) and *vav* (*w*) sometimes unpredictably marking the vowels *i*, *o*, and *u*. Certain consonants could be pronounced more than one way, depending on the grammatical form of a word; thus, for instance, the letter *bet* could sound either like our letter *b* or like our *v*. Phrasing, too, was a challenge: no system existed for punctuation, nor did Hebrew possess uppercase characters to mark the beginning of a new sentence. At best, a single dot might act as a comma or period in non-biblical texts. A child would have to memorize how to pronounce the words, and master a chant for breaking them into phrases and sentences. This might not have been so difficult when Hebrew was the Jews' mother tongue, but it was much harder when that was no longer the case. Chanting was of the essence, as the Talmud provocatively put it:

> If you recite Scripture without melody and Mishnah without song, this verse applies to you: "And I [God] have given them laws that are bad and statutes by which they shall not live." (Ezekiel 20:25)

Chanting, in turn, is also doubtless a powerful aide-mémoire. Gradually, as you were taught the sense of what you were reading, you could begin to anticipate how to pronounce the words and how to divide them. You would also memorize a chanted translation in Aramaic. Working together, a team of instructors would have memorized the pronunciation and chanting of four thousand verses of the Torah plus more than ten times that number of verses for the rest of the Bible.

The other major items in a young man's curriculum, Midrash and Talmud, would often be studied by heart with a professional reciter (a human memory bank) and a teacher. This was an "essentially oral world," in Yaakov Elman's phrase.[1] Whereas the Bible was read from a written text, here you would need to memorize wording as well as pronunciation, phrasing, and meaning. Dots and dashes (*nikkud*) representing vowels and other fine points of pronunciation had not yet been invented.

Did mastering this system require prodigious minds? Or did it actually produce them? The latter, probably. The same is no doubt true of the seven thousand to eight thousand characters learned by Chinese students today.

All the while, however, a chain of events was unfolding that threatened this entire system of perpetuating Judaism's sacred texts. Following the Arab conquests of the Middle East that began around the year 630, Arabic of some sort rapidly eclipsed Aramaic, becoming within a century the prestige language across most of the region and by 900 its main Jewish colloquial. While Hebrew, Aramaic, and Arabic all belong to the western branch of the Semitic language family, Hebrew has much more in common with Aramaic—especially the Aramaic dialect spoken by Jews—than it does with Arabic. Furthermore, Hebrew and Aramaic shared an alphabet, while Arabic had its own. Soon Hebrew was as foreign to an Arabic-speaking Jewish schoolboy as German is to English speakers. Even skilled cantors were having problems with the intricate poems they had to recite in the synagogue. No doubt adding to the confusion were the period's Jewish migrations and social change.

The guardians of Hebrew's textual memory felt impelled to act. And so a historic project was launched: to commit to writing every detail necessary to preserve the biblical text—an immense combination of fieldwork, textual evaluation, and linguistic analysis. It was called the *masorah*, or "transmission." For some three centuries, teams of scholars, known as the *baaley masorah* or Masoretes, based in Tiberias, Jerusalem, and Babylonia, worked with the best available manuscripts and professional chanters to create an authoritative biblical spelling, pronunciation, phrasing, and chanting. The task required them to devise notational systems to capture it all, while analyzing patterns for predicting stress placement, inflections, and the vagaries of Hebrew pronunciation.

And they didn't stop there: they counted the verses, words, and letters of every book of the Bible and the patterns of occurrence of any noteworthy word or feature (of which there were thousands). Talmudic texts were also attended to. This wealth of data created a fail-safe against copying errors. The Masoretic Bibles, in addition to including the diacritics and cantillation marks, annotated each biblical verse with "Masoretic notes": alerts of various kinds as well as

FIGURE 5. Job 37–38 with the old Babylonian-Jewish pronunciation marks (nikkud), as preserved in a 9th–10th century text from the Cairo Genizah.

linguistic and spelling statistics. Open a scholarly Bible and you will see them in arcane mouseprint, a rambling database to guard against the text ever being corrupted. Few readers (other than scribes, printers, or grammarians) ever notice these Masoretic notes, but they are the joists and foundations upon which the entire edifice of the Hebrew Bible has endured—although, as we will soon see, not without some cracks.

Just standardizing the pronunciation and chant was a tall order; there were many reading and chanting traditions, and hosts of variations in pronouncing individual words. To devise an orthographic system that preserved the original spellings was another challenge. (Imagine devising a system to capture the vowels in *courage* and *courageous* if you had never seen the two words in writing. Or the different tones for saying the word "so.") How should one encode just enough phonetic or musical detail but not too much? How should pronunciation *and* chanting marks be fitted legibly into the letters? Partially marked-up Bible passages discovered in the famed Cairo Genizah, the medieval repository for discarded texts in a Cairo synagogue, have offered glimpses of how the system evolved. It took generations of trial and error.

By the year 1000, the groundwork was fully established. At least four rival systems of diacritical marks had been developed for pronunciation and two for the chant. All but one soon vanished (not to resurface until the nineteenth or twentieth century). The deserving winner was the so-called Tiberian system, with its dots and dashes (*nikkud*) for pronunciation and its cantillation neumes (*taamey neginah*) simultaneously marking chant, phrasing, and accentuation. These markings appear above or below the letters, thus preserving the integrity of the original text. Perfected by the Ben-Asher dynasty of Masoretes in Tiberias, it elegantly and ingeniously conveyed the reading tradition they considered the most authentic. Although the pronunciation in biblical times remains a mystery, most modern scholars consider the Tiberian Masoretic text a remarkable preservation of how the Hebrew Bible was pronounced in synagogues in the first or second century of the Common Era.

The Masoretes rightly occupy a special place in Jewish history. They preserved both the living sound and shape of biblical Hebrew

FIGURE 6. From Deuteronomy 28 in the Aleppo Codex, the authoritative Jewish Bible text, ca. 930 CE, Tiberias.

and the biblical text itself as canonized by the Rabbis two thousand years ago. Thus they ensured that Jews across the Diaspora would study from (more or less) identical copies.

The Sequel: Corruptions and Derring-Do

Majestic copies of the Masoretic Bible were sent on their perilous way to communities in Spain, Germany, Persia, and elsewhere in the Diaspora. Few from that first precious crop have survived, either whole or in part. The oldest intact copy, now in the National Library of Russia, is the Leningrad Codex (ca. 1008), upon which many modern scholarly editions of the Bible are based.

But another copy of the Bible, much older, achieved greater fame—and misfortune. This is the so-called Aleppo Codex. It was produced around 930 in Tiberias with diacritics, cantillation symbols, and full Masoretic notes in the hand of Aharon ben Asher himself, supreme Masoretic authority—"lord of scribes and father of sages," as a later dedication hails him. Transferred to Jerusalem, the codex was pillaged by the Crusaders and ransomed to Egypt; and there, in the twelfth century, its fame began. The revered scholar Moses Maimonides (1135–1204), perturbed by the rampant disparities among Torah scribes in making section breaks, recognized the codex as the handiwork of Aharon ben Asher and adopted it as the basis for the Torah scroll he himself was writing. His version soon gained universal acceptance.

Alas, not all scribes are perfectionists. The Masoretic notes were widely compromised, and today few Torah scrolls or printed Hebrew Bibles accurately reflect the spelling, vocalization, and chanting notations in Ben Asher's master Bible. Indeed, a recent study of one hundred complete medieval Hebrew Bibles found that just fifteen, almost all of them by Sephardi or Oriental copyists, were consistent with more than 75 percent of the Masoretic notes, and only one, the Aleppo Codex (more below), was 99 percent consistent.

Did it matter, in the long run, whether Torah scrolls and Bibles were perfectly identical and accurate? From a religious perspective, apparently not. Notwithstanding the strict requirements of halakhah (Jewish religious law) that every letter of a Torah scroll be legible and intact, rabbinic consensus accepted the creeping inaccuracy of the text as long as it did not interfere with plain meaning or halakhic interpretation. The discrepancies that copyists had created—a vowel letter here, a chant mark there—fell beneath the semantic radar.

One such discrepancy, for instance, was the spelling of the word *mezuzot* (doorposts) in Deuteronomy 6, where the Torah text used by the medieval commentator Rashi seems to have lacked a letter *vav* (used as a vowel) that is present in today's editions and scrolls. A rough parallel would be occasionally spelling *labor* as *labour*—a proofreader would make sure it was spelled consistently but perhaps no more than that. However, other misspellings (say, *two* for *too*) could change the meaning of a sentence and therefore could not be tolerated. For much the same reason, those today who chant the Torah in synagogues have generally been allowed to sing a wrong note (or more than one wrong note)—except where doing so would subvert the syntax. Both rabbinic and popular Jewish sentiment has focused on preserving the *meaning* of the sacred texts, not their precise lettering or sound per se.

A bittersweet fate befell the great Aleppo Codex itself. Brought for safety by Maimonides's great-great-grandson from Cairo to Aleppo, Syria, it was placed under lock and key by the local Jewish community for over five hundred years. Few knew it existed. It was the non-Jewish printer Daniel Bomberg's great *Rabbinic Bible* (Venice, 1524/25) that became the model for all Jewish printed Bibles since then, even though it only loosely matched the *masorah*.

When, finally, the Aleppo Codex was spirited out of Syria to Turkey in 1957, by a Jewish cheese merchant who hid it in a washing machine, some two hundred of its five hundred pages—almost the entire Five Books of Moses—went missing, probably to be sold on the black market. They are still unaccounted for. Tragically, no facsimile copy had ever been made. What remains of the Aleppo Codex is today held by the Ben Zvi Institute in Jerusalem, and only recently has this Bible of Bibles become the basis for a popular printed edition.

The Experts Say One Thing, the Public Does Another

Whatever its use as a channel of communication, medieval Hebrew carried a strong symbolic charge. Languages often do, literary languages even more so. Hebrew could evoke times past and shared values. But equally, as we will see, it embodied differences, changes, creativity. One might speak of two poles in constant flux and tension. The Masoretic system of diacritical marks—developed to standardize and conserve—paradoxically also helped foster longstanding divisions. So did two other early medieval developments to which we will soon turn: the new technology of the Hebrew book itself and the first prayer books (*siddurim*).

The Masoretes' labors yielded a valuable by-product: a sense of Jewish unity. For a Diaspora now evolving new cultural identities, an authoritative biblical text plus a simple key to reciting it offered a hope that the Jewish exiles would adhere to their heritage and soon be ingathered to the land of their fathers. However, Jewish communities also celebrated their individuality. Local custom had long been a tenacious force in Jewish practice. Hebrew scripts varied. Communal pronunciations and chanting styles were also tenacious. Pedigree played a part: Spanish, Italian, and Yemenite Jewry claimed to originate with very ancient Jewish exiles. In fact, regional Hebrew accents had existed in earlier times, as both the Bible and the Talmud attest. How much more so now, when Hebrew existed in tandem with so many vernaculars.

We have a broad idea about some of the major medieval Hebrew "reading pronunciations." Here are three:

(1) Where: Apparently brought from the land of Israel to early medieval Spain and Italy, and thence to France and Germany; ancestor of the dominant Israeli vowel system today.

What: five full vowels: *i, e, a, o, u.*

(2) Where: Apparently in use in Babylonia, from where it made its way to Yemen.

What: five full vowels: *i, ey, a, o, u*—with *a* where Israelis say *e* and point it with a *segol*, but *ey* where Israelis say *e* and point it with a *tzeyre*, thus *kalav* for "dog" and *seyfar* for "book."

(3) Where: Apparently cultivated in the city of Tiberias (northern Israel); adopted somehow in late medieval Ashkenaz; used until recently by most American and British Ashkenazim.

What: seven full vowels: roughly *i, ey, e, a, o, oh,* and *u,* thus *yisro'eyl* "Israel."

There were many other differences, almost certainly far more than the many of which we are aware (see table 3.1). For instance, the Jews of the early medieval Rhineland said a raspy *ḥ* (thus *ḥayyim* "life") for the letter *ḥet,* while the Jews of Bavaria and Austria said *h,* thus *hayyim,* and the two were known, respectively, as the *Bnei Ḥes* and the *Bnei Hes* "the people of Heth" (with a wink to the biblical Hittites in Genesis 23:3). In Yemen and Baghdad, until recently, the letter *daled* at the end of a word was pronounced not "d" but "th" (as in "clothe").

TABLE 3.1. A few words in selected medieval Hebrew pronunciations (approximation)

Spanish	ya'akov	moshe	david
Italians	Yañkov	moshe	david
Some Yemenites	ya'akev	mesha	dowith
Some German Ashkenazim	yaakauv	maushe	dovid

In fact, pronunciations often varied between formal recitation and, say, quoting a phrase in a study-hall discussion. Personal names had their own vagaries, thus Yankev, Yankevitch preserving something of the old throaty letter *ayin* of Yaakov; so too the Hebrew words embedded galore in the Jewish vernaculars, thus Yiddish *yontef* (holiday) as against *yom tov* in Hebrew proper.

The Masoretes never reached a consensus about which pronunciation was best and which diacritic system (*nikkud*) was best suited to transcribe it. Instead, as noted earlier, they produced at least four systems of *nikkud*, of which only two, the Tiberian and the Babylonian, caught on initially. The Babylonian *nikkud* eventually joined the others in well-deserved oblivion. But this is where Jewish diversity or perhaps social realities intervened, in ways that often defy simple explanation. For example, the Jews of Spain and the western Mediterranean—possessors of that simple five-vowel *pronunciation* system—adopted the seven-vowel Tiberian system of *nikkud*, a total mismatch; for instance, they pronounced both the *patah* (meaning "open") and the *kamatz* (meaning "closed") vowel symbols as *a*. Perhaps the prestige of the Tiberian scholars sold them on it. Meanwhile, the Yemenites, who have preserved their own complicated vowel pronunciation, went in the opposite direction by adopting the five-vowel Babylonian *nikkud* to transcribe it in the Middle Ages. And how did the Ashkenazim, who in the early Middle Ages seem to have pronounced just five vowels, end up with the seven-vowel pronunciation that Orthodox traditionalists still maintain today? Another mystery.

Where a language is passed down in the normal way, one expects "popular" practice to have a strong diversifying pull. But Hebrew was different: it was a learned language, passed down from teacher to pupil. And yet here too, popular practice put a big spoke in the Masoretic wheel.

More Standardization or Less? The Book and the Prayer Book

The eighth and ninth centuries brought a technological revolution: the introduction of the book. The rewards for literary cultures were immense. In place of unwieldy scrolls, a copyist could now write a book—or, strictly speaking, a codex (a handwritten book). Soon thereafter came vellum codices, then paper ones. Hebrew codices duly multiplied. The rich amassed large libraries. Jewish knowledge in particular stood to gain as the vast oral Torah—Talmud, Midrash, liturgy, and their commentaries in Hebrew and Aramaic—was increasingly being committed to writing.

But the old oral system did not simply collapse: as in Islamic and Christian academies, memorization continued to vie with written texts in the large rabbinic academies of Babylonia, North Africa, and the Rhineland that were responsible for perpetuating the Talmud and Midrash. Early medieval religious scholarship, as well as popular religion, rested on memorization—part of a "fundamentally memorial" culture, as Mary Carruthers has put it.[2] Hebrew, then, though not a spoken language in the usual sense, was constantly on the tongues of Jewish scholars and students in the early Middle Ages. It was also a language not just of reading but of writing, used to express new thoughts and ideas.

Memory, of course, has its limits, and the wording of the Talmud and Midrash was treated somewhat fluidly and not subjected to word counts, linguistic analysis, or the other controls that Masoretes applied to the Bible. But now, with books becoming common, some no doubt worried about a deleterious effect on the art of memorization. And memorization indeed began to retreat, even from where it was most hallowed and necessary, namely, in worship. Increasingly, then, the major prayers, which Jews had hitherto memorized and often improvised, were written down and circulated in synagogues. Soon it was the turn of the entire Hebrew liturgy to be codified—the Siddur (order [of prayers]), as it came to be known.

The first *siddurim* (prayer books) were compiled in the ninth or tenth century by Babylonia's *geonim*, leading rabbinic scholars who at the time served as rabbinic authorities for the entire Diaspora. Most notable were the scholar-poets Amram ben Sheshna (d. 875) and Saadiah (882–942). Their stated goal was to ensure rabbinically approved prayer in the synagogue and to respond to appeals for liturgical guidance that they had been receiving from as far afield as Spain and southern Arabia. No doubt they had other motives, too. Codifying the prayers would contribute to the authority of the *geonim* and help stem the inroads being made by a radical, antirabbinic religious movement, Karaism, of which more in the next chapter.

The new prayer books spread rapidly across the Diaspora, and their legacy is reflected to this day in every Jewish prayer book, Hebrew or translated. In the tenth century, their impact on knowledge of Hebrew was dramatic. To be able to read the standard prayers, and to do so in Hebrew, was now widely considered a duty for every man and boy, and in some locales for women and girls as well, whether or not they understood what the Hebrew meant. But there was also a downside: a stifling of the creativity of the synagogue service.

And yet, the prayer book, like so many things rabbis have tried to regulate, would evolve defiantly local variations. Distinctive regional liturgies always existed, of which today's Ashkenazi, Sephardi, and Mizrahi liturgies are the chief heirs. And while there was never a linguistically regional flavor to their wording, they were particularly resilient, resisting constant attempts at correction by well-meaning scholars who were often unlearned in the rabbinic style in which the prayers were written and of which vestiges survive today. For a thousand years, until well into the nineteenth century, the *siddur* was the average Jew's main Hebrew menu, and a varied one: a feast of rabbinic prose, biblical poetry, talmudic passages, mystical chants, and obscure virtuoso verse (*piyyutim*).

In the next chapter, we will see how Jews living in different and distant communities sustained Hebrew as a language of intellectual creativity and put it to new and sometimes surprising uses.

4

The Sephardic Classical Age

Aesthetics and Cultural Selves

The era to be discussed here—from 900 to the fateful year 1492—includes some of the most vibrant, creative, and even anomalous moments of Jewish cultural history, moments that would provide a sophisticated momentum for Jewish life thereafter. At its heart was Sepharad, as Spain was proudly known in Hebrew.

One of the most important trends of this period was the increasing differentiation of Diaspora identity. As major Jewish cultural and demographic centers sprang up in Europe and North Africa, these communities began to develop their own distinctive customs, attitudes, and temperaments, laying the foundation for later divides among Ashkenazim, Sephardim, and Mizrahim. In the previous chapter, we touched upon this diversification in terms of how Hebrew was pronounced and spelled, but the various communities also developed their own Hebrew styles and attitudes toward the language itself.

Jews reared in the rising Arab civilization of Spain, North Africa, and the Middle East began pressing for a "purification," a renewal of a biblical Hebrew aesthetic and a reining-in of the rabbinic mode. At the same time, as we will see in the following chapter, a very different spirit held sway under Christian rule: first in Byzantine southern Italy and later in Provence, northern France, the Rhineland, and central Europe, a rabbinic Hebrew aesthetic continued to thrive. In tandem with it, a pragmatic new concept of Hebrew made itself felt in southern Italy: Hebrew as a medium of science and technology. As so often, this last development was the sum of many forces, some springing from deep within Jewish tradition and some from without.

A Hebrew Metaphysics

What ideas did medieval Jewish thinkers hold about the spirit of the Hebrew language? Did an ideology or metaphysics of Hebrew underpin its actual use? It was agreed that it was a holy tongue, but what made it holy?

Some espoused a bare-bones, rationalist approach. In his immensely influential (and controversial) philosophical work, the *Guide of the Perplexed*, Moses Maimonides (1138–1204) proposes a straightforward explanation as to why the talmudic Sages called Hebrew "the holy tongue." The reason is natural and moral rather than metaphysical: Hebrew, says Maimonides, has no literal words for things crude or erotic, only euphemisms. Most medieval Jewish rationalists followed Maimonides in regarding Hebrew's sanctity as derived from its natural functions rather than from its association with the mystical or the divine, its normality, as Menachem Kellner puts it.[1] God does not "speak," Maimonides argued, and no words or thinking can come close to expressing what He is.

But there was also broad rabbinic opposition to this approach. "May God forgive him," murmured Rabbi Yom Tov Ishbili (Spain, 1250–1330) in response to Maimonides's explanation of Hebrew's sanctity (*Sefer HaZikaron*). Rabbi Moses Naḥmanides (Spain, 1194–1270), whose scriptural exegesis combines esoteric allusions with analysis of the plain sense of the text, set out what eventually became the dominant view:

In my view, the Sages call the language of the Torah the "holy tongue" because it is the language in which the Torah, Prophets, and all of Scripture was given, the language in which the Almighty speaks with His prophets and His people . . . the language of the holy names by which we call Him . . . and He used it to create His universe. (Commentary on Exodus 30:13)

To Naḥmanides, Hebrew's sanctity came directly from God.

Hebrew was also generally considered the mother of all languages (though an opinion in the Talmud credits Aramaic with this honor) and therefore "the most perfect and fittest for self-expression," as the great philosopher-poet Judah Halevi (Spain, twelfth century) puts it in his philosophical masterpiece, the *Kuzari*. But Halevi and Naḥmanides were talking about Hebrew in its original or ideal form. And even in its later form, the logical elegance of its grammatical architecture, seemingly undisturbed by other tongues, would move the philosopher and grammarian Profiat Duran (Spain, ca. 1350–ca. 1415) to recognize Hebrew as the motherboard of all human languages: "nothing less than a universal grammar," as Josef Stern has put it.[2] True, grammar does not a language make—and Halevi spoke for many medieval Jewish writers in lamenting that Hebrew had "shared the fate of its bearers, degenerating and dwindling with them." And yet, for Duran, this same "universal" Hebrew was in turn but a reflection of the ultimate language, the biblical text itself (in modern terms, not *langue* but *parole*). And in the Bible's Hebrew text, Duran, though forced to forswear his faith, saw the magical prospect of "a renewal of Jewish consciousness, education, and culture," to echo Maud Kozodoy.[3]

The ancient esoteric speculations about Hebrew mentioned in the previous chapter continued to occupy famous figures, at times quite publicly but at times in secretive writings, some of which have

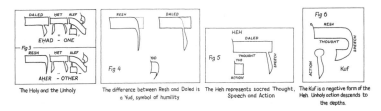

FIGURE 7. From a traditional Hasidic mystical commentary on the Hebrew letters.

still not been published. In his grammar *Sefer Tsaḥot* (1141), the astronomer-astrologer polymath Rabbi Abraham ibn Ezra sought spiritual significance in the vowels themselves, according to the Masoretic system:

> The seven major vowels match the seven great heavenly bodies: Saturn, Jupiter, Mars, the Sun, Venus, Mercury, and the Moon, which in turn match the seven words in the first verse of Genesis.

In sixteenth-century Prague, the mystical philosopher Judah Loew (known as Maharal, 1525–1609) would see a different set of meanings. To him, the same seven vowels match the seven divine "voices" that, according to the Midrash, were heard at Sinai, radiating into the world's seventy languages and filling all space: six vowels filling the six directions of three-dimensional space, the seventh (*shurek* or *kubbuts*, representing the sound *u*) occupying the center. Each also is shaped in a way that mimics how the mouth moves when it is uttered—at least when articulated with an Ashkenazi accent. Hence, said Maharal, "the Ashkenazi vowel-pronunciation alone corresponds to the [mystical] truth."

Some circles of mystics took their belief in the sanctity of the Hebrew language to even greater extremes, whether by "opening up" existing texts or by generating their own. In twelfth- and thirteenth-century Germany, a new midrashic method evolved for crafting infinitely variable interpretations of the Torah through the letters' shapes, names, numerical properties, occurrences and absences, and so forth. The divine names were subjected to unending analysis. Naḥmanides spoke of the entire Torah as consisting of hidden divine names, if the words could be suitably redivided. Mystical circles in southern Europe, where Kabbalah first emerged in its present form, created a midrashic symbolism in such works as *Shiur Qomah*, *Sefer ha-Bahir*, and the *Zohar*. Initiates imbued Jewish practices of study and prayer with mystical dimensions. Some kabbalists also believed that chanting permutations of Hebrew sounds could work miracles, or even instill prophetic power in the reciter.

Ancient Golem techniques also surfaced in the Sephardi and Ashkenazi world, inaugurating a long and varied legacy of ecstatic visualization and materialization of humanoid forms—the voice amplifying the resonance of every limb to the divine emanations through the twenty-two Hebrew letters, seeking to attain, in Moshe Idel's words, "the experience of the creative moment of God."[4] Speaking Hebrew on the Sabbath was instituted in the circle of Rabbi Isaac Luria of Safed (Egypt and Israel, sixteenth century) as an act that might hasten the Messiah. In sum, as Gershom Scholem observes, "the fact that God expressed Himself is far more important than any specific 'meaning' that might be conveyed."[5] Remarkably, this openness to the text put the mystic in the same boat as the untutored masses who could only mouth their prayers and waived the right to understand them.

Did Aramaic share any of these powers? After all, the *Zohar*, the seminal text of Kabbalah, was itself written almost entirely in Aramaic. In the world of the Kabbalah, there was indeed an intricate balance between Hebrew and Aramaic, essential to cosmic stability: Hebrew was the lofty language, suited for formal petitions to God, while Aramaic, considered a degraded, diasporic language, paradoxically provided a pathway to a more intimate communion with the *Shekhinah* (in the kabbalistic system, the "lowest" and most accessible aspect of the divine presence). For this reason perhaps, they thought, the ancient Kaddish prayer had been set in Aramaic: to proclaim God's name in a way that outdoes the power of any conventional Hebrew blessing.

And another apparent paradox: In the light of these beliefs about the power of Hebrew, one might have expected strong opposition to using it for mundane matters. But such was not the case. It was taken for granted that the holy tongue could also be a mundane tongue, for correspondence, business, and the like. Had not Hebrew, after all, once been the language of mundane life in the age of the Bible and the Second Temple?

Mirror, Mirror: Going Head-on with Arabic

Let us turn from the metaphysical to the this-worldly. We begin again in the aftermath of the Arab conquest in the seventh century. The new rulers of the Middle East and North Africa not only brought a new religious, linguistic, and political order; they also brought new ideas about language itself. Arab intellectuals adored Arabic, thrilled to its poetic meters, and boasted of its riches and rarities. The Arabs scorned the languages of their conquered peoples; for Muslims, moreover, the Arabic of the Quran was sacred.

Jewish everyday affairs and even Jewish scholarship were soon being conducted in Arabic. The religious leadership in Babylonia (the *Geonim*) began couching legal responsa and commentaries in Arabic. Judah ibn Tibbon (Provence, twelfth century), a leading Arabic-to-Hebrew translator, would retrospectively defend this decision:

It was the language that people understood, and it is an adequate
and rich language for any topic and any need—direct, lucid, and
capable of rendering your thoughts so much better than Hebrew.
(Introduction, Bahya ibn Pakuda, *Ḥovot ha-Levavot*)

Virtually every Jewish grammarian and philosopher during the
golden age of Arabic learning (roughly 800–1200) wrote in the Arabic language (albeit in Hebrew script), beginning with the towering
figure of Saadiah Gaon, whom we encountered briefly in the previous chapter as, among other things, the compiler of a standardized
prayer book. Saadiah—philosopher, linguist, poet, politician, rabbinic authority, and head of one of the great talmudic academies of
Baghdad—both harnessed and deflected the Arabization of Jewish
life, paving the way for a golden age of Hebrew arts. Under the influence of Islamic philosophy, he also laid the foundations of medieval Jewish rationalism.

Babylonia was then the seat of Arab power and culture and the
nerve center of the Jewish Diaspora. Acculturation and Islamic rationalism were in vogue. Jews, while remaining a people apart, had
discarded Aramaic for Arabic as their day-to-day language. Saadiah
was convinced that it was possible to be loyal both to rabbinic Judaism and to the demands of rationalism, and to this end he under-
took a risky linguistic venture: an elegant Arabic rendition of the
Torah, the *Tafsir*, that captured the plain meaning of the text in a
manner in keeping with Jewish tradition. At the same time, he set
aside the enigmatic and colorful midrashic interpretations, reserv-
ing them for more advanced study.

This was a bold move: religious authorities had long opposed
publishing any Arabic translation precisely because they were
afraid it might replace the rabbinically approved, deeply midrashic
Aramaic translations. But with the *Tafsir*, Saadiah managed to en-

hance the knowledge of Hebrew: native Arabic speakers could easily compare the translation with the Hebrew text, and learn new words and grammatical forms. (This could be difficult with the Aramaic versions, where no clear line distinguished the word-for-word translation from rabbinic interpolation.) Saadiah's *Tafsir* became a classic in Arabic-speaking Jewish communities, and his plain-sense (*peshat*) approach to exegesis would be adopted all around by Rashi, Maimonides, and most other medieval interpreters. It remains a standard point of Jewish access to the Torah even today.

Beyond his commitment to reason and his philosophical works on God and the soul, Saadiah's own soul stirred to the Hebrew language of the Bible, and to the contrasting linguistic poverty of his contemporaries:

> I saw that many of our own people do not even understand simple biblical Hebrew, let alone a difficult phrase. Their recitations are riddled with errors, and when they attempt a poem they barely manage the commonest of ancient words. (Introduction to *Sefer Ha-Egron*)

Saadiah was in part responding to the Karaites, a new Jewish sect that had emerged in Muslim Babylonia. Rejecting Midrash and rabbinic authority, they advocated a plain-sense, if often idiosyncratic, interpretation of the Bible. (*Karaite* may be traced to the Hebrew word *mikra*, scripture, or **kara**, scriptural reciter/expounder.) In order to make the case that their interpretations stood on firm ground, they began systematically researching the grammar of biblical Hebrew, blaming rabbinic Judaism for impoverishing it and undermining its very credibility. Midrashic interpretation, they pointed out, deviated from linguistically correct readings of the biblical text.

Saadiah (and his successors) admitted that midrash, by definition, deviated from the straightforward meaning of scripture; nevertheless, the Karaites held no monopoly on linguistic analysis, and their interpretations, too, could be far-fetched. But most of all, Saadiah was vexed by *Arabiyya*, the Arabs' religious and national pride in their own tongue. Since, according to Islam, Allah had chosen Arabic to be the language of his final and most perfect prophecy, recorded in the Quran, Arabic must be the most perfect of languages. Saadiah and other Jewish thinkers drew the obvious conclusion: since the Quran was false and the Hebrew Bible true, and since God had chosen Hebrew as the language in which to reveal the Torah to Moses, what Muslims believed about Arabic must be equally false—and instead it must be true of Hebrew. This new notion about Hebrew's perfection went well beyond the views of previous generations of Jewish thinkers.

For Saadiah, then, the sad state of Hebrew did a disservice to its superior sanctity. He lamented:

> We have been exiled to the ends of the earth. We have learned its languages, and [the Gentiles'] jargon has engulfed our own lovely words. . . . Our language is mocked in the land of our captivity. . . . We can no longer express our thoughts in sanctity and strength, and Hebrew's visions and pronouncements are a sealed book.

In 902, Saadiah had had a vision of how Hebrew should be revived, more sweeping than anything that would be dreamed a thousand years later by Eliezer Ben-Yehuda, the "Father of Modern Hebrew." He wrote:

> It is incumbent on us, and all of God's people, to study and explore [Hebrew] at all times, man, woman, and child. It must constantly be on our lips, for it affords us an understanding of the Divine Law. [It must be] spoken by all Jews in their goings-out

and comings-in and in all their work, in their bed chambers and with their infants.

The results would be messianic and global:

> If only the nation would return to Hebrew, it would ultimately become the language of humankind, by which "all nations shall call on His name and worship Him in unison." (Zephaniah 3:9)

This was Saadiah's popular message to his people. But its practical impact was no doubt minimal. He was just twenty years old at the time.

However, Saadiah also had a more specific message, one intended for the poets of Israel. Jews could not hope to excel in Arabic poetry; they were not schooled in the intricacies of the language. But to the aesthetic principles of Arabic poetry and the ideology of *Arabiyya*, Hebrew could pose a counteraesthetic and counterideology. Saadiah dubbed it *tsahut halashon*—or simply *tsahut*, a word found in Isaiah 32 as *tsahot*, denoting "purity" or "clarity" of language. For Saadiah, the word embodied the antiquity, spirituality, and linguistic beauty of biblical Hebrew.

The rhetoric of *tsahut* soon became a staple of Jewish resistance to Arab claims for the superiority of their language. It was the strongest statement of Hebrew purism since the revolt against Rome so long ago.

Like many advocates of linguistic purity after him, Saadiah wanted biblical Hebrew to be restored as *the* model for Jewish creativity, complete with its puzzling syntax and lexical richness and precision, as well as its parallelisms and stylistic nuances. The rarer a feature, the more *tsah* it was, making for a quintessentially classical aesthetic. However tiny its word inventory when compared with Arabic, Hebrew was *not* inadequate; this tiny cruse of oil could burn forever. Setting aside his persona as a rabbinic scholar, Saadiah proceeded to take on a poetic persona of his own. In place of the rabbinic extravaganzas and enigmas in the usual synagogue *piyyutim*, his own poetic output brimmed with *biblical* obscurities. This was the way to counter the charms of Arabic and its claims to sanctity: demonstrating Hebrew's antiquity and superiority by going back to the Bible.

Easier said than done. Unlike Arabic, Hebrew had no dictionaries, no style guides, and no systematic grammars. Saadiah, unfazed, thereupon composed two groundbreaking reference works. First came a Hebrew rhyming dictionary, the *Egron*, for anyone who desired to write "riddles, tales, compositions, and rhyming verse." Then came *The Book of Elegance of the Language of the Hebrews*, a guide to making the most of what the biblical language could offer, with special attention to the rare and the irregular. This work also included the first extensive, systematic grammar of Hebrew.

Indeed, it was as a grammarian—better, a linguist—that Saadiah left his most lasting mark on the Hebrew language. Like modern scholars, Saadiah asked fundamental questions about language, its origins, and the principles of phonology—questions that did not concern the Masoretes. In fact, he took an interest in all forms of Hebrew: rabbinic, paytanic, and biblical. His own works on language, ironically, were largely forgotten, superseded by such famed successors as Jonah ibn Janah (Spain, ca. 990–1050) and David Kimhi (Provence, 1160–1235), but his model of linguistic study would be indispensable to the Hebrew arts and to the study of Torah.

In the ninth–tenth centuries Babylonia and Persia saw a burst of Hebrew creativity. One gem was *Meshalim* by Saʾid ibn Babshad (ca. 1000), a rhyming essay on perfection and pages of rhymed proverbs. Suffused with Jewish, Arab, and Greek thought, it demon-

FIGURE 8. Children's alphabet primer (11th–12th century) preserved in the Cairo Genizah.

strates the "breadth of vision and openness of mind,"[6] in Yosef Tobi's words, achieved by Jewish writers of the East. Lost and forgotten like most works of the age, this wisdom would be rediscovered centuries later in the Cairo Genizah.

Moses Maimonides was in many ways Saadiah's successor—a giant of rationalism who sought to synthesize Greco-Islamic philosophy and science with Torah, and to standardize halakhic practice. Much like Saadiah, he, too—a product not of Babylonia but of Andalusia and Morocco—was torn between two languages. All of his philosophical and medical works are in Arabic; so, too, his first great rabbinic work, the commentary on the Mishnah, a fact he later bitterly regretted. (He did not have any regrets, however, about writing his philosophical works, including the *Guide of the Perplexed*, in Arabic.)

But when it came to creating the first-ever systematic code of Jewish law and custom, the *Mishneh Torah* (literally, The [oral] Torah restated), streamlining the talmudic erudition needed for apprehending the substance and pith of the law, Maimonides was in no

FIGURE 9. Maimonides' code of Jewish practice, the *Mishneh Torah* (late 12th century).

doubt. He framed it neither in contemporary Arabic nor in contemporary Hebrew-Aramaic legalese, but instead went right back to the classic of rabbinic literature, the Mishnah. The Hebrew of the Mishnah was simplicity itself, a mirror (as noted earlier) of the everyday Hebrew of the masses. Maimonides's goal, he wrote, was that his book be "easily understood by the majority." He had no use for the linguistic acrobatics of the *paytanim*. His choice of Hebrew style was a key weapon in achieving his goal: to make talmudic law and Jewish doctrine accessible to anyone with just a basic Jewish education, eliminating the need to wade through the discursive style, lengthy presentations of opposing opinions, tangential discussions, and unhelpful structure of the Talmud—not to mention its coextensive use of Aramaic, which by this time was no longer a common Jewish vernacular but a scholarly language known only to the erudite.

Maimonides's back-to-the-sources approach to Hebrew also embodied his approach to law itself, in which he consistently tried to draw a straight line from the Torah, through the Talmud, to contemporary practice, without any reference to posttalmudic jurisprudence. The Hebrew of the *Mishneh Torah* was "a new virtuoso creation," as Isadore Twersky has observed, "a designer style for a work combining law, jurisprudence, and philosophy in a way that was lucid, brief, and open to oral memorization, but also variously muscular and authoritative or soft and decorative, stirring to the call of the biblical verse."[7]

Despite much initial opposition on nonlinguistic grounds to his overall project in the *Mishneh Torah*, Maimonides's code rapidly became authoritative—and enduringly popular. But he also stands with Judah the Patriarch and the Bible commentator Rashi as a *linguistic* genius: achieving brevity and simplicity in a web of complexities. Unfortunately, although his style influenced many, it had few true imitators. The style of subsequent legal writing would continue to oscillate between his crisp, simple language and Hebrew-Aramaic legalese.

We have now watched medieval Hebrew being tugged this way and that between intellectual poles: ancients and moderns, the restrictive and the untrammeled, or—to risk an anachronism—the classical and the romantic. Saadiah's linguistic legacy was deeply classical. In fact, he owed a great debt to the purism of two arch-competitors, the Arabs and the Karaites. Maimonides's linguistic legacy also looked back, but in his case to what we may call classical rabbinic Hebrew. Meanwhile, what was unfolding in Iberia was something else: a mix of the classical and puristic approaches to Hebrew in a spirit that was in every way contemporary.

The Golden Age of Andalusia

In tenth-century Andalusia in southern Iberia, at the other end of the Jewish-Arab world from Babylonia, an emerging Jewish community was seeking a religious and cultural identity of its own, and took up Saadiah's aesthetics of *tsaḥut* and his plain-sense approach to biblical interpretation. Out of this came the Andalusian golden age of Hebrew poetry and linguistics.

The story begins around 950, with a fierce quarrel over the authentic nature of Hebrew. It featured Spain's first two great Hebrew poet-linguists, Menaḥem ben Saruq and Saadiah's own disciple, Dunash ben Labrat. The issue: does *tsaḥut* allow outside influences, or indeed anything from outside the Bible?

This was not a religious controversy but an aesthetic and scholarly one. Menaḥem seems to have been averse to any contamination of the holy tongue with foreign vocabulary, or even neologisms. To make his point, he produced a comprehensive biblical dictionary, probably the first, using only the Hebrew and Aramaic of the Bible as evidence to explore the meanings of words.

For Dunash, however, biblical and rabbinic Hebrew was all one whole. Dunash was also prepared to mine its sister languages, Aramaic and Arabic (in over 150 cases!), for clues to the meaning of obscure words, since he believed them to be corrupted offspring of Hebrew. Most linguists today readily employ the same technique, though they would hardly agree with Dunash as to why.

The debate between Menahem and Dunash, and their disciples, raged on many other fronts as well. Could the root letters of Hebrew words sometimes be abstract, invisible, as Arab grammarians were saying about Arabic? Were root letters inviolable or did they sometimes interchange? Is it proper to write Hebrew verse in Arabic meter? Dunash authored the popular Sabbath poem *Deror Yikra* (among many others) in such an Arabic meter, to the distaste of some coreligionists.

These disputes may seem arcane, even bizarre, but what would the medieval Hebrew legacy in religious scholarship or science or poetry have looked like without the knowledge of Hebrew grammar? This is not a rhetorical question. While serious grammatical study remained almost unknown in the Ashkenazi world, Sephardi rabbis considered it a necessity. The scholar Jonah ibn Janah, a disciple of Menahem's disciples and arguably the greatest Hebrew grammarian of all times, insisted that such knowledge was the key to the gates of Torah. Ashkenazi rabbis, who generally rejected this view, nonetheless produced monumental works of scholarship and even some great devotional poetry. But they were never able to subject the Torah to the same rigorous linguistic analysis as did their Sephardi brethren, and the accomplishments of Ashkenazi poets paled in comparison with their Andalusian counterparts. Those achievements depended upon a grasp of biblical grammar and semantics—the complexities and vagaries of verb and noun inflections, the subtleties and ambiguities of vocabulary, the significances of a root. And to fathom the obscure Greek and Aramaic words in the Talmud and Midrash, even that was not enough. Grammatical manuals and dictionaries were essential.

Where did the study of Hebrew grammar come from? The Rabbis of the Talmud and Midrash, though they were always making linguistic points, did so out of an intuitive sense of the system. They had almost no terminology for roots, tenses, verb forms, and so forth. Saadiah and his successors thus began to borrow terms and concepts from Arabic grammar, which has much in common with Hebrew, including its distinctive system of roots. In the eighth century, Islamic scholars in Mesopotamia—inspired by Greek and Roman exemplars—developed a formal science of grammar based on an intricate theory of three-consonant roots that effectively explained Arabic's daunting variety of forms.

It took some time before this system was properly applied to Hebrew. In fact, the most prominent dispute between Menaḥem and Dunash revolved around the correct method for identifying the root consonants. Anyone studying Hebrew today quickly learns that Hebrew words are built on a frame of three, occasionally four, consonants, some of which can sometimes disappear when a verb is inflected. But the earliest generations of Hebrew grammarians would assign four, three, two, and even one consonant to a single verb. It was one of Menaḥem's disciples, the Moroccan-born grammarian Judah Ḥayyuj, who finally solved the problem. Writing in Cordoba around 990, he figured out how to apply the Arabic three-consonant theory to Hebrew, and to unlock the logic in the more puzzling Hebrew inflections. It was now at last possible to have an

TABLE 4.1. How Ḥayyuj saw three underlying consonants in every verb
(and we still do)

Hebrew verbs	Ḥayyuj's root
kamti (I arose), *akum* (I will arise), *kum* (arise!)	k-w-m [vav was *w*]
sabboti (I turned), *esov* (I will turn), *sov* (turn!)	s-v-v
natati (I gave), *eten* (I will give), *ten* (give!)	n-t-n

organized Hebrew dictionary searchable by root—provided you
first knew how to identify the root.

Jews of a nonphilosophical nature often eschewed the study of
grammar, seeing it as a distraction from the real meat of Torah
study or, worse, as a nefarious foreign body imbued with the Greek
or the Arab spirit. (Grammar was one of the seven liberal arts
on which classical philosophic education was based.) Indeed,
many learned Jews believed worldly studies were a slippery slope
leading from a pragmatic acquaintance with Aristotelian astronomy or linguistics to dangerous beliefs about the origin of the
world. Jonah ibn Janaḥ (Ḥayyuj's successor as dean of Judeo-
Spanish grammarians) bitterly described such attitudes in
eleventh-century Saragossa:

> Sheer envy toward present-day scholars, particularly in this re-
> gion, leads many people to attack them for some new insight that
> conflicts with the Midrash but in no way affects Jewish law. They
> claim, "This conflicts with what the rabbis taught," blowing [the
> conflict] completely out of proportion and distorting the truth.
> (Introduction to *Sefer Ha-Rikma*)

The work of the grammarians did have one unfortunate consequence: determined to impose a semblance of order on biblical He-

brew, they greatly narrowed the range of what was acceptable. The rules they formulated still underlie the grammar taught in Israeli schools and sanctioned in the media today, which has no doubt made literary Hebrew trimmer and easier to master. But in the process they drove a host of biblical and rabbinic words and forms to extinction.

A Golden Age of Poetry

The golden age of Andalusian Jewry, which lasted into the twelfth century, is best known not for its grammar but for its poetry—which the study of grammar made possible. It was a time when religious bigotry was in relative remission, the courts and the garden parties of the Muslim ruling class were open to (some) Jews, and a few rose to be court poets, viziers, and even generals. Modern scholars gasp at the broad synthesis of Jewish and Arab learning. Much, indeed most, of the poetry was still deeply pious, but much—the kind that modern scholars tend to like—was worldly, aristocratic, and rather Arabic in spirit: hymns to wine and love, paeans to patrons, put-downs of foes, lonesome plaints, vignettes and tableaux, parodies (of doctors and cantors, for example), aphorisms, riddles, and the occasional battle song.

None better embodied, in life and poetry, the fusion of Jewish values and aristocratic worldly duties than Shmuel ben Yosef, known as Shmuel ha-Nagid ("the Prince," 993–1056), talmudist, grammarian, poet, vizier to the Muslim king of Granada and (incredibly) his commander-in-chief. In this aphorism, he paints the glories of love and war with an irony bathed in biblical wisdom—and a brilliant play on the word *lesaḥek* (cavort, joust), evoking both the jousting in Saul's and David's armies and the Israelites cavorting with the Golden Calf. (Except where indicated otherwise, translations of poetry in this chapter are mine.)

Battle begins like some gorgeous girl
Of whom all dream of partaking [lit. cavorting, jousting],
But it comes to a close like an odious hag,
Her suitors all blubbing and aching.

With wit and inventiveness, the Spanish Hebrew poets deployed Hebrew's two great modes of allusion: playing on the Jewish sources and playing with words. Take this vignette from the *Book of Taḥkemoni* by Judah al-Ḥarizi (thirteenth century Spain/Provence):

And the lightning plays on clouds
Like a racing warrior never tired or faint,
Like a watchman of the night who slumbers and opens
His eye so slightly and shuts it in a trice.

There is a powerful graphic charge here in the two metaphors and the comic clash between racing warrior and slumbering watchman—not to mention the ironic twist on the famous "watchman of the night" of Isaiah 21:11. The Hebrew words for "racing" and "never tired or faint" also add playful allusions to biblical imagery of the sun and the Creator, while the word for the "playing" lightning echoes a verse from 2 Samuel: "Let the young men arise and *joust*" (2:14). Meanwhile, the word for "tired," *yiʿaf*, anticipates the watchman's droopy eyes (*afʿaf* is an eyelid).

Poets like al-Ḥarizi strove for a delicate synthesis: to appear contemporary while fostering Jewish sensitivities and even pieties. The lyrics of Judah Halevi (ca. 1075–1141), perhaps the era's greatest and most celebrated Jewish poet, set the old yearning for Zion against the comforts of Spain, using the power of rhyme to magnetize the words for "West, delight; Arabs, ruins":

My heart is in the East and I at the farthest West.
How can I taste what I eat and find delight?

How can I pay my oaths and vows while
Zion is in Christendom and I in Arabs' chains?
Forsaking the bounty of Spain would be as trifling
As it would be precious to see the dust of the Temple ruins.

The distinction between "sacred" and "worldly" verse (in Hebrew, *kodesh ~ ḥol*) is embedded in everything written about the
golden age, and indeed in what the poets themselves thought about
it—as plain, seemingly, as night and day. And yet, there is much that
is elusive, even illusory. In the communities of Andalus, untrammeled by the old authorities and talmudic erudition of the East,
synagogues rushed to commission the best poets to compose elegant *sacred* verse for Sabbaths and holidays in the new "classical"
spirit of *worldly* verse—with its purely biblical language, its Arabic
rhyme schemes and meters, and its simplicity. But religious tradition has a dynamic of its own. The sacred verse that emerged was an
uncertain mix of the old rhymes and meters and the new, biblical
language strung to traditional acrostics, midrash, and allegory a-
plenty. No doubt, many agreed with the poet Abraham ibn Ezra
(1092–1167) when he denounced the old poetry as obscurities and
impurities, but even he maintained a special synagogue style. Andalusian sacred verse is truly, to use Ezra Fleischer's phrase, "an equal
component in the artistic system."[8]

Philosophers often favor verse (or aphorisms) for its tightness,
complexities, gnomic qualities, and its hold on the reader. The Hebrew sacred verse of the golden age tuned itself to the philosophical
agenda of the time as the *paytanim* had never done. Solomon ibn
Gabirol (Spain, 1022–ca. 1068) must rank with Friedrich Nietzsche
and Alexander Pope for his metaphysical genius, in both prose (Arabic) and verse (Hebrew). Often ascribed to ibn Gabirol is the still-

favorite synagogue hymn *Adon Olam*, so very familiar—but so poorly understood.

> Master of eternity, who reigned
> Before any entity was yet formed,
> It was when at His behest all was made
> That His name was proclaimed King.

This first stanza (of five) opens on a grand paradox: God the transcendent king without subjects! But then in what sense king? King by courtesy of the relationship His creatures build with Him. The solitary monarch is a lyrical image that would one day redefine man's relationship to God in ḥasidic thought. *Adon Olam* is a gem both lyrically and philosophically.

Many poets sang of deeply personal troubles, of the sort that might afflict anyone. Abraham ibn Ezra, famed astronomer-poet-wit, bewailed his employment prospects.

> If I made shrouds
> No one would die,
> If I sold lamps
> Then in the sky
> The sun for spite
> Would shine at night
>> (Abridged translation by Nathan Ausubel,
>> *Treasury of Jewish Humor*)

At times, highly respected poets like Moses ibn Ezra (ca. 1060–1138) could invoke a sensuality seemingly at odds with Jewish proprieties but dealing, in Raymond Scheindlin's words, "not with sex but with beauty"[9] in an abstract manner, highly conventionalized and impersonal. Biblical Hebrew, a small pool of words and images but a rich source of allusions, was perfect for the role. In a manner that would never have occurred to Shakespeare (or to Andrew Marvell, author of "To His Coy Mistress"), ibn Ezra declares his submission to his lover's wrath in the same idiom as a dispirited Moses (Numbers 11:14) imploring God, "Kill me":

> Consume me not in wrath, my beauty,
> Show me wondrous favor, my love,
> And kiss your love and do his desire!
> If you wish me to live, give me life,
> Or if you desire to kill, kill me.

Running beneath the Arab themes and tropes the poets made their own were the host of complex rhythms and meters they learned from Arabic verse. One of ibn Ezra's last great compositions, as a refugee in the Christian north, was a treatise (in Arabic) on Spanish-Hebrew poetics, designed to induct the Hebrew poets there into the worldly art of Andalusia.

Thus far, we have dwelt on poetry as the medieval artistic medium par excellence. But what of narratives? There were no epic Hebrew poems like *Beowulf* or the *Song of Roland*, but there was a wealth of Hebrew prose stories—a tradition reaching back to the Talmud and the Bible itself. We find them in Babylonia in early medieval collections such as the (so-called) Midrash of the Ten Commandments and the Alphabet of Ben Sira. They pop up everywhere, in memoirs, legal opinions, midrashim. Some were original; some reworked Jewish or non-Jewish tales. There were the *maḥbarot*, rollicking medleys of adventure stories (*maqamot*) in a rhymed prose. Most celebrated was the fifty-episode *Book of Taḥkemoni* (ca. 1215), a dazzling display of Hebrew by the wandering Spanish poet al-Ḥarizi. Another, a sort of Hebrew *Canterbury Tales*, was the *Book of Delights* (*Sefer Shaʾashuʾim*) by the twelfth-century Barcelona physician Joseph Zabara (also known for his less delightful Hebrew treatise on urine). A century later, in southern France, there was the *Book of Tales* (*Sefer Hama'asim*). Hebrew readers in Christian Europe also snapped up translations of Oriental favorites like *Kalila and Dimna*. For the first time, with cultural windows opening in southern Europe, Hebrew fiction was being designed to entertain rather than to instruct. A *maḥberet* was even authored in deeply traditional Yemen.

There were also the ad-lib stories that you heard from your mother or friends or a visiting merchant: in other words, folktales. These included tales of rabbis, demons, historical moments, moral exempla, and many a romantic novella where a girl gets her man. Of course, they were usually told in the local language. But the language that Jews used for transmitting them (say, from Arabic to Italian) and preserving them was Hebrew, "the principal medium of creation and dissemination," as Eli Yassif has put it.[10] The Hebrew folktale would continue for centuries, culminating in the stories of the Ḥasidim.

And in the background, especially outside the Arabic-writing world, traces remain of another Hebrew genre, private and often ephemeral: the letter, from everyday correspondence to lofty ethical wills. Here (in my translation) is some wisdom from one that was preserved:

> Show respect and affection to your bosom wife, address her positively and pleasantly. Others will thereby respect her, and from her honor you will earn status and honor. (Judah ibn Tibbon, ca. 1180)

The end of the golden age came suddenly, in the mid-twelfth century, when the Jews of Andalusia and the Maghreb were forced to choose Islam or death. Many fled to Christian Europe, bringing their knowledge with them. They were the crème de la crème, they thought, and so did others. The Andalusian worldly aesthetic duly spread around the Mediterranean and beyond. North Africa, Provence, Italy, Byzantium, even Yemen adopted the Sephardi (Spanish) style and set a new tone for Hebrew verse. In Italy, to the dismay of some and the quiet pleasure of others, it produced many a ribald Hebrew tale in *maqama* form—featuring cuckolded men with faux-pious wives, damsels wed to old codgers, and so forth, often fleshed out with a rabbinic moral. The Vatican Library houses a Hebrew Arthurian romance from 1279, *Melekh Artus*, with the Holy Grail judiciously changed to a *tamḥuy* (a talmudic charity plate): "Then King Artus ordered that all the events befalling the knights who went on the Quest of the Plate (*tamḥuy*) should be recorded."

This worldly aesthetic has been seen in very different lights: as an enduring "anything you can do, we can do better"—indeed, a model for modern Jewish culture—or alternatively as a chimera, a blind alley in Jewish cultural history. Maimonides scorned such poetry, and he was not alone. Particularly enigmatic is the mélange of sensual and sacred. Judah Halevi and Moses ibn Ezra were apologetic in their latter years, "compunctious poets" in Ross Brann's phrase,[11] but was this a merely literary pose? A genuine symptom of the stress of Jewish parvenus in an alien culture? Without doubt, it also stemmed from a philosophical attraction to the beauty of opposites—and a cherished but problematic erotic heritage: the biblical Song of Songs.

What remained of this worldliness all but perished in the expulsion of 1492. Iberia had been home to more Jews than anywhere else in the Diaspora. In North Africa, where many now found refuge, another aesthetic took hold, a pious culture of popular *piyyut*: the poets sought to speak to the masses, not the muse, in plain rhyme rather than rhythmical complexity, with the words sung to familiar Jewish and Arab melodies. There was a turn from worldly wit to Kabbalah and themes of exile and redemption, as the nation contemplated its destiny. Many poets pivoted from the Bible to the words of the Sages, their *bakashot* (songs of supplication) fusing Hebrew with kabbalistic Aramaic. Similar currents swept Italy and Yemen. Here is the climax of a poem traditionally chanted at the start of the Yemenite Sabbath-evening meal:

ARAMAIC STANZA:

Seated in the study house, blessing the Holy One,

Morning and evening, glowing like fire,

On every head a sacred crown,

And a craving to know the mystery sublime.

HEBREW STANZA:

Fulfill, O Lord, the words of the prophets,

Make haste with king, prophet, and priest,

Let us ascend Zion like a lion,

And let us build the Temple in magnificence.

As we will shortly see, a parallel Hebrew sacred culture had been flourishing in Ashkenazi Europe. Both would eventually find themselves marginalized by modern secularism and Jewish nationalism—only to reclaim a very "contemporary" place in Jewish and Israeli culture.

So much for Hebrew as a language per se. But a written text could also convey other visual layers of significance, especially in the choice of lettering itself: cursive hand for the quick or commonplace, square letters for codices and printed books, a typographic cursive (popularly dubbed "Rashi script") that became iconic for rabbinic texts, elaborate scribal and typographic calligraphy—all in a plethora of regional styles but all one big visual family, at least

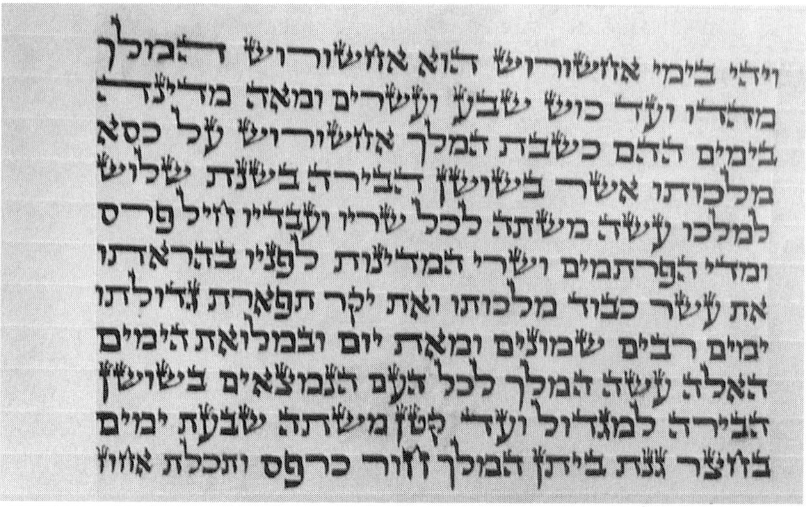

ויהי בימי אחשורוש הוא אחשורוש המלך

מהדו ועד כוש שבע ועשרים ומאה מדינה

בימים ההם כשבת המלך אחשורוש על כסא

מלכותו אשר בשושן הבירה בשנת שלוש

למלכו עשה משתה לכל שריו ועבדיו חיל פרס

ומדי הפרתמים ושרי המדינות לפניו בהראתו

את עשר כבוד מלכותו ואת יקר תפארת גדולתו

ימים רבים שמונים ומאת יום ובמלואת הימים

האלה עשה המלך לכל העם הנמצאים בשושן

הבירה למגדול ועד קטן משתה שבעת ימים

בחצר גנת ביתן המלך חור כרפס ותכלת אחוז

FIGURE 10. The first verses of the biblical Book of Esther in a scribal script.

until modern fontography crashed the scene. The scribal arts still live on in the ornamental *ketubah* (marriage contract) and above all in the work of the sacred scribe, the *sofer*, laboring on parchment with feather quill and special-formula black ink, to write Torah scrolls, *mezuzot*, *tefillin*, and writs of divorce as Jewish law dictates— each Hebrew letter in its customary form, and every letter *shin*, *ayin*, *tet*, *nun*, *zayin*, *gimel*, and *tzadi* significantly adorned, by talmudic decree, with tiny crowns.

Hebrew had another, humbler presence in the Jewish-language ecosystem and the Jewish imagination, more visible and in some ways more inclusive: in the everyday vernacular. Almost everywhere, Jews wrote the vernacular in the Hebrew aleph-bet, and everywhere, Hebrew words and expressions added a haphazard but vital ingredient—the yeast that helped produce a Jewish variety of Arabic, Persian, Spanish, German, Italian, and whichever other Diaspora languages Jews spoke, from the Middle Ages and into modern times. These Hebraisms might be religious (*bar mitzvah*), emotive (*meshugge*, "crazy"), cautionary (*ganavear*, "steal" in Ladino); in talking Torah, they could generate an impenetrable lingo. Sometimes, notably with Judeo-German and Judeo-Spanish, geographic and linguistic drift produced distinct new Jewish languages: namely, Yiddish and Ladino. We will return to this.

5

Medieval Ashkenaz and Italy

SCIENCES, SONNETS, AND THE SACRED

Hebrew as a Language of Science in the Christian Mediterranean

The appearance of Andalusian-style poetry in Italy, but with northern European subject matter, was not an isolated occurrence. The tale of King Artus that we encountered in the previous chapter was a typical product of what we might call the afterlife of the Andalusian golden age. Fleeing earlier waves of persecution—by Islamic rulers—in the eleventh and twelfth centuries, many Andalusian Jews had resettled in the Christian lands of Italy, Provence, and northern Spain, bringing secular learning and their unique Jewish culture with them.

The combination of Andalusian influence with local Jewish intellectual traditions proved particularly fertile for the Hebrew language. In these lands, Hebrew came to perform a sweeping array of functions as nowhere else in the Diaspora: not only in religious scholarship but also in the sacred and secular arts, everyday management, and—most remarkably—the sciences. In Muslim Spain, scientific texts had been available in Arabic, and Jews and non-Jews could read them easily. Not so in the Christian world, where Jews had an impetus to transform Hebrew into a language of science—with fruitful results.

This part of our story begins in ninth-century southern Italy, before the arrival of the Andalusians. At the time, the foot of Italy was still under Byzantine rule; Jews there had traditionally used Greek in speech, writing, and prayer. (Even in Roman and pre-Roman times, southern Italy was largely Greek-speaking.) Hebrew lived on the margins. Then, in the ninth to eleventh centuries, Hebrew began to blossom, in unprecedented ways: in a wealth of poetry—not only the old, familiar liturgical *piyyutim* but also mystical poetry and worldly verse; in collations (e.g., *Yossipon*, 953) of Philo, Josephus, and other classical sources, providing generations of medieval Jews with a nonrabbinic window onto their history; in high-flown miscellanies of sacred, informative, and fun reading, most famously Yeraḥmeʾel's *Sefer Hazikhronot* (twelfth century); in a family chronicle like *Megillat Aḥimaʾatz* (1054), set in a rhyming prose modeled on the Arabic rhymed epistle. And then there was Hebrew's greatest contribution to early medieval Italy: a scientific-technical literature.

Shabbatai Donnolo was the first European Jew known to us who wrote scientific works in Hebrew. He left a brief bio. Having received a traditional talmudic education in southern Italy as it was being overrun by the Saracens, he engaged a Baghdadi gentleman to instruct him in Arab astronomy and records his surprise on discovering that it corresponded with what he had learned of astronomy in the Talmud—although none of his talmudic tutors had understood such things. Where Donnolo's search for wisdom took him he doesn't say, but he went on to produce a string of scientific writings: *Sefer Ḥakhmoni* (ca. 946), on astrology, medicine, and much else, and *Sefer ha-Mirkaḥot* (The book of mixtures, ca. 970) on pharmacology—probably Europe's oldest known Hebrew medical text and Italy's first medical text in the half millennium since the fall of the Roman Empire. He likely also wrote the *Practica* on diseases and therapies, as well as *Sefer ha-Mazalot* on astronomy.

How did Donnolo write science in Hebrew? He employed an elegant biblical-rabbinic idiom, with technical terms often transliterated from the Greek or Latin: *stomakhus* (stomach), *trigon* (triangle), *diametron* (diameter). No fewer than three hundred hebraized Greco-Latin botanical and pharmacological terms appear in the *Practica*. His preface to *Ḥakhmoni* says nothing about his choice of language, as if it were perfectly natural and easy to write scientific treatises in Hebrew. Perhaps it was; maybe there were other Hebrew scientific writings, since lost, that inspired him. Donnolo frequently cites the oldest Hebrew medical encyclopedia to have survived, *Sefer ha-Refuot*, attributed to a physician named Asaf and likely composed between 300 and 700 in the land of Israel, before the rise of Arab medicine. *Sefer ha-Refuot* was a survey of Near Eastern medical wisdom in quasi-biblical Hebrew, with a plethora of transliterated Greek terms. Was it also part of a lost scientific-philosophical Hebrew literature from talmudic times? Or was Asaf just seeking to pass off his own book as an ancient Hebrew work? We cannot be sure.

And why Hebrew in the first place? Donnolo himself probably spoke Greek, but might not have been able to read or write in it. And Byzantine Jews in general, even if they had access to high-level Greek schooling, which is unlikely, were a marginalized group. As for the focus on medicine, Christian medicine in Europe was still in its infancy and Arab medicine not yet widely known. When medieval European kings and princes needed a doctor, Jewish physicians filled the gap, and most of their knowledge came in Hebrew. At Salerno, the first medical school in Italy (founded in the ninth century), instruction was in Hebrew, Arabic, Greek, and Latin. In the Provençal medical schools of Arles, Narbonne, and Montpelier, Hebrew was actually the official language of instruction in the ninth and tenth centuries, the curriculum being taken from Hebrew, Syriac, and Arabic translations of Hippocrates and Galen. This was no ad hoc arrangement; with hoary classics like Asaf's encyclopedia to its credit, Hebrew initially had the status of a language of ancient medical wisdom, the equal of Greek. Donnolo was by no means an eccentric anomaly.

As a result, spoken Hebrew could again be heard. Aside from its routine appearance as a language of instruction in early medieval medical schools, it remained essential for Jewish physicians excluded from Latin or Greek. (Of course, it also served as a Jewish lingua franca for communication among merchants, travelers, and, inevitably, refugees.) But Christian medicine eventually weaned itself off Hebrew, and for a time a linguistic iron curtain would divide Christendom from the Islamic realm in which Muslims, Christians, and Jews alike studied science in Arabic.

Then, in 1148, forced conversions to Islam sent Muslim Spain's Jewish intelligentsia fleeing to the relative safety of Christian Spain, Provence, and Italy—and suddenly the iron curtain was pierced. Accustomed to writing in Arabic and working professionally in non-Jewish society, Andalusian Jews who found themselves in Christian lands were now excluded from their former professions. Simultaneously, however, they found that their skills were much in demand from resident *Jewish* intellectuals eager for Hebrew translations of Greco-Arab science.

Within a century, the entire body of Greco-Arabic science had been rendered into Hebrew—everything from Galen and Averroes to Euclid and al-Khwarizmi—as well as (discreetly) a large part of Christian science. The nineteenth-century bibliographer Moritz Steinschneider lists more than 500 Hebrew translations by over 150 named translators across three centuries.[1] The largest demand was in Italy; in 1279, the first Hebrew version appeared in Rome of Avicenna's medical magnum opus, *The Canon*, to become perhaps the most widely read Hebrew scientific work of the Middle Ages.

Here is a tiny snippet from volume 30 of the tenth-century Andalusian physician Abulcasis's *Kitab al-Tasrif*, a key work in the development of European surgery, which Shem Tov ben Isaac rendered into Hebrew in Marseilles around 1250:

> The section of the two arteries in the temples gives relief for chronic migraine and severe headache and constant ophthalmia and the flow of acrid superfluities into the eyes.[2]

Shem Tov was a Hebrew loyalist. For "ophthalmia," he has *efer ha-eynayim* (ash of the eye), a calque from the Arabic. For "asthma" he has *ginnuah*, from the biblical *ganah* (to groan). Abraham ibn Ezra, too, made a point of sourcing his astronomical and mathematical terms from the Bible. Meanwhile, in Provence and Aragon, an emerging "indigenous" Hebrew technical syntax was being created in the simple rabbinic style of the Mishnah.

True, many translations were rush jobs, and their syntax sounded more like Arabic than like Hebrew—a sort of "translationese." But in their defense, many technical translators thought it a virtue to stick closely to the original. And many also continued to admire technical Arabic as far superior to Latin or Hebrew. Maimonides's own translator, Judah ibn Tibbon, quoted earlier, hailed Arabic for its "exact and lucid vocabulary, reaching the heart of all matters, far beyond what Hebrew can do" (Introduction, Bahya ibn Pakuda, *Hovot ha-Levavot*).

Hebrew translationese was father to the first technical prose standard that Hebrew had had since the Mishnah, and one of much greater complexity and precision. Dubbed *leshon tekhunah* (astronomese), it became the hallmark of philosophical luminaries like Levi Gersonides of Provence and the kabbalistic literature emerging at that time. Not only its vocabulary but also its syntax bore an unmistakable stamp of Arabic influence.

And yet Hebrew was not felt to have been de-Judaized. Although wording and syntax had been cut loose from the hallowed moorings of the past, they were not perceived as any less authentic. "Astronomese" was to Mediterranean Jews rather like what technical rabbinic Hebrew became to Ashkenazim: a functional medium. The message counted more than the niceties. Astronomese remained in use in philosophical and scientific texts for centuries, and eventually even rabbinic authors saw its vocabulary and style as an established source on a par with the Hebrew of the Mishnah or Maimonides. Not until the late nineteenth century was it abandoned—not so much because it was abstruse and Arabic-sounding but because the Hebrew Enlightenment realized the value of forcing Hebrew into a more European style. To Hebrew readers today, medieval astronomese sounds not just foreign but weird.

Some Hebrew technical translators put their knowledge of Arabic to work in two other, quite remarkable ways: producing medical-scientific poetry and acting as intermediaries between Arabic and Latin. On the former point, Solomon ben Abraham ibn Daud (1233) tried his hand at a Hebrew verse translation of Avicenna's great *Urjūza fī al-tibb* (Poem on medicine) by which so many physicians memorized their skills. Here are a few memorable facts about the color of urine:

> The color white is among the signs that indicate excess food
>   and drink,
> or indigestion as well as phlegm and also cold; or that watery
>   flow or obstruction of the liver has occurred.
> If the urine is a little yellow, it indicates bile, in a small amount.
> If the color is the color of fire, it shows an excess of bile active. [3]

When it came to helping with the transition from Arabic to Latin, the master translator Jacob ben Makhir ibn Tibbon (great-grandson of Judah) had a nice system: he would translate aloud from the Arabic text into the Provençal vernacular, which a Christian scholar would then render on the spot into Latin. Soon enough, though, Christians were able to dispense with such middlemen and to produce Arabic-Latin translations of their own.

In many ways, the twelfth and thirteenth centuries marked a high point of Hebrew technical literacy—spurred not just by scientific curiosity but also by a desire to compete with the literate Latin and Spanish culture emerging in Christian Spain; it would take another six hundred years before Enlightenment Hebrew would compete with German and Russian with equal passion. But in the fourteenth and fifteenth centuries, the persecutions (now by Christians rather than Muslims) and eventual scattering of Spanish and Provençal Jewry destroyed their entire scientific ethos. The refugees who reached Italy or Muslim lands turned to other fields, and the memory of Hebrew as a language of science would be all but erased.

In 1518, Petrus Mosellanus, rector of Leipzig University, declared that "there lies hidden in the libraries of the Jews a treasure of medical knowledge so great that it seems incapable of being equaled by the books of any other language."[4] Thousands of such Hebrew medical manuscripts were destroyed through expulsions and book burnings; an estimated fifteen thousand survived in world libraries. And there, alas, this literature still remains hidden.

Yellow Stars and Hebrew Sonnets

Italy, the birthplace of Hebrew scientific writing, was also, as we have seen, the home of Europe's first Hebrew poets. By the tenth century it had been eclipsed by Spain, but in the fourteenth century it would regain its prominence as the site of a poetic revival. By this time Christian Spain, Provence, and northwestern Europe were becoming increasingly inhospitable to Jews; England had already expelled its Jews completely, and France was on the way to following suit. Jews from all of these places took refuge in the patchwork of principalities and fiefdoms that was Renaissance Italy, which became a microcosm of the Diaspora experience: Jews were treated now with unusual tolerance, now with venom, often shut in ghettos and forced to wear the yellow badge of shame.

Unlike anywhere else in premodern times, Italian Jews wrote for the arts in both Hebrew and the prestige vernacular. Italy was a multilingual society in which Jews felt honored to play their part. They were also impelled by the new respect in which Hebrew was held by many Renaissance Christian scholars. Adopting new vernacular meters into their poetry, Italian Jews produced Hebrew terza rima, ottava rima, and sonnets that rivaled the best the Renaissance and the Baroque could produce. Here in my translation is the opening of a sonnet by Immanuel of Rome (thirteenth–fourteenth century), a master of bawdy and attitude and a kaleidoscope to his times:

> Two years now since I took
> A man—and he lives, but life has no joy.
> I would be sovereign among the fairer sex
> Were he but struck by a bolt or thunderclap.
>   (*Maḥberot Imanuel*)

And there was the stage. Members of the Italian Jewish elite were active in Renaissance acting and dance. For Purim, in or around 1550, the accomplished Jewish producer-playwright Leone de' Sommi of Mantua was inspired to write and stage a full-scale comedy in biblical-talmudic Hebrew, *Tsaḥot bediḥuta de-kiddushin* (A comedy of betrothal), mixing *commedia dell'arte*, Jewish communal satire, and a talmudic tale in a Romeo-and-Juliet drama worthy of the Bard himself. An Italian-Hebrew dramatic tradition was born.

It all came quite naturally. Literary Hebrew and literary Italian were both artifices, demanding extreme attention to linguistic niceties and ancient sources. After all, until at least the fourteenth century, what we call Italian was simply considered garbled Latin; no effort had yet been made to form a standard language out of the dozens of local dialects. Italian poets were creating their language as they went along; in this sense they were not unlike Jewish poets stretching and experimenting with Hebrew to make it serve new poetic purposes.

The flowering of this poetic revival extended into the seventeenth century and beyond. Here, for instance, are the first and last stanzas of a sonnet of exquisite logic and balance by Immanuel Frances (ca. 1618–ca. 1703):

> When I behold Hannah in the shining light,
> When I recall Naomi in full splendor,
> For Hannah my being verily burns,
> And for Naomi my spirit catches fire. . . .
> I say to thee, O Love, with arms outstretched:
> Either grant me two hearts side by side
> Or rend the heart that I have in twain.[5]
>   (My translation)

The Italian-Jewish symbiosis also extended to the religious sphere, as in the synagogue music of Salamone Rossi (Mantua, ca. 1570–1630) and in the allegorical pastoral dramas of Rabbi Moshe Ḥaim Luzzatto (1707–1747), the revered mystic and moralist of Padua.

Indeed, a generation later, Luzzatto would be hailed by the German-Jewish Enlightenment as the father of modern Hebrew—his pastoral dramatic verse was so very "contemporary" and his Hebrew so stunning. This was a fitting climax to Italy's distinctive thousand-year Hebrew poetic tradition, "unparalleled for length and continuity in the Jewish world," in the words of Dan Pagis.[6] Ironically, as we will see, the so very "modern" Luzzatto drama discovered by the Enlightenment would eventually be consigned to oblivion, while his handbook of piety, *Mesilat Yesharim,* a best seller in the yeshivas of pre–World War II Poland, is still popular in Orthodox circles today.

Hebrew in Medieval Ashkenaz: A Holy Language par Excellence

In treating the early medieval period, I spoke about leading rabbinic figures in the westernmost part of Europe who believed that Torah study had to be founded on knowledge of grammar. At the end of the Middle Ages, in the easternmost part of Europe (except for Russia itself, off-limits to Jews until the eighteenth century), the Polish halakhic authority Moses Isserles confessed to a colleague, "I have never studied the discipline of grammar" (Responsum 7). How to account for the difference?

There is more than one way to learn a second language. You can imbibe Hebrew texts all day, every day, from an early age, read the commentators for ad hoc help, never study formal grammar—and yet master the writings of the Rabbis. You would also be able to write a passable prose. Torah education has flourished in this manner, and still does. Call it Hebrew literacy by osmosis. This was the strategy employed by the Jews of northern and central Europe who later spread eastward to Poland, Lithuania, and Ukraine.

For these Jews, broadly known as Ashkenazim, Hebrew was a language primarily intended for religious purposes—though also useful for correspondence, business transactions, and record keeping. Ashkenazi scholars wrote religious poetry as a vehicle for linguistic creativity, but lightheartedness and wit had no place in their art, and the only mention of love was in connection with the love of God. Indeed, reading literature for entertainment was often condemned, regardless of its language. In everyday speech and writing, medieval Ashkenazim resorted to a Judeo-German (Yiddish) or Judeo-French vernacular, which contained admixtures of Hebrew and was written in Hebrew characters. Ashkenazim had virtually no access to Gentile schooling or any communal interest in acquiring Gentile literacy until the eighteenth or nineteenth century. As for Latin, the language of European scholarship, one generally had to be a Christian to be schooled in it. When Jews did at times contrive to engage in scholarly interaction with Christians, especially during the twelfth-century "Little Renaissance" in northern France, such interaction was entirely oral.

Let us begin with northern France, the Rhineland, and the Danube valley in the eleventh and twelfth centuries—Tzarfat (as Jews called northern France) and Ashkenaz (Germany), the cradle of the Ashkenazi heritage. These clusters of small communities were able to create an enduring machinery of Jewish religious study that would spread across the entire Jewish world. It rolled upon the biblical and talmudic commentaries of Rashi (Solomon ben Isaac, 1040–1105) and those of his disciples, known as the Tosafists (France and environs, twelfth and thirteenth centuries).

Rashi's commentaries on the Bible and Talmud—the latter written in a blend of Hebrew and Aramaic—were monumental; yet they were feats of elegance, brevity, and clarity, in contrast to the complex and florid style of the Ashkenazi *paytanim*. Rashi's style has been venerated as nothing short of miraculous. Generations of students have been reared to seek significance in his every word. He doubtless had in mind the talmudic dictum "Always impart teachings to your disciple concisely." In this respect, his style adumbrated that of Maimonides while, within the Ashkenazi world, it rapidly became the gold standard of Hebrew prose. Only later, and most likely thanks to the dual influence of Rashi and Maimonides, would it become the norm for Jews elsewhere.

Aside from their sheer content, Rashi's commentaries opened a new era in Hebrew prose—a medium heretofore neglected by the poetry-intoxicated authors (both Muslim and Jewish) of the Arabic-speaking world. First, Rashi's Bible commentary is in pure Hebrew, rendering abstruse and Aramaic-laden midrashim into the simple style of the Mishnah. He thus made serious study possible for those with only a modicum of rabbinic education. Independently of the new linguistics being developed by Sephardi Hebraists, he infused his commentaries with grammatical and above all syntactic insight. He also coined hundreds of words to facilitate his project. Rashi's entire Torah commentary uses just 263 foreign (medieval French) glosses; for him, explaining Hebrew terms and phrases *in Hebrew* was superior to translation. Even the glosses usually appear alongside explanations in Hebrew.

There was also an Ashkenazi poetry. Unlike the Jewish poets of medieval Spain, who wrote both sacred and worldly verse, Ashkenazi poets devoted themselves to sacred perspectives. Most celebrated were the poems they wove into the synagogue liturgy for every special time and season: hymns for the High Holy Days, laments (*kinot*) for fast days, pleas and confessionals (*selihot*), prayers for winter rain and summer dew, and much more—all in the erudite, intricate *piyyut* style inherited from the ancient poet Kallir, refracting a thick potion of biblical and midrashic sources. Yet they would become the artistic accompaniment to the Jewish calendar for the ordinary man. These poets also created a host of proud local liturgical traditions: the Mainz liturgy, the Worms liturgy, and so forth.

The modern Ashkenazi prayer book represents a synthesis of these local customs. One example is *Shir Hakavod* (The song of glory, popularly known as *Anim Zmirot*), swingingly sung in many modern synagogues—but originally the passionate plaint of a mystic unable to "see" beyond the prophets' imagery of the divine presence to the Creator Himself. Drawing on the rich significations of *rosh* (head), *pe'er* (splendor, head of hair), and anagrams like *shir* (song) and *rash* (pauper), it concludes with an enigmatic allusion to the talmudic Rabbi Ishmael, who visualized God sadly shaking His head over the destruction of His temple and then imploring him, "Bless Me, My son":

> May my blessing ascend to the Nourisher's head (*rosh mashbir*),
> Who conceives and begets a mighty saint.
> And with my blessing to You, nod Your head to me
> And accept it like prime incense (*besamim rosh*).

Inseparable from liturgical poetry and prose were cherished chanting modes (*nusah*) and melodies, some of which were thought to go right back to the Revelation at Sinai. It is ironic that, come the nineteenth century, these very same words would be reset to melodies in the style of contemporary opera, performed by operatic *hazanim* (cantors)—and enthusiastically adopted by the Jewish masses. This was a popular music as virtuoso as the words themselves. For the Ashkenazi communities across Europe, synagogue worship was an icon of their identity.

Within the religious subject matter of medieval Ashkenazi writing, there was a surprising diversity of genres: travelogues like the

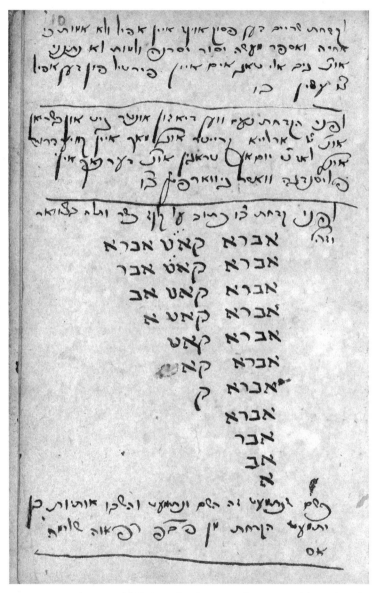

FIGURE 11. Hebrew-Yiddish cure (16th century). Uttering the Talmudic formula "abracatabra" [sic] decrementally was meant to decrease the illness.

Journeys of Rabbi Petaḥiah of Regensburg; graphic elegies and chronicles of the Crusades; grammatical studies; legal codes and cases; theology and psychology of the soul; esoteric guides to textual interpretation by Rabbi Eleazar of Worms and his circle; the hugely influential narrative vade mecum on piety known as *Sefer Hasidim.* There was a wealth of morality tales, often rabbinic in origin but forever morphing with time and place and their challenges. The *Encyclopedia of the Jewish Story* records 36 versions across the centuries of "The Jewish Pope" and no fewer than 106 (in Hebrew or other Jewish languages) of the "Seduction of Joseph," with Joseph variously portrayed as a classical stoic, a chivalrous hero, a Hasid, a Maskil, and a tormented secular Jew.[7]

Thirteen Hebrew tales from northern France recently published from a manuscript in the ducal library of Parma, Italy, offer a glimpse of the penalties and temptations, in Rella Kuschelevsky's words,[8] that beset early Ashkenazi Jewry: "Why do the righteous suffer?" they ask, or "What will we find in heaven or hell?" But as in any good medieval yarn (Jewish or Christian), there's a dragon and a warrior, a ghost and an angel, a modest and faithful bride, a seductress, a prostitute, a king, three thieves, a scholar, and Satan. A little softer are the charming animal fables of Berakhiah, a thirteenth-century Anglo-Jewish Aesop:

> A rooster once scratched at a dunghill, seeking worms for his supper. But what did he find but a pearl? He stopped his pecking and flicked away the pearl. Said he: "I thought my work would earn me a nice juicy worm or fly, but all I found is a pearl. You're enchanting, I warrant, and some rich man will seize you and set you in gold, but what use are you to me? To a rooster, better a worm, even half a worm, than a precious pearl." (My translation)

Sadly, however, the Hebrew muse soon seems to have flown. Expelled in the thirteenth and fourteenth centuries from France, England, and much of Germany, and migrating east to Poland and other Slavic lands, Ashkenazi Jewry for four centuries produced little religious poetry or other creative writing in Hebrew. Rhymed book prefaces and communal elegies were among the few modest genres that persisted. One reason was the declining interest in studying the Bible and midrashic narratives, the inspiration and linguistic wellspring of most great Hebrew poets. Instead, young men threw themselves into Talmud and law codes. Grammatical knowledge was likewise ignored, even scorned, despite campaigns for school reform by luminaries like Judah Loew ("Maharal") of Prague and Rabbi Jacob Emden (1697–1776).

Every tourist in Prague today is shown the statue of Maharal, creator of the legendary Golem. But Maharal was a talmudist and radical thinker, a product of an exceptional moment in the sixteenth century when Renaissance science reached Poland and, more important, Prague. It was also espoused by such leading rabbinic figures as Moses Isserles (Krakow, 1520–1572), author of a commentary on a standard astronomical textbook but better known as the supreme legal authority for Ashkenazi Jewry, and David Gans (Germany and Prague, 1541–1613), an associate of the astronomers Johannes Kepler and Tycho de Brahe. Before long, geometry and algebra primers were increasingly appearing in Germany in both Hebrew and Yiddish.

The same Renaissance culture also influenced Yomtov Lippman Heller of Prague (1578–1654), who alongside his seminal works of talmudic learning composed a grammar book, a memoir in prose, and two poems about Jewish deliverance during the Thirty Years' War. And some time later, a long-forgotten genius: Tobias Cohen (1652–1729), native of Metz and Krakow, graduate (like generations

FIGURE 12. Construction of the body, from *Maaseh Tuviya*, a textbook of the sciences (1707).

of Ashkenazi young men) of the medical school of Padua in Italy, and a guest of the Ottoman Empire, where he was free to produce (in David Ruderman's words) "the most influential early modern Hebrew textbook of the sciences,"[9] *Maaseh Tuviya* (Venice, 1707). The Ashkenazi-Sephardi divide could be a porous one.

Ironically, the European Renaissance, which gave rise to this Ashkenazi renaissance, also contributed one catalyst to its demise: the spurt in Hebraic scholarship among Christians, which is the subject of our next chapter. In the long run, though, the Renaissance served dialectically to reinforce Ashkenazi rabbinic suspicion of linguistic and biblical learning. By the mid-seventeenth century, religious aversion to "Gentile wisdom" was so intense that even Hebrew-language scientific works widely fell into disfavor. The serious reading of an educated Ashkenazi male was usually Hebrew religious scholarship and ethical literature—not much different from what it had been when the Middle Ages began. As for women and the less educated, they entertained themselves by reading Yiddish.

But eventually the Renaissance, in a way, almost had the last word. In the late eighteenth century, Jews in central Europe began to revolt against the long freeze in cultural and religious values. This was the Haskalah (Jewish Enlightenment) movement. As we will see in chapter 8, it took just a slight opening of Christian society to the entry of Jews for the dam to burst. Within two generations, Gentile Enlightenment values would be lapping at the last bastions of traditional Jewish culture—and at what remained of Hebrew.

Even so, however, all would not be lost; Judaism and Hebrew culture would find new resources from within, in the form of ḥasidic and antiḥasidic revivalism. And even as the Haskalah was just beginning to unfold in Germany, a genius of talmudic learning in the traditionalist heartland of Lithuania, skeptical of anything that smacked of Haskalah, philosophy, and Gentile influences, would initiate a revival of grammar as a tool of talmudic scholarship. His name was Elijah, better known as the Gaon (prince, prodigy) of Vilna (1720–1797).

Lost and Found

The medieval Hebrew works discussed in these chapters were the lucky ones. They were either recopied and preserved in Jewish hands or, just as often, swept up for some ducal or ecclesiastical archive and perhaps eventually cataloged, rediscovered, and finally published. Hundreds of sacred poems got passed down in the various liturgies. But most works were lost, burned, or simply forgotten. Only with the revelation of the Cairo Genizah is the vastness of this sacred poetry slowly emerging.

We've observed that Jews in Christian Europe wrote almost everything in Hebrew, whereas those in Arab lands generally used Arabic for matters scientific or philosophical. The difference turned out to be crucial: well before this era ends, the great age of Jewish and Arab secular learning had also ended. Few Jews wished any longer to read its Arabic-language products, and few preserved them. These great works faced oblivion unless translated into Hebrew and brought to Christian Europe. And often even that did not save them.

By contrast, fortune favored the Hebrew worldly poetry of the golden age, brought north by Sephardi refugees. Although it held little attraction for pious Ashkenazi and Sephardi readers, manuscripts sometimes found their way into Jewish or Christian collections—and eventually into the eager hands of Jewish "enlighteners." The nineteenth century saw the publication in Germany of many great works of the golden age, even though often garbled and/or misattributed. These swiftly took an honored place in the "enlightened" modern-Jewish bookcase.

Who Held the Keys to Culture?

Jewish cultural history has often dwelled on the educated male. In reality, running through medieval Jewish life was a three-way divide among the shoulds, the could-nots, and the should-nots.

A minority of Jews, often a large one, comprised educated males. They, the shoulds, were expected to be at home in Hebrew and religious literature (generally the Pentateuch and Talmud with commentaries and, after the seventeenth century, kabbalistic works—and, in the Sephardi realm, some Bible, Mishnah, and Midrash). Remarkably, in medieval Ashkenaz, the tutor with his one-room school was the "central figure in the educational process," as

Ephraim Kanarfogel puts it,[10] until a boy was sent away to talmudic academy. Another minority was made up of less literate males, the could-nots.

That left half the population: the should-nots—in other words, women. Almost everywhere, women were generally precluded from studying the Torah in depth (if at all), being exempt by talmudic law itself. In the influential words of the twelfth-century *Sefer Ḥasidim*:

> One must teach one's daughters the practical rules for *mitzvot*.
> The sages' statement that "Teaching one's daughter Torah is like teaching her impropriety" refers to in-depth study, talmudic reasoning, and the esoteric.

Accordingly, few women could attain a command of Hebrew. In Europe, however, they were commonly taught to read enough Hebrew to know their prayers (though there were also specially composed women's prayer books in Yiddish). They were also taught to read and achieve literacy in the Jewish vernacular, typically Yiddish or Ladino, which was everywhere written in Hebrew script. One deleterious effect on Hebrew of the advent of printing in the fifteenth and sixteenth centuries was the boom in popular books in Yiddish and Ladino, ostensibly for womenfolk but in fact for men as well. Since these were written with a mass readership in mind, they had much wider appeal than scholarly works in Hebrew. And that set the stage for a prolonged struggle between Hebrew and the Jewish vernacular for the loyalty of the masses. In the late 1930s, as World War II began, the struggle was still raging.

The gap between the sexes can be overstated. Some major central European communities did school their girls in Torah and Hebrew, and there were remarkable cases of erudite women like Eva Bacharach (Germany, d. 1651), a member of a noted rabbinic line. In the Arab world, too, while Jewish and Arab women were mostly illiterate, girls without brothers would sometimes be given a textual education. The traveler Petaḥiah of Regensburg reported of Samuel ben Eli Gaon (influential head of the Baghdad Academy, twelfth century):

> He has no sons, only one daughter. She is expert in Scripture and Talmud. She gives instruction in Scripture to young men, through a window. (*Travels of Rabbi Petachia*)

Male and female literacy among Jews probably well exceeded that of non-Jews in most medieval societies. In the Middle Ages and as late as the eighteenth and nineteenth centuries, Jewish literacy served to emphasize the gulf between Jew and Gentile, affording many Jews (women as well as men) a sense of empowerment in their powerlessness, while providing anti-Semites with yet another cause for envy and suspicion.

When All's Said and Done

The period from the closing of the Talmud in the seventh century until the beginnings of the Haskalah or Enlightenment in the eighteenth century was a time during which religion dominated Jewish life and Hebrew was primarily a religious language. Yet, despite the thread of religious and textual continuity, we have found Hebrew being put to many purposes that, while not secular (as scholars often render the Hebrew word *ḥol*, "worldly"), could also not be labeled religious, and taking many novel linguistic forms that had no scriptural or other textual precedent. In the long-running struggle for religious and ethnic survival, Hebrew played key roles in transmitting knowledge and expressing national pride. These were strong vital signs, as written languages go. At the same time, as noted, non-Jewish and especially Arab practices left an indelible mark on methods of textual study and even choice of language.

Modern scholars like to laud some parts of the medieval record, such as grammatical study or the Andalusian golden age, while lamenting or neglecting others. What we have seen here should serve as a corrective. Did the era see advances? Without a doubt: *nikkud* (diacritics), a systematic Hebrew linguistics, the simple lucid prose styles of Rashi and Maimonides. Then came what many would justifiably see as a decline, with the waning of the High Middle Ages and the great expulsions from western and central Europe. The Jewish Enlightenment, which we shall encounter in greater depth in chapter 8, would bring fresh advances on many fronts, even if against these must also be set some staggering losses.

6

Hebrew in the Christian Imagination, I

MEDIEVAL DESIGNS

Introduction

Many languages have held a special place in the Christian mind: Aramaic as the tongue of the apostles (not to mention Jesus himself); Greek, Latin, Syriac, Old Church Slavonic, and others as the languages of revered Bible translations. Moreover, the Church has always regarded the Hebrew Bible, the "Old Testament," as itself sacred, and as testifying to the veracity of the New. Might it not then be expected that the Hebrew *language*—or at least the Hebrew text of the Bible—would occupy a special place of honor?

At times it did, even intensely, and such moments will be the focus of this and the following chapter. However, for most of two millennia, both the Hebrew language and the Hebrew text of the Bible have been marginal to Christianity or even deliberately repressed. We will ponder this as well.

From early Christianity down to the Renaissance, what interest there was in Hebrew was almost invariably religious in nature. At times, it was associated with a quest for the transcendental. More often, it was the product of efforts to cast new light on the meaning of the Bible. From time to time, Hebrew also served as an ideological tool or symbol for promoting religious reform. And, persistently, the Church sought to employ it for the practical business of converting the Jews.

With the Renaissance and Enlightenment, Christian Europe suddenly developed a passion for exotic languages—and for Jewish culture. The latter in turn generated new ideas about language, sending aficionados to their Hebrew Bibles and dictionaries. New forms of "Hebraism" surfaced in the political science being developed in Britain and the Netherlands by Thomas Hobbes, Hugo Grotius, and others, and in new twists on old beliefs like millenarianism. But by the early nineteenth century, with the dawning of a new secular age, religious and ideological interest in Hebrew among Christians had precipitously waned. Today, it rarely makes a headline or a budget line.

Christian and Jew almost always came to Hebrew from different directions, although sometimes with similar goals in mind. Christians were rarely reared on Hebrew texts. Nor did they generally take much interest in composing or speaking the language. As we will see, theirs was a very different linguistic and cultural ecosystem, one in which Latin (and later other European literary languages) played a role similar to that played by Hebrew among Jews. At the same time, Christians and Jews were sometimes conscious of their converging linguistic interests and even reached out to one another. Christian Hebraism eventually made some lasting contributions to the Jewish study of Hebrew, if not exactly by design.

We will now retrace our steps through history, going back to the rabbinic period but this time looking at Hebrew's reflection in a Christian mirror.

Early Christianity, Origen, and the Ghost of Hebrew

Most Christians in the year 100 CE would not have encountered a Hebrew version of the Bible. Nor would they have heard or seen the Hebrew language. They were typically Gentiles, often living alongside Jews in cities like Antioch (in modern-day Syria) or Sardis (in modern-day Turkey), but in quite separate social and religious spheres. It was primarily to Gentiles that the early Church addressed its theological message, presenting itself as a religion separate from Judaism and doing so in the Greek language.

Yet the Jewish scriptures were ever present in some form or other, interpreted symbolically in confirmation of the Christian message. For the most part, they were known as they appear in the Greek Septuagint or in Syriac; most later translations were based on one or the other of these two. (Syriac, a close relative of Aramaic, was written in its own alphabet and was an important language of early Christian scholarship.) Rarely during Christianity's first millennium were churchmen seized by a desire to know and study the Hebrew Bible in the original. The two outstanding exceptions were the Church Fathers Origen and Jerome.

In early third-century Caesarea, a mixed Gentile and Jewish city between present-day Haifa and Tel Aviv, an Alexandrian theologian named Origen decided to lay out the entire Jewish Bible in parallel Greek and Hebrew columns. He filled an estimated six thousand pages. Besides the Hebrew text and that of the Septuagint, he included a transliteration of the Hebrew into Greek letters and three alternative translations into Greek. The final product is thus known as the *Hexapla* (sixfold). Alas, only fragments survive.

Origen, whose Hebrew was shaky, probably had Jewish help when it came to the transliterations. He also shuffled the order of the Greek Septuagint and sprinkled it with brackets and interpolations to enable his readers to compare the Greek and Hebrew versions word for word.

Why? Origen writes of wanting to clear up the worrying discrepancies among different Greek versions of scripture and to establish a reliable and authoritative translation. This could be done only through reference to the Hebrew. The *Hexapla* could also assist Christians in their disputations with Jews, enabling them to quote the Hebrew, albeit from a transliteration. Origen may also have been interested in unlocking the esoteric power of the Hebrew divine names by pronouncing them aloud, or merely gazing upon them. The Near East had long been saturated with such practices. But this rationale alone does not explain the immense labor he put into the effort. He must surely also have believed that a reference guide to each Hebrew word would help Christian preachers in their pursuit of allegorical interpretations of the Jewish Bible. But neither his contemporaries nor his disciples took the study of Hebrew any further; what Origen had done was more than sufficient.

Back to the Hebrew: Jerome Rewrites the Latin Bible

Around the year 375, in the Syrian desert, a young ascetic named Jerome was studying Hebrew as a linguistic mortification of the mental flesh (as James Barr has put it).[1] He had been fascinated by theology and grammar while a young man in Rome, but then withdrew to the desert where, he records, he was smitten with a more carnal desire, assuaged only by his learning Hebrew:

> My mind still raced with evil thoughts. To tame its turbulence, I sought out a brother hermit, a former Jew, and asked him to teach me Hebrew. I, who was once so much at home with the flow of Cicero and the softness of Pliny, was learning my letters all over again and producing words guttural and harsh to the ear. What labor I invested, how often I despaired—anyone who lived with me will tell you. But, thank the Lord, from the bitterly sown

seed I am plucking sweet fruit. (Letter 125, Ad Rusticum §12. My translation. Slightly abbreviated.)

The "sweet fruit" was the creation of a new Latin translation of the Jewish Bible, directly from the Hebrew. (Jerome would also render the New Testament from its original Greek into Latin. The two translations, together known as the Vulgate, remain the standard Latin Bible for the Catholic Church.) The translation from Hebrew took a mere fifteen years (390–405), during which Jerome received considerable help from local rabbis he approached while living in Bethlehem. He also penned copious Latin commentaries on the biblical text. In the commentary on Jeremiah, for example, one scholar has counted explanations for over seventy-five Hebrew words and thirty proper names.[2]

Jerome's driving purpose seems quite clear: he was repelled by the hodgepodge of Latin and Greek versions in circulation, and he had a profound reverence for the Hebrew of scripture. Several years spent rendering the Septuagint into Latin had left him disillusioned with the Greek. Only through the Hebrew original, the *hebraica veritas* (Hebrew truth), as he called it, could one engage with the Holy Spirit that had given these works to man. In particular, Jerome wanted to get at the plain-sense meaning: only by this route could one approach the deeper, figurative meaning that the Church saw in the Jewish Bible.

Beneath all this, one can discern other strange forces at work. Jerome was in love with the Hebraic and the Oriental, those aspects of Christianity (and of Judaism) that made it so foreign to the Greco-Roman spirit. To undertake a translation was therefore no easy task: Greeks and Romans were not given to learning exotic tongues, or to equating any literature or rhetoric with their own. Compared with the Latin that Jerome adored, the style of the prophets, he wrote, "had once seemed raw and repugnant" (Letter 22, Ad Eustochium, § 30). He had forced himself to love it.

Jerome had no love for Jews or for Judaism. He routinely disparaged Jews and caricatured the very rabbis who taught him. But the Hebrew language was, to him, distinct from actual Judaism: it was part of *Verus Israel*, the "true Israel" of which the Church now proclaimed itself the sole legatee. His attitude prefigured the love-hate relationship felt by a long line of medieval and Renaissance churchmen for the Jews who taught them Hebrew.

Jerome's *hebraica veritas* was enough to upset Augustine (354–430), greatest of early Church theologians. Who needed a translation from the Hebrew? he tartly asked Jerome, not least because the existing translations were the work of men wiser than he, and even they did not always match the Hebrew text. Indeed, Augustine asserts in *De doctrina christiana*, the seventy translators who created the Septuagint "enjoyed so much of the presence and power of the Holy Spirit in their work of translation that among that number of men there was but one voice" (bk. II, chap. 15).

Nonetheless, in that same work, Augustine felt compelled to concede that "Latin speakers . . . need two other languages for the knowledge of Scripture, Hebrew and Greek, so that they may have recourse to the original texts if the endless diversity of the Latin translators throws them into doubt" (bk. II, chap. 11). Self-contradictory assertions of this kind will recur in this chapter. In the meantime, Augustine's objections notwithstanding, Jerome's translation from the Hebrew steadily became the standard Latin version.

For medieval Christendom as a whole, Jerome's Vulgate had a far-reaching impact that he himself could not have imagined or wished for. Like the Greek Septuagint, the Vulgate came to be seen, as Jerome Friedman has put it, "not as a translation but as the

Latin voice of God."[3] It was not that Jerome's Latin was so beautiful, but rather that the Church and its flock became accustomed to treating the particular Bible version they grew up hearing as the original. The spoken word has a peculiar power. It was thus the *latina veritas*, not the *hebraica veritas*, that exercised so deep an effect on Western civilization.

Twelfth-Century Paris and a Fleeting Romance

Seven hundred years would pass before the study of Hebrew again had a place in Christian intellectual life. Once Jerome's translation cleared away the thicket of earlier translations, the Western Church could comfortably accept his rendition of the plain sense and focus on allegorical, symbolic, and mystical interpretations. And the few who did care about the plain sense or the etymologies of biblical names could similarly rely on Jerome's translation and commentaries. Now and then, an individual churchman might acquire Hebrew and study Jewish mystical texts, or a Jew knowledgeable in the Bible might be consulted either by a bishop seeking to discredit the Rabbis or by an outstanding scholar—like Alcuin of York (735–804), adviser to Charlemagne—wishing to clear up the endless textual corruptions generated by copyists or second-rate translators trying to pass themselves off as Jerome. But these cases were exceptional. Jews had little part in Christian engagement with the Jewish Bible.

The twelfth century, however, saw a rare meeting of Christian and Jewish minds. Burgeoning cities, the growth of commerce, and improved transportation went hand in hand with ecclesiastical reforms and the founding of urban colleges and libraries. During this period, known to historians as the twelfth-century Renaissance, interactions between Christians and Jews seem to have been relatively easy. For a few fleeting decades, in Paris, Troyes, and other northern French centers, Bible scholars of the two faiths set aside their differences to conduct a dialogue on a new, rationalistic agenda that each was independently developing for studying the Hebrew Bible.

On the one side were the yeshivot (academies) of the disciples of Rashi, dedicated to plain-sense biblical interpretation and text-critical analysis of the Talmud. On the other were the Victorines, British and French scholars centered at the new Collegiate Abbey of Saint-Victor, founded in Paris in 1108. Both groups used the tools of literary, historical, and linguistic analysis to advance understanding of the plain sense-in-context of the Hebrew Bible. In delving into the meaning of biblical Hebrew, the Victorines went far beyond Jerome.

This brief comment on the firmament (Genesis 1), by Andrew of St. Victor (d. 1175), embodies the Victorine agenda:

Leaving aside such issues as whether the firmament is pure fire, whether it moves, and what it serves as a representation of, we will limit ourselves to seeking a literal explanation. (Commentary on Heptateuch)

The same words could have come from the pen of Rashi. Indeed, the Victorines and their followers were not afraid to draw on the popular Jewish translations (*pitronot*) into French and Latin, or the latest rabbinic commentaries produced by Rashi's successors, the latter of which they heard firsthand or found circulating in Latin translation. Andrew of St. Victor stands out, with 140 of his 248 references to the Hebrew coming from contemporary Jewish sources.

Leading practitioners of Hebraic scholarship in England included Herbert of Bosham, who could even read Rashi's commentary in the original, and Stephen Langton, archbishop of Canterbury and author of a Hebrew-Latin lexicon. They were undeterred by the critiques of Christianity in which contemporary rabbinic commentaries sometimes engaged. Even the mystically oriented Cistercian order consulted the rabbis in revising the Psalter. The Jews, for their part, monitored Christian exegesis, sometimes even in Latin, and may have emulated some of its methods.

This is not to say that the Jewish interpretation was deemed *the* authoritative interpretation, or that Jews were on a "telephone line to the Old Testament," as Beryl Smalley jokingly put it,[4] if only for the simple reason that there were frequently more Jewish interpretations than one. Christian scholars reserved the right to follow their own taste or reason in choosing some over others. They could also heap scorn on those they disliked.

Were the Victorines pushing the envelope? Socially, yes. To conduct business with Jews was one thing, but to consult regularly and seek guidance quite another. Religiously, too, their efforts to seek the plain meaning of the text broke the Christian mold, which valued typological exegesis—understanding Old Testament texts as prefigurations of the New—over all other readings. But ultimately the Victorines were looking not to acquire knowledge for its own sake but to understand their own faith more fully. If that meant reining in anti-Jewish thinking, so be it. In fact, the whole project turned on mutual trust: Christian trust that the Jews had an authentic text and interpretive tradition that they were purveying honestly, and Jewish trust that what they were disclosing would not be used to disparage or convert them.

Such a detached commitment to *hebraica veritas* proved unsustainable. By the close of the twelfth century, Christian perceptions of Judaism were shifting ominously. The very contact with Jews that had given Christians some insight into the Jewish reading of the Bible triggered anxieties among those theologians, as well as among their coreligionists, and sharpened the sense of difference. And the entire enterprise was riven by disputes and self-doubt. Richard of St. Victor, a radical in his own right, sharply criticized Andrew, insinuating that he was a Judaizer—a grave accusation:

> In many places [in Andrew's work] the Jewish opinion is given as though it were not so much the Jews' as his own! On that passage [in Isaiah], "Behold a virgin will conceive and bear a son," [Andrew] gives the Jewish objections [to the translation "virgin"] without even refuting them.[5]

The writing was on the wall. In 1168, the canon-law authority Rufinus condemned the Hebrew text as less reliable than Jerome's Latin. In 1198 the Cistercians recanted and prohibited Hebrew study with Jews.

Mysteries of an English Abbey and an Oxford Alchemist

In England, they did things differently. One thirteenth-century monastery was captivated not only by the Hebrew Bible but by the Hebrew language itself, and invested immense effort in producing sophisticated linguistic manuals. Whom they were for, and how the monks were able to create them, remains a mystery.

Longleat House, the stately home of the Marquis of Bath in the Wiltshire countryside west of London, preserves a unique two-hundred-leaf medieval manuscript. Its contents include a thirteenth-century dictionary of biblical Hebrew and a Hebrew grammar written in Hebrew and Latin. Recently published in all its splendor,[6] the dictionary is perhaps the greatest accomplishment of medieval Christian Hebraism. Embracing the entire biblical vocabulary and more, it is most likely the product of a generation's work, copied by three Christian scribes and probably completed at the Benedictine abbey in Ramsey in central England.

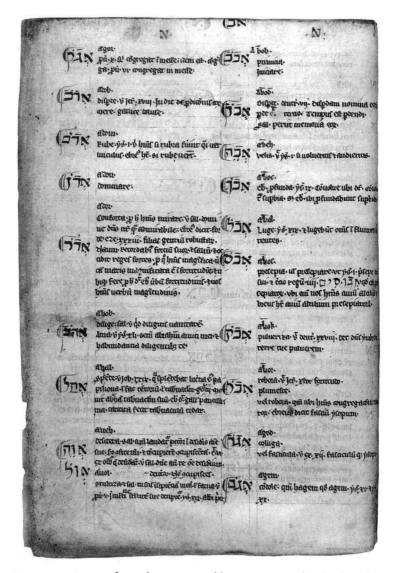

FIGURE 13. A page from the Ramsey Abbey Dictionary (England, 13th century).

The verb section lists 1,392 Hebrew verbs, many with several subentries, and all listed (for the most part correctly) in the imperative form—a feat of organization and grammatical analysis by itself since in the Bible only one in ten of these verbs occurs in the imperative, and there would seem to have been no other similarly organized Hebrew lexicon that the authors of this one could have imitated. Each entry is glossed in Latin and, often, in French, with a biblical citation as illustration. The authors frequently drew on Rashi's commentaries for their definitions. There is no evidence that Jews (or converts) were directly involved, but, after Spain, medieval England had some of the best Jewish scholarship in Hebrew.

Less fortunate than the Ramsey dictionary was the *Ars loquendi et intellegendi in lingua hebraica* (The art of speaking and understanding Hebrew), listed in the abbey's ancient catalog. Were medieval Jews and Christians actually conversing in the Holy Tongue? Sadly, the manuscript has not survived to tell us, but no fewer than twenty-five Bible manuscripts written by Jews have also been found, with Latin translations added by Christians.

Meanwhile, in Oxford, a remarkable philosophy of Hebrew was taking shape in the mind of the Franciscan scientist, alchemist, and polymath Roger Bacon (1214–1294). Synthesizing Aristotelian philosophy of language with Christian doctrine, Bacon's hypotheses about Hebrew anticipated many great questions of the Renaissance. (In some ways, they also resembled ancient and medieval Jewish thinking about Hebrew.) If it was the language of divine revelation, Bacon posited, Hebrew must possess explosive powers for good and evil. And if it was the mother of all languages, surely all languages shared a universal grammar, differing only superficially but pointing the way to universal scientific knowledge. And surely the plain sense of the Hebrew (and Greek) of the Bible was the key to this scientific understanding. No translation could help; the Bible had to be studied in the original. Plus, there was a practical, if secondary, benefit: knowing Hebrew could help Christians convert the Jews.

In sum, what was happening in thirteenth-century England pointed to the first organized attempt by Christians to make Hebrew studies their own. But the opportunity was lost: in 1290, Edward I became the first European monarch to expel the Jews from his kingdom en masse. Not until 1656 could they return.

Fear and Reprisal

> Certain friars were tutored in Hebrew with the goal of mastering the mischief and the falsehoods of the Jews, so that they might no longer have the effrontery to deny the true text, as had been their wont, nor the glosses of their own wise men who concur with our saints in these affairs.
>
> —Anonymous fourteenth-century biographer of Pablo Christiani

Fear gripped the Church of Rome in the thirteenth and fourteenth centuries. Unheard-of Aristotelian theologies, rumors of doomsday, religious dissent, and nightmarish visions of Christendom as an organic body upon which Jews were feasting like zombies were challenging its stability. The Church responded with aggressive evangelism. Friars formed themselves into missionary armies, with a powerful linguistic weapon: Hebrew knowledge. For the first time, the language became strategic territory on which their theological battles would be waged.

While these centuries saw bloody attacks on Jews becoming increasingly common, the Dominican and Franciscan orders preferred using the tactics of persuasion laid down by Thomas Aquinas: Jew and Muslim must be addressed, mildly if possible, with reference to their respective sacred tongues, and shown that they had misunderstood their own scriptures. Tactics included public disputations and church sermons—both compulsory. To this end, Dominican colleges were founded across Spain in the 1250s and 1260s to train friars in Hebrew and Arabic—the first such foreign-language schools in Christendom.

The friars, then, were trying to turn the tables on the Jews. Where the Victorines felt some respect for Jewish learning, and where the Hebrew language held a clear fascination for some Christians in England, the friars were seeking to challenge Jewish authority over the language. But the conversion campaigns failed, as did the Hebrew-teaching institutions. Few Jews were swayed by Christian arguments, however Hebraically informed. Mass conversions of Spanish Jewry came only in the late fourteenth and fifteenth centuries—and then as a result not of suasion but of violence.

Woe to them, for they corrupt the text

The Church's growing demonization of rabbinic literature, especially the Talmud, opened another angle of attack on Jewish Hebraic authority. An inexorable logic was at play here: since Jews and Judaism were bad, but their scripture was holy, their evil had to come from elsewhere. And what did the Jews have that Christians did not? The Talmud. In 1239, Pope Gregory IX ordered that all Jewish books in western Europe be confiscated and, if found un-Christian, burned. The French king obliged, but first, chivalrously, staged a disputation in Paris between Friar Nicholas Donin and four French rabbis. In actuality, the disputation took the form of a trial in which the Talmud was the defendant and the rabbis its attorneys. The clerical court found the Talmud guilty; over ten thousand volumes (a staggering number in itself) are said to have been consigned to the flames.

Christian scholars now began to recognize the rabbinic classics, the Talmud and Midrash, as the engines of Jewish faith. These scholars (typically, zealous ex-Jews) eagerly anthologized the texts in Latin so they could pillory them as distortions, fantasies, and examples of Jewish "self-heresy." Talmudic and midrashic interpretation of the Bible, they declared, ignored the plain sense that the Jews themselves had so long defended.

And then there was the Hebrew Bible itself. Ever more frequently, the old accusation was repeated that exclusive knowledge of Hebrew had enabled the Jews to corrupt scripture in order to mask the Christian truth. (Muslims adopted a similar explanation to address uncomfortable discrepancies between the Bible and the Quran.) The Jews, it was said, had even censored later Jewish texts—the Talmud, the Midrash, and Josephus—to remove information about the Christian savior. The twelfth- and thirteenth-century chronicler Giraldus Cambrensis records with pleasure:

> Master Robert, Prior of St. Frideswide at Oxford [the core of the future Oxford University] . . . was a literate man erudite in the Scriptures, with a knowledge of Hebrew. He sent to various towns and cities of England where Jews resided to gather large numbers of Hebrew copies of Josephus. . . . And in two of them he found testimony about Christ written fully and at length, but as if recently scratched out, while in the others it had been entirely edited out. . . . The Jews were duly convicted of this malicious fraud. (*Works* 8:65–66)

This suspicion that the writings and writers on whom Christianity was existentially dependent were infinitely capable of dissimulation was a prescription for extreme psychological reactions. Such accusations would reach fever pitch with the Christian discovery of Kabbalah in the Renaissance.

7

Hebrew in the Christian Imagination, II

FROM KABBALISTS TO COLONIALS

Kabbalah Uncovered

European culture during the fifteenth and sixteenth centuries can be summarized in three words: humanism, renaissance, and reformation. Motivating proponents of all three was a desire to reach back to a simpler, more spiritual past: whether the intellectual and artistic world of classical antiquity or the "purer" Christianity of the Bible and Church Fathers. *Ad fontes!* (to the sources) was the motto of the age. Latin authors, of whom there were still many, sought to imitate the style of Virgil and Cicero rather than the accepted conventions of medieval Church Latin. The rediscovery of ancient Greek—the knowledge of which had long lapsed in western Europe—created great excitement. Inevitably, this interest in the past led to a curiosity about the early Church and about Hebrew, which appeared to some as a third classical language.

The interest in ancient languages took many forms: aesthetic, philosophical, esoteric, and even magical. It accompanied a new attitude of syncretism, the greatest proponent of which was the Florentine philosopher Marsilio Ficino (1433–1499), one of the founding fathers of Renaissance humanism. Ficino was convinced that the thought of all ancient thinkers—Plato, Zoroaster, Pythagoras, Hermes Trismegistus, Moses, and Jesus—shared one essence, and devoted himself to capturing it. Under these various influences, Renaissance Christian Hebraists would begin to turn to a genre largely ignored by their medieval predecessors: kabbalistic texts.

In 1486, Ficino's disciple Pico della Mirandola, a twenty-three-year-old Renaissance wunderkind, was planning a spectacular symposium in Rome on universal truth. Inducted into Jewish esotericism and Hebrew by obliging Jewish acquaintances, Pico was convinced that the literature of Kabbalah was the *true* transcript of what Moses heard at Sinai. Thus Christianity and Judaism were one, with Kabbalah as the point of connection. Differences between Judaism and Christianity were superficial, apparent only at the exoteric level.

Pico took seriously kabbalistic ideas about the theurgic powers of the Hebrew language and, synthesizing them with his other occult investigations, concluded that it could be used to unleash the divine and bring salvation. "There are no letters in the Law," he wrote, "which in their forms, combinations, separations, contortion, direction . . . do not manifest the secrets of the ten sefirot" (*Conclusiones cabalisticae* I.28.33. My translation).

Prior to the symposium, Pico unwisely published his findings, with studied obscurity, in a set of nine hundred Latin theses. The pope promptly banned the event. Not that anyone would have understood much. Thesis 70 speaks of the infinite meanings produced by conjoining the biblical consonants with different vowels; in his commentary on the first word of Genesis, *bereshit* (in the beginning), he finds no fewer than twelve anagrams, strings them together, and discovers a message about the Trinity.

This episode of European intellectual history might have been forgotten but for Johannes Reuchlin, Pico's star student. Reuchlin (1455–1522) was probably the most brilliant German humanist of his time. Writing in a Latin embroidered with scores of Hebrew words, he set out to prove that the truths of Christianity were encoded in the Hebrew Bible. To this end, he employed three decoding tools encountered in rabbinic esoterics: *gematria, notarikon* (reading words as acrostics), and *temurah* (systematically exchanging each letter for another).

Thus, permuting the forty-two letters of the first two verses of Genesis, Reuchlin thought he, too, like Pico, had detected a message about the Trinity. Similarly, in his dialogue *De arte cabalistica* (1517), a fictional Jewish philosopher explains that the mysteries of Hebrew can provide unassailable power for good. Leading the Latin reader through the fifty gates of understanding and thirty-two paths of wisdom "whose great power can raise us to a virtually uninterrupted communion with the angels, the lofty, and the divine," he divulges seventy-two mysterious three-letter Hebrew strings and asserts, "By these symbols the angels are summoned and bring help to mankind." Reuchlin thus engaged in a sort of linguistic alchemy, transforming Jewish texts into Christian ones.

Did Reuchlin's approach to Judaism affect perceptions of Jews? Reuchlin himself had an unusual sympathy for the Jews of his day, campaigning vocally for Jewish rights. "I know that my opponents find me hard to bear," he wrote, "for calling the Jews 'our fellow citizens.' Now I would like them to go crazy and burst apart when I say that the Jews are our brothers" (*Defensio* [1513]. My translation). And anger them he did; few of his contemporaries embraced this message, although a number of scholars and intellectuals jumped on the Kabbalah bandwagon, either by reading Reuchlin or by gaining access to the sources themselves. Unfortunately, the newly discovered kabbalistic wisdom was pressed into the service of converting the Jews. Proselytizers presented Kabbalah as a Christian message of "pure love," contrasted with the alleged talmudic ethos of "legalism."

This interpretation gained adherents. Many of the people snapping up Latin translations of kabbalistic texts were staunch Catholics. Medieval authority was failing, the papacy was discredited, and faith seemed threatened. Pope Sixtus himself was amassing a Kabbalah library. And why not? The Jews had no doubt perversely concealed their own ancient Israelite Christian wisdom. The needs of theology, in Moshe Idel's acute phrase, trumped the facts of philology.[1]

Christian Kabbalah: A Theology of Its Own

Christian Kabbalah (soon to become post-Christian Kabbalah) began to seek meaning in every paralinguistic and metalinguistic dimension of Hebrew esotericism, employing the techniques of Reuchlin but also analyzing the names and shapes of letters, diacritics, cantillation marks, and scribal adornments. While stemming from Kabbalah and beliefs about Hebrew, Christian kabbalism was widely perceived on all sides as a distinct set of values, ideas, and practices.

This new kabbalism focused not on worship of God but on mystical enlightenment and the limitless powers that *gnosis* or esoteric knowledge could grant to man. Manipulations of the Hebrew language, speculative numerology, and other theurgic techniques promised practitioners limitless intellectual power, untrammeled by the Church. By the cunning of history, this quest to control the natural world by means of the supernatural world would profoundly influence those who sought to control the natural world through knowledge of nature itself. Students of Christian Kabbalah would eventually include such scientific rationalists as Francis Bacon, Giordano Bruno, Gottfried Wilhelm Leibniz, and Isaac Newton. Indeed, Christian kabbalism could be said to have sup-

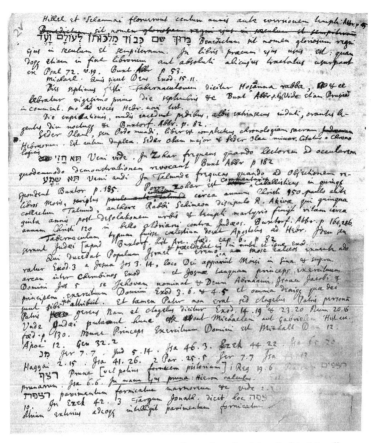

FIGURE 14. Isaac Newton's own Hebrew handwriting in his *Miscellaneous Notes and Extracts on the Jewish Temple* (ca. 1680).

plied much of the intellectual confidence that underwrote early modern science.

Jewish, Christian, and pagan or Hermetic esotericism mingled freely in the minds of Renaissance syncretists. In Italy, there was Giulio Camillo, who labored at building a seven-level "memory theater" representing the seven *sefirot* (in Kabbalah, divine emanations), seven planets, and a plethora of kabbalistic and Greek-

FIGURE 15. Articulation of the letter *tet* in Helmont's *Short Sketch of the Truly Natural Hebrew Alphabet* (Germany, 1667).

language imagery. His hope was to provoke in his audiences an experience of déjà vu, bringing to the surface the knowledge of the Creator and universal truths embedded in what we might now call the subconscious. These would then impart the art of transforming matter, word, and soul.

In Germany, there was Francis Mercury van Helmont, described by Allison Coudert as "the most famous (or infamous) Christian kabbalist of the 17th century."[2] His *Short Sketch of the Truly Natural Hebrew Alphabet* (also known as *The Alphabet of Nature*, 1667) claimed that deaf-mutes could be taught Hebrew, and that he had rediscovered the key to peace on earth in the shape and sound of the Hebrew letters. But his fixation with Hebrew made him the outlier. Increasingly, Christian kabbalists dismissed Hebrew altogether, looking instead to the magical and theosophical power of numbers.

Despite the massive output of Christian kabbalists, and their influence on some of the greatest minds of the early modern era, their works lost their appeal in the eighteenth century as the Renaissance gave way to the Enlightenment. Christian Kabbalah eventually found its place, as Frank Manuel has put it, in "a corner in the cemetery of Baroque learning."[3]

Humanism, Eden, and Babel

The Renaissance, wrote D. C. Allen, "loved language as other ages have loved wealth and power."[4] Renaissance humanists also sought those things that bind humanity together. It might be the Greco-Roman classics or other ancients, or it might literally be a "first language," or *lingua humana*. Here, as Roger Bacon had noted two centuries earlier, Hebrew had a distinct advantage.

Motives varied for seeking the *lingua humana*: to discover the perfect language that might resolve controversies and prevent wars; to explain the ever-growing diversity of languages that seafarers were discovering; or to make sense of biblical accounts of Eden and Babel. Sometimes the rational and the esoteric mingled; it was an age when religious authority was under attack and the esoteric was knocking on the door. And for many, this first language could only have been Hebrew. Indeed, in a world where the Bible was generally accepted as true, no other language had such a persuasive claim to primacy.

Perhaps no single thinker applied more of these reasons at once than Guillaume Postel (1510–1581). This French Hebraist, a pioneer of comparative lexicography, was torn between the view in Plato's

Cratylus that language was "conventional"—that is, a product of human interactions—and the view that it went back to an Adamic Hebrew given by God and still charged with sanctity. As evidence for the latter, he offered word correspondences, including such gems as the similarity between the Hebrew *valad* (offspring) and French *valet*—not quite an example of systematic comparative linguistics.

But Postel was also a practitioner of the Hebrew esoteric. Moved by a belief that if only humankind would speak Hebrew, an undifferentiated knowledge of the Lord would fill the world and peace would reign, Postel writes of his own mystical ascent to a Hebrew alphabet spanning the heavens.

Postel was not alone in finding evidence of Hebrew in European languages. A contemporary of his, the pioneering Viennese historical cartographer Wolfgang Lazius (1514–1565), suggested that after Babel the earliest Hebrews had migrated from Mesopotamia to Germany, hence such Hebrew-German correspondences as *lev* (heart) and *leben* (to live), *sovev* (turn) and *schweben* (hover). By contrast, the seventeenth-century Jesuit polymath Athanasius Kircher found the best evidence of the Hebrew-first theory in the simplicity of the language's triconsonantal roots.

Notwithstanding the strength of these arguments, the theory of Hebrew primacy had some prominent critics. Both Dante and Milton expressed skepticism. Bishop John Wilkins shrewdly noted that language rapidly "degenerates," so how could the Hebrew of the Bible have been that of Adam? In 1690, John Locke's treatise "Of Words or Language in General" (in his *Essay Concerning Human Understanding*) dodged the issue altogether, claiming that "God, having designed man for a sociable creature . . . furnished him also with language, which was to be the great instrument and common tie of society."

Hebrew, the Humanist Curriculum, and the Jews

With their mastery of written (and spoken) Latin, Christian scholars were well equipped to master Hebrew despite its alien grammar, lexicon, and script—and to plunge headfirst into the Hebrew Bible and even into rabbinic texts. Lack of vowel markings and punctuation was little deterrence to a classical scholar. The humanist passion for Greek and other strange languages stirred them still more.

One genre of classical learning in which the humanists outshone their Jewish counterparts was the systematic training in the art of Hebrew correspondence, culminating in the *Institutio epistolaris Hebraica* by Johannes Buxtorf the Elder (1564–1629), "a tool of immense utility for any learned Christian with basic Hebrew who wanted to communicate with contemporary Jewish scholars and booksellers," in Theodor Dunkelgrün's words—and, indeed, with fellow humanists.[5] Though not drawn to write Hebrew poetry or science, Christian Hebraists created a rich epistolary legacy.

Interest in Kabbalah or in the Hebrew language, of course, did not necessarily translate into positive attitudes toward Jews. In this regard, Reuchlin was more the exception than the rule. Desiderius Erasmus (1466–1536), the father of European humanism and one of the great proponents of *ad fontes*, believed it necessary for students of theology to know Greek and Hebrew, scraping off the centuries of Church Latin to find the Hebrew original beneath. To Erasmus, however, Hebrew was not a Jewish language but a classical language for all mankind. Thus he had no qualms about damning the Jews themselves.

Europe's Jews themselves had mixed responses to Christian Hebraism. The abuse of Jewish texts to malign or missionize made

them understandably reluctant to offer their books or their knowledge. Divulging mystical or rabbinic interpretation was also ex-
pressly prohibited in rabbinic law. It was from baptized Jews or fellow scholars such as Reuchlin that the humanists acquired most of
their Hebrew. Nonetheless, some Jews rejoiced when a Christian
came and said, "Teach me." Eminent rabbis, grammarians, and kabbalists in Italy and the Rhineland, including Obadiah Sforno, Elijah
Levita, and Naftali Hertz Treves, broke ranks to tutor Christian humanists. Treves penned a Hebrew letter around 1520 to the Augus-
tinian monastic leader Caspar Amman, promising to lend him a volume of Midrash:

> O Doctor Caspar Amman, famed for knowledge of Hebrew and
> grammar and immersed in Bible and prophetic tradition. . . . I
> shall do your bidding as far as I can. Just write to me in good
> spirit in Hebrew or Latin, may it please you.[6]

The paradox did not escape the French humanist Joseph Scaliger:
"It is peculiar how Buxtorf is adored by the Jews, though he so of-
fends them [. . .]" (*Secunda Scaligerana*, 249).

Following the horrors of the 1492 expulsion from Spain, the ex-
plosion in Christian Hebraism may well have confirmed Jewish
hopes of the arrival of the Messiah. Rabbi Abraham Halevi, an exile
from Spain, wrote as much:

> God has changed the hearts of many nations in the lands of the
> Christians to study Hebrew and Jewish literature, which they do
> thoroughly to the best of their ability. There is no doubt that they
> and many like them will return to the God on high, as the true
> prophets have testified.[7]

But neither Jews nor humanists could rest secure. In 1509, the
Holy Roman emperor Maximilian mandated the confiscation of all

Jewish books with a view to eradicating what remained of Judaism in his realm. The idea was the brainchild of Johannes Pfefferkorn, a convert to Christianity and Judeophobic propagandist. Pulling the strings was an unholy alliance of universities, churches, and the Inquisition.

Jews protested the emperor's edict; so did humanists. Brought in to adjudicate, Johannes Reuchlin wrote a sweeping vindication of Jewish literature: not only was it permissible, he averred; it was a civilizational treasure, worthy of study. European opinion on the subject became polarized. The assault on Hebrew became a proxy for a general counteroffensive against humanism. Pfefferkorn branded Reuchlin a heretic and Jew-lover who could read Hebrew no more quickly than an ass could climb a staircase.

For several years, poisonous tracts were traded; indictments and appeals ensued. One episcopal court even assessed the Inquisition for costs. In 1520, days after signing the first papal condemnation of Martin Luther, Leo X found against Reuchlin. By his death in 1522, Reuchlin had established Christian Hebraica, in Jerome Friedman's words, as "a *cause célèbre* of liberal Christian scholarly circles,"[8] but his efforts could not save the Talmud: in 1553, Pope Julius III issued a bull consigning all copies of the Talmud to the flames.

The thousands of Jewish books that burned in Rome's Campo de' Fiori and soon in scores of Italian cities reflected the hysteria stirred in Counter-Reformation minds by the spread of printed Hebrew books and by the ever-growing interest of Protestant Hebraists in the works of the Rabbis. In the vast new system of Church and state censorship, printers could expect pre- and postpublication audits, and specially trained inquisitors scoured rabbinic writings for insults to Catholicism. Venice banned possession of Hebrew books altogether. Inevitably, given the acute ambivalences, the very Hebrew letters in Hebrew books came to manifest a "conjunction between the sacred and the demonic," as Amnon Raz-Krakotzkin has put it.[9]

Martin Luther and Protestant Hebrew

Hebrew's part in the Renaissance has largely been forgotten. By contrast, its impact on the Reformation and the Early Enlightenment is better known, perhaps because here its influence was more enduring. The great Protestant Bible translations (Luther's German Bible and the King James Version) based themselves on the Hebrew original; Puritans and colonial Americans embraced biblical Hebrew; and, in a lesser known development, some of Europe's greatest jurists began to appeal to rabbinic civil law and governance as the basis of a free society.

Among the Reformation's key doctrines, which rapidly spread across sixteenth-century Europe, was that every Christian should be able to read the Bible for himself (or even for herself). For this to be possible, the Protestant reformers would have to provide their followers with vernacular translations. And just as they sought to return to a pristine, pre-Catholic version of Christianity, they sought to reach back past the Vulgate, basing their translations on the Hebrew, Aramaic, and Greek originals. Thus the Reformation added its own religious voice to the humanists' cry of *ad fontes!*

But there was more at play than rejecting the Vulgate, which the Cambridge Hebraist Edward Lively declared "in infinite places erroneous and faulty." The Reformation was a fight to reclaim the literal sense of the biblical text. Its overarching hermeneutical principle was that, through historical and literary insight, believers could recover the truth about ancient Israel and the ancient Church, and thus the proper worship of God. Even distinctly Christian readings of the Old Testament (Christological allegory, for example) had to be anchored in the plain Hebrew sense and its context. Hebrew scholarship, in short, was central to forging Protestant theology.

Among the tight-knit groups at the helm of the German Reformation in Wittenberg (where Luther spent most of his career), Switzerland, and the Rhineland were Hebraists like Conrad Pellican, Sebastian Muenster, Huldrych Zwingli, and Wolfgang Capito. Luther's team completed a grand German Bible translation in 1534 and then revised it unceasingly. To understand context and render it reliably into an effective German required a great deal more than mastering the grammar of Hebrew and its lexicon; it meant negotiating realistically with the limitations of sixteenth-century German. This was a goal far beyond anything the Victorines had attempted four hundred years earlier.

Hebrew could also give historical insight into Christian scripture itself. What could the Last Supper mean, asked one Protestant scholar, without a grasp of the Jewish blessings over food? As Luther put it,

> Without this language [Hebrew] there can be no understanding of Scripture, for the New Testament, although written in Greek, is full of Hebraisms. It is rightly said that the Hebrews drink from the fountains, the Greeks from the streams, and the Latins from the pools.[10]

Luther meant what he said. He had acquired a fair amount of Hebrew, digesting Reuchlin's Hebrew textbook and soon thereafter acquiring the confidence to disagree with both Reuchlin and Jerome. Jerome had translated the Hebrew term *rakiʾa* in Genesis as *firmamentum*, but Luther, mindful of the verb *raka* (to stretch), preferred *expansio*. Reuchlin translated the noun *ḥefets* as *voluntas* (will), but Luther insisted on *beneplacitum* (pleasure), preserving a

FIGURE 16. Reuchlin's musical notation for the Torah chant in his *De Accentibus et orthographia linguae hebraicae* (Germany, 1518).

subtle nuance of the Hebrew. But Luther also claimed to rely as much on his own theological and poetic instincts as on careful linguistic analysis, declaring pointedly, "I am no Hebraist in matters of grammar, for I do not hold myself to the text. Instead it passes through me" (*Table Talk* 314:12).

Luther and his "Sanhedrin" (as he called his team of translators) consulted rabbinic sources regularly. The theologian Johannes Mathesius recalled witnessing meetings of the translation committee when he boarded at Luther's home in 1540:

> The Doctor [Luther] came into the committee with his old Latin and new German Bible, and with them at all times the Hebrew

text. Mr. Philippus brought the Greek, Dr. Kreutziger the Hebrew along with the Chaldean. The professors had their rabbis [rabbinic commentaries] to hand. (*Thirteenth Sermon*)

But Luther and his fellows were hardly philosemites, and their faith in their Jewish sources was limited. Were Jewish elucidations reliable? Were they not tainted by Jewish beliefs? Were rabbis really any better than Christian grammarians? Skeptical, the Reformers adopted a selective methodology for translating the prophetic books of the Hebrew Bible, shunning rabbinic interpretations and even the plain sense of the text itself when it offended their Christian sensibilities.

All told, Luther's translation owed more to the Greek or Latin than to rabbinic opinion. When it suited his purposes, he even questioned the reliability of the Masoretic vowel points. Nonetheless, he recognized that knowledge of Hebrew, even Jewish knowledge of Hebrew, was a necessary component of his grand endeavor. And Hebrew left a deep imprint on his translation, which in turn did more than any other text to shape modern standard German. As we will see presently, the English language owes Hebrew a similar debt.

Inevitably, Hebrew scholarship, however de-Judaized, provoked charges of "Judaizing," especially in the heresy-sensitive climate of sixteenth-century Europe. Catholic and Protestant scholars hurled the term at each other, and many Protestants railed against humanist Hebraists and against Jews themselves. When he was not working on his famous Rabbinic-Latin Bible, Sebastian Muenster was writing rabidly anti-Semitic tracts with such passages as this:

Today the Jews, though living freely among Christians, abuse their venerable tongue and spout blasphemies. These perfidious people would have been banned from Christendom, had not the Redeemer himself wished them to survive.[11]

Was a "Hebrew anxiety" triggering some neurotic disorder? Perhaps an Oedipal hatred? Or a collective, religious version of "anxiety of influence" (in the term of the literary critic Harold Bloom)? Luther, in *On the Jews and Their Lies* (1543), called for all Jews to be expelled before they could poison more wells and ritually abuse more children. In *On the Last Words of David* he cursed himself for having used so much rabbinic exegesis in his translations.

But Luther's legacy of Hebraism endured. Wittenberg would become Europe's third-largest Hebrew printing center, and nineteenth-century German Lutherans the dominant academic voice in Hebraic studies.

"And behold it was good": English Dons the Spirit of Hebrew

They will say it cannot be translated into our tongue, it is so rude. It is not so rude as they are false liars. . . . The properties of the Hebrew tongue agree a thousand times more with the English than with the Latin.

—William Tyndale, *Preface to The Obedience of a Christian Man* (1528)

With these words, William Tyndale signaled the start of a special relationship between the Hebrew and English languages. His English translation of the Pentateuch (1530), the first-ever English translation from the Hebrew, would provide the fabric for the 1611 King James Bible and inject a Hebraic quality into the syntax and phraseology of English literary and religious usage without parallel in any European culture.

In the fifty years before Tyndale published his translation, twenty-two Bible translations had appeared in European vernaculars. (England lagged behind because its bishops forbade alternatives to the Latin Vulgate—a prohibition Tyndale boldly defied.)

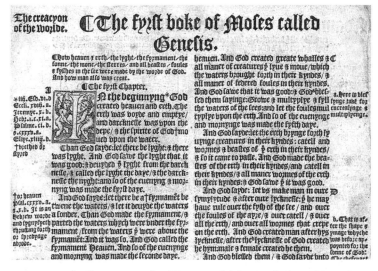

FIGURE 17. The first verses of William Tyndale's translation of Genesis.

Now the Continental Reformation translators, with whom Tyndale had ties, strove to capture the *sense* of the original Hebrew and Greek. Their German or French renderings were not meant to *sound* Hebraic, but rather to render the meaning of the Hebrew as closely as possible into idiomatic French or German. Tyndale, however, strove for more.

Take, for instance, his rendition of Genesis 1:4, *va-yar elohim et ha-or ki tov*: "And God sawe the lyghte that it was good." Here, Tyndale's translation was patently *not* in agreement with idiomatic English (whether that of the sixteenth century or that of the twenty-first). Rather, it shadowed the syntax of the Hebrew. Instead of placing the word *that* (his rendition of the often ambiguous Hebrew *ki*) in front of "the light" to accord with English syntax, he left it where it was. And even the Hebrew construction is an uncommon, suggestive one; behind the literal sense, "God saw that the light was good," are echoes of another biblical adage, "He [God] is good." In the best spirit of humanism, Tyndale wished his readers to puzzle over the original and to sense that it presented no single, self-evident meaning.

Tyndale could also convey biblical prosody. Take Genesis 3:15, where God, after Adam and Eve have eaten of the forbidden fruit, tells the serpent that there will be eternal hatred between his descendants and humankind. Here the text engages in characteristic wordplay, taking advantage of the similarity between the underlying words *nashaf* (bite) and *shaf* (strike or tread):

> And I will put enmity between you and the woman, and between your seed and her seed; he will strike (*shaf*) you on the head, and you will bite (*nashaf*) him on the heel.

Luther translates similarly to what I have done here; rendering *nashaf* as *beissen* (bite). But Tyndale was determined to capture the resonances of the Hebrew: "and that seed shall tread thee on the head, and thou shalt tread it on the heel."

Tyndale wished to forge a Hebraic consciousness, unlike so many twentieth-century translators trying to make readers forget they are reading a translation. The result was English that was at times even more "crude" than Renaissance English was generally thought to be. But Tyndale was not willing to sell his English birthright for a mess of Roman rhetoric.

Tyndale lived to complete only two-thirds of his Bible translation. The English regime, for unrelated reasons, hunted him down in Belgium, where in 1536 he was strangled at the stake, still in his forties. A letter in Latin to the prison governor survives, pleading for a lamp, "for it is tiresome to sit alone in the dark, but above all . . . [for] the use of my Hebrew Bible, Hebrew grammar, and Hebrew lexicon . . . that I might spend my time with that study."[12]

The King James Bible (1611), and the flood of new English Bible translations that fed into it, carried Tyndale's notion of a Hebraic

English scripture further still. Take these verses from Exodus, which had sounded maddeningly simple and disjointed to men trained in the style of Cicero:

> And Pharaoh sent, and behold, there was not one of the cattle of the Israelites dead. And the heart of Pharaoh was hardened, and he did not let the people go. (Exodus 9:7)

With the frequent use of the humble word *and*, King James's fifty translators, almost all of them Oxford and Cambridge humanists accomplished in Hebrew, Greek, and other disciplines, felt they had captured the biblical style and structure better than even Tyndale. And rather than shunning repetition—a basic tool of Hebrew style— they embraced it:

> This now is bone of my bones and flesh of my flesh. (Genesis 2:23)

They also aimed for consistency, trying as far as possible to re- produce the sparse biblical lexicon rather than render words differ- ently in different contexts. Thus every *lev* was rendered "heart" and every *nefesh* "soul." They were able by this means to re-create bibli- cal imagery in such passages as "and in the hearts of all that are wise-hearted I have put wisdom" (Exodus 31:5). Their passion for literalness was also unconstrained by tastefulness. Whereas the New English Bible (1970) speaks of killing "every mother's son," King James renders, more faithfully, "him that pisseth against the wall" (1 Samuel 25:22). "As I finde in the Hebrew," wrote Edward Lively of Cambridge, a contributor to the King James Version, "so I have Englished, that is, the truthe of interpretation, be it under- stood as it may."[13]

This massive Hebraic project occurred without any direct Jew- ish involvement. England, after all, had been *judenrein* since the late thirteenth century. Nonetheless, the King James humanists appreciated Jews, especially the baptized Hebrew tutors they imported from Europe. Edward Lively was lyrical about rabbinic Bible scholarship:

> They alwaies preserved . . . the knowledge of the Hebrew tongue among them by the benefit of art and learning . . . and therefore the Hebrew text they placed faire in the midst like a Queene with the translations about it as it were handmaids attending on her.[14]

Through the stylistic tradition that links the King James Bible, John Donne's seminal sermons, the Book of Common Prayer (1662), the choral scores of Purcell and Handel, and the Revised Standard Version (1952), some of the most canonic English literature and oratory we commonly read today has been imbued with a Hebraic quality that rivals the syntactic complexities of the Latinate style of Austen or Dickens—from the rhymeless rhythms of Walt Whitman's *Leaves of Grass* or Emily Dickinson's hymn forms to the three-part structures in John F. Kennedy's inaugural address and Martin Luther King Jr.'s "I Have a Dream."

Hebrew Enters Politics: From Puritan England to Colonial America

The history of seventeenth-century England is above all the story of a struggle for religious and political liberties. Modern histories often portray this struggle as one of secularism versus religion. But in fact, as the historian Eric Nelson has shown, much of it was anchored in the Hebrew Bible and its rabbinic interpreters.[15]

In the midst of an extended social and political crisis, English jurists and political theorists turned to Judaism and the Hebrew Bible as a source of wisdom. This new fascination led to such works as *Uxor Ebraica* (The Jewish wife, 1646) on the theory and practice of Jewish marriage and divorce law, and—shortly after the execution

IOANNES SELDENUS
·Jureconfultus.

FIGURE 18. John Selden (1584–1654), British jurist, Talmudist and Hebraist.

of Charles I—*De synedriis et praefecturis juridicis veterum Ebraeorum* (1650–1655), on the ancient rabbinic supreme court and its authority to control the ruler.

The author of these works was John Selden (1584–1654), hailed by John Milton as "the chief of learned men reputed in this land" (*Areopagitica*). The first talmudist in England since the expulsion of the Jews—and, more surprisingly, a philosemite—Selden recognized the humaneness of Jewish marital law and found in Deuteronomy and the Talmud a model for the proper relationship between the judicial and executive branches of government. Selden and his circle represented the high-water mark of humanist Hebrew-Aramaic erudition. Among the beneficiaries were Ben Jonson and Milton, Thomas Hobbes and John Locke.

But in England (as across Europe) the ideal of a trilingual humanist culture in Latin, Greek, and Hebrew rapidly waned. A major factor was the educational system: until the late nineteenth century, the curricula of elite schools and colleges revolved around Latin alone (plus Greek for advanced students). There were also religious prejudices and distaste for an alien Semitic tongue. Hebrew studies retreated to the religious seminary and the ivory tower.

But the English Protestant spirit lived on in the unique circumstances of Puritan New England. There, Hebrew entered the Christian public domain in an unprecedented way. The settlers who built New England saw themselves as latter-day Israelites brought by Providence to a second promised land, where the "new heaven and new earth" foretold by the prophets would unfold. In this drama, the Old Testament took center stage and with it, Hebrew.

The Hebrew of the Bible supplied the colonists with many of their personal and place names: Ezra, Nathanael, Abigail, Goshen, Salem. Names of Christian saints were a rarity. The Old Testament itself was unceasingly studied; the New England meetinghouses, like synagogues of old, were houses of study.

The first book printed in America embodied the powerful symbolism of American Hebraism: the *Bay Psalm Book* (1640) was the Massachusetts Bay colonists' own translation of the book of Psalms, directly from the Hebrew. It was briefly surpassed in popularity by the edition of Henry Ainsworth. ("Hee had not his better for the Hebrew tongue in the universitie [of Leiden] nor scarce in Europa," reported William Bradford, governor of Plymouth Colony.)[16] Ainsworth's glosses sought to bring the nuances of the Hebrew directly to the masses. One psalm, for instance, uses four terms for lions:

128   PSALME. LXXXIV.

all worlds, *Isa.*44.6. that he giveth *being* or exiſtēce unto all things, and in him all are and conſiſt, *Act.* 17.25. that he giveth *being* unto his word, effecting whatſoever he hath ſpoken, whether promiſes, *Exod.*6.3. *Iſa.*45.2,3. or threanings, *Ezek.* 5.17. and 7.27. It is in effect the ſame that *Ehjeb, I will be,* or *I am,* as God calleth himſelfe, *Exod.*3. 14. Of this the Gentiles named the greateſt God, *Iove,* and *Iu-piter,* that is, *Iah father,* (of the ſhorter name *Iah,* mentioned *Pſal.* 68.5.) and *Varro* the learnedeſt of the Romanes, thought *Iove* to be the god of the Iewes. *Auguſt.l.*1.*de conſenſ.evan.c.* 22. Hereof alſo in Greeke writers he is called *Iao, Diodor.Sicul.l.*2.*c.*5.*Clem. Alex.ſtrom.l.* 5. *Macrob. l.*1.*Saturnal.c.*18. But in the Greeke tongue the name *Iehovah* cannot rightly be pronounced ; and for it the Greeke Bibles haue *Lord,* which the new Teſtament followeth, as *Mark.*12.29. from *Deut.* 6.4. and elſewhere uſually ; and the Hebrew Text ſometime putteth *Adonai, Lord,* or *Ælohim, God,* for *Iehovah* ; as *Pſal.* 57.10. compared with *Pſal.* 108.4. 2 *Chron.*25.24. with 2 *King.*14.14. When *Adonai, Lord,* is joyned with it, it is written *Iehovih,* as *Pſal.*68.21. then the Iewes read it *Ælohim, God,* as at other times they read it *Adonai, Lord* ; and pronounce not *Iehovah* at all at this day ; though in ancient dayes it appeareth to be otherwiſe. The Greeke hiſtory of Baruch, ſeemeth to uſe in ſtead of it, *Aionios,* that is, the *eternall,* or, *everlaſting, Bar.*4.10, 14,20,32,24,35. and 5.2. See the Annotations on *Gen.* 2.4. *onely thou* or, *onely thine,* that is, which onely haſt *Iehovah* for thy name ; for the true God hath onely *being,* and *Idols* are *nothing in the world,* 1 *Cor.* 8.4. and *Angels,* and *Magiſtrates* are called *Elohim Gods, Pſal.*8. and 82. but *Iehovah* is peculiar to very God alone. And this is that name (I ſuppoſe) which the authour of the booke of Wiſedome calleth *incommunicable, Wiſd.* 14. 21. Yet this is the name of Chriſt, called *Iehovah our juſtice, Ier.*23.6. for *Gods name is in him, Exod.*23.21. and *he is very God, and eternall life,* 1 *Iob.*5.20.

PSAL. LXXXIV.

The Prophet longing for the communion of the Sanctuary, ſheweth how bleſſed they are that dwell therein. 9 *He prayeth to be reſtored unto it.*

1 To the maſter *of the muſicke* upon Gittith, a Pſalme to the ſonnes of Korach.

2
3   HOw amiable *are* thy dwelling places, O Iehovah of hoſts! My ſoule longeth and alſo fainteth for the courts of Iehovah ; my heart and my fleſh
4   doe ſhout unto the living God. Yea the ſparrow findeth a houſe, and the ſwallow a neſt for her, where ſhe laieth her young ; thine altars Iehovah of hoſts, my King and my
5   God. O bleſſed *are* they that abide in thine

---

houſe, ſtill they ſhall praiſe thee Selah.   O
6   bleſſed *is* the man whoſe ſtrength *is* in thee, they in whoſe heart, *are* the high-wayes. They *that* paſſing thorow the vale of Baca,
7   put him *for* a well-ſpring, alſo *with* bleſſings the raine covereth. They ſhall goe from
8   power to power, he ſhall appeare unto God in Sion.   Iehovah God of hoſts, heare thou
9   my prayer: give yeare, O God of Iakob, Selah.   See thou, O God, our ſhield, and looke
10 upon the face of the Anointed.   For, bet-
11 ter *is* a day in thy courts than a thouſand: I have choſen to ſit at the threſhold in the houſe of my God, rather than to remaine in the tents of wickedneſſe. For Iehovah God *is*
12 a Sunne and a ſhield, Iehovah will give grace and glory, he will not withhold good from them that walke in perfection.   Iehovah of
13 hoſts, O bleſſed *is* the man that truſteth in thee.

Annotations.

1   Ittith] ſee *Pſal.*8.1.
2   Verſ.2. *dwelling places*] or *habitacles,* : ſee the Notes on *Pſal.* 43.3.
3   Verſ. 3. *for the courts*] that I may come into them : for the Prieſts onely went into the Temple, the people ſtood in the courtyards which were two, 2 *Kings*11.5. See *Pſal.*65.5.   *ſhont*] to wit, for deſire to come unto God.
4   Verſ. 4. *the ſparrow*] or *bird,* in Chaldee, *the dove* ; the Hebrew *tſippor* is generally any *bird, Pſal.*11.1.*Gen.*7.14. ſpecially the *ſparrow,* when other birds are named, as here and *Pſal.* 102.8. for ſuch haunt mens houſes.   *ſwallow*] or, *free bird,* called in Hebrew *dror,* of *libertie* which this bird ſeemeth to have above others, flying boldly and neſtling about houſes : ſo *Prov.*26.2. The Greeke takes it here for the *turtle dove,* (which hath in Hebrew another name, *Pſal.* 74.19.) ſo alſo doth the Chaldee, adding this reaſon, *becauſe her young are lawfull to be offered on thine altar.   thine al-tars*] to wit, are the places where the birds neſtle neere unto them, in houſes or trees, which ſometime were by Gods tabernacle, *Ioſ.* 24. 26. or underſtand as before, (*I long for*) thine altars.
6   Verſ.6. *the high wayes*] or *cauſeyes* ; namely, which lead to thy houſe : that is, they which affect heartily, long after, and delight to goe up to thy houſe.   Spiritually theſe *wayes* or *pathes* are made by preaching of the Goſpell, *Eſa.* 40. 3. and 35. 8. and 11.16.
7   Verſ.7. *They that paſſing*] or, *of them that paſſe. of Baca*] that is, *of mulberie trees* ; which uſe to grow in dry places. The Greeke ſaith, *vales of teares.* Both meane that through wants and afflictions we muſt come into the kingdome of God. This valley was neere unto Ieruſalem, as may be gathered by 2 *Sam.*5.22,23.*Ioſ.*15.8.   *put him* or

---

FIGURE 19. From Henry Ainsworth's *Annotations upon the Booke of Psalms* (London, 1612).

FIGURE 20. The coat of arms of Yale University: *urim ve-tumim* (light and truth).

> Lions of sundry-kinds have sundry-names. . . . *Laby*, that is Harty
> and couragious. *Kphir*, this lurking, couchant. . . . *Shakhal*, of
> ramping, fierce nature; and *Lajith* of subduing his prey.

In New England public schools and meetinghouses, a reading knowledge of biblical Hebrew was for a time widely imparted—the only such attempt in the history of Christianity. Although familiarity with Hebrew never became widespread among the masses, it was quite common among the intelligentsia and the better-trained of the clergy. At Harvard, Yale, Princeton, and the seven other colleges created to train these educated ministers and God-fearing gentlemen, all students had to devote substantial time to Hebrew (not always willingly), a distinction reserved in Europe for Latin. They were also encouraged to produce Hebrew compositions and orations—a practice borrowed from the teaching of Latin and Greek. Harvard theses regularly addressed such issues as "Aleph with the function of a point has the sound of all vowels."

Harvard's first two presidents were Hebrew scholars, as were the first president of King's College (later Columbia) and the first president of Yale University, Ezra Stiles. A world-renowned intellectual, Stiles was also the leading American Hebraist of the era. He was also a prominent supporter of the American Revolution. This epitomizes the fact that the study of Hebrew marched hand in hand with the Enlightenment principles of the American founding—a tradition going back to Milton and Selden. Like Selden, Stiles was a philosemite, even if he still hoped for the conversion of the Jews. But unlike his intellectual forebears, he counted Jews among his friends. He learned much about Hebrew and Judaism from his friend Rabbi Hayim Carigal. In an elegant Hebrew letter to Carigal describing the 1775 Battle of Bunker Hill, Stiles beseeched him for a reply in Hebrew: "May I hope for one in answer to my long Hebrew letter of 1773." And oh yes, his son, Ezra, was taking Hebrew at the University of Connecticut.

Of altogether loftier significance—for some—were the native Indians. Could they be the Ten Lost Tribes of Israel? Were their languages descended from Hebrew? Elias Boudinot, president of the Continental Congress in 1782–1783, a revolutionary and later a member of Jefferson's administration, certainly believed so. Persuaded by the linguistic and cultural evidence of James Adair's *History of the American Indians* (1775) that the Indians were Jews, Boudinot in *Star in the West* assigned them a central role in the millennium, which he believed imminent. They would, he predicted, return to the land of Israel with all other Jews. Jefferson and Adams thought otherwise. Little more was heard of the Jewish Indian theory, until the Book of Mormon (on which see the next section).

Even as revolution stirred, school curricula were becoming noticeably more secular. After the defeat of the British "Pharaoh," millenarianism faded; so did the Puritan vision of a new Canaan. By 1800, the Harvards and Yales were no longer turning out men of the cloth but graduates in the arts and sciences. And Hebrew henceforth would have little place in the American public domain.

Zion, Mormon, and the New Evangelism

Repeatedly in this chapter, we have seen the deep impact on Hebrew of political, social, and technological change—the Renaissance, the printed book, and the Reformation are among the more obvious landmarks along the way. But the advent in the nineteenth century of safer and speedier passenger ships and the phenomenon of tourism brought the Holy Land closer to every Christian. In tandem, and not entirely by coincidence, came Zionism: the desire to reestablish Jewish sovereignty in the ancient land. There were both Jews and Christians that entertained this vision, but with somewhat different goals in mind.

The so-called Second Great Awakening in early nineteenth-century America moved millions of Christians to turn to Bible study—in the vernacular but often with a minister eager to display his Hebrew. They also enthused over pictures and reports from the new tourist-travelers to the Holy Land. Some spoke of a new Hebrew ingathering to Zion—committed (as ever) to converting the Jews, but leaving it to them to learn how to be "born again."

In 1836 the Anglican Mission to the Jews unveiled a grand Hebrew version of the Book of Common Prayer; soon, a second, fully vocalized edition appeared in three thousand copies. Evangelists pressed ahead with the modernization of Hebrew vocabulary in the hope of communicating with Jews in a contemporary vein. Germany too saw substantial missionary interest in Hebrew (and Yiddish), and in 1900 the founder of the Leipzig Institutum Judaicum predicted that Zionism would mean the revival of Hebrew, "the most important means of promoting the evangelization of Israel."

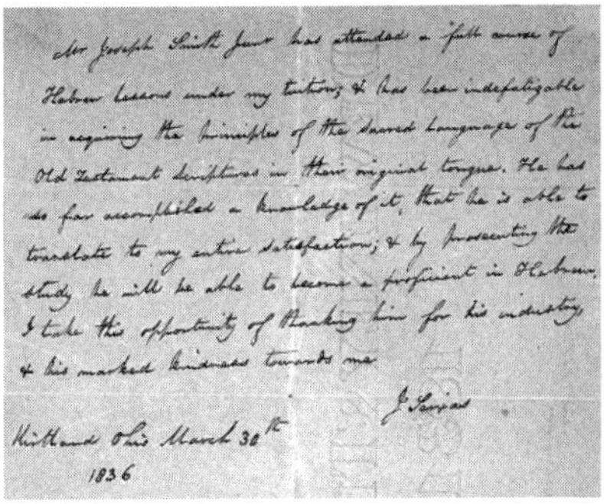
Mr Joseph Smith Junr has attended a full course of
Hebrew lessons under my tuition; & has been indefatigable
in acquiring the principles of the sacred language of the
Old Testament Scriptures in their original tongue. He has
so far accomplished a knowledge of it, that he is able to
translate to my entire satisfaction; & by prosecuting the
study he will be able to become a proficient in Hebrew.
I take this opportunity of thanking him for his industry
& his marked kindness towards me.

J. Seixas

Kirtland Ohio March 30th
1836

FIGURE 21. Joshua Seixas's letter of commendation to the Mormon leader, Joseph Smith, 1836.

Also desirous to see the return of the Jews to ancient Judea were the Mormons. Mormon belief holds that the Book of Mormon (1830) contains prophetic memories vouchsafed to Joseph Smith by descendants of Jewish exiles living in pre-Columbian America. These had been couched in Hebrew and in Egyptian script but then translated into English. (The originals were taken back to heaven.) In 1836, Smith and other Mormon leaders had received two months' instruction in "the language of the Lord" from Joshua Seixas, son of the senior rabbi of New York. A certificate discovered in the Salt Lake City archives states:

> Mr. Joseph Smith Junr has attended a full course of Hebrew lessons under my tuition; & has been indefatigable in acquiring the principles of the sacred language of the Old Testament Scriptures in their original tongue. He has so far accomplished a knowledge of it, that he is able to translate to my entire satisfaction; & by prosecuting the study he will be able to become a proficient in Hebrew.

However, the Mormon church has taken little interest in Hebrew per se.

Conclusion

Religious aspirations have been the chief driving force of Hebrew as
an element in Christian life. Whenever Hebrew has entered the
Christian conversation, it has always done so in the service of a conscious purpose, often in order to fill a particular niche in what
might be called the linguistic ecosystem. For most Christians, who
were generally unaware of the Hebraic scholarship that went into
producing the Bibles they read or that were read to them, Hebrew
was of course a mainly invisible presence. (Colonial New England
was the exception to this rule.) But in the linguistic ecosystem of
the religious elite, it could at times be a very palpable presence,
playing a supporting role in correcting or elucidating the Greek or
Latin Bible or figuring more prominently in certain distinctive
"subplots" (unlocking the Kabbalah, for example). But its most persistent role, fading in and fading out across the centuries, was as an
accessory in the enterprise of converting the Jews—or, if that
wouldn't work, discrediting their books and challenging their understanding of the Hebrew Bible.

Meanwhile, in the wider Christian intellectual sphere, the roles
assigned to Hebrew, though more limited, could be occasionally exhilarating and even seminal. For serious writing and research, Latin,
and more recently the European vernaculars, have always been the
languages of choice. But there was one major moment in European
social and political history when Hebrew scientific or philosophical
writings attracted the best and brightest: in the seventeenth century when, as we have seen, British and Dutch thinkers studied and
applied the legal-political writings of rabbinic authorities. On a different level, as we have also seen, Hebrew spoke to the metaphysical dreams of Renaissance, millenarian, and Christian-Zionist fig-

ures eager to undo Babel or defeat Satan and tap into the symbolic capital of an original *lingua humana*.

Of course, these generalizations do not capture the inner conflict, and often the fear and rage, felt in some periods of European history by Christian scholars who saw a need to go to the Jews for the keys to the meaning of the Old and even the New Testaments.

As times changed, some passions cooled while others were ignited. And as Christian scholarship mastered biblical Hebrew, there was also less reason to "go to the Jews"—or Jews became too hard to find. Hebraic scholarship gravitated to the universities, which themselves were generally becoming less denominational, and attitudes toward Jews and Judaism likewise morphed and shifted. But traces of an orientation to Hebrew and Hebrew sources in European thought, the English language, and the American political system can still be seen today.

8

Can These Bones Live?

HEBREW AT THE DAWN OF MODERNITY

Two Tickets to Modernity: Enlightenment and Ḥasidism

In 1780, two books appeared, one in Berlin and one seven hundred miles to the east in the tiny Ukrainian town of Koretz. What appeared in Berlin was the first volume of a magnificent new edition of the Torah, the *Biur*—with the ancient Hebrew rendered into an elegant modern German by the philosopher Moses Mendelssohn. What appeared in Koretz was the first work of ḥasidic thought. Each of these two books, so very dissimilar, would help change the future of the Hebrew language.

Let us begin with Mendelssohn (1729–1786). He believed that the glorious Hebrew of the Bible deserved the best: a glorious German translation. For too long, he felt, Ashkenazi Jews had neglected their linguistic and literary heritage. They had no interest in studying Hebrew grammar or in penning Hebrew poetry; when they wrote in Hebrew, it was a crude mishmash. As for religious scholarship, almost all of it revolved around the Talmud and its medieval commentaries. Their schooling was mired in the past, ignoring science, mathematics, and non-Jewish languages. And when they studied the weekly Torah portion for the Sabbath, they disgraced it, in his view, by rendering it into the local Yiddish dialect.

In truth, almost all Germans, Jew and Gentile alike, spoke in dialect. Modern Standard German was a new and artificial language written by the great figures of the emerging German intelligentsia like Gotthold Lessing, Immanuel Kant, and Johann Wolfgang von Goethe. Mendelssohn and his small Jewish avant-garde wanted his coreligionists to join this new German culture at the ground level. There was an upwardly mobile group of Jewish merchants who were seeking to assimilate the ways of the bourgeoisie; a group of Jewish intellectuals eager to take part in the German Enlightenment; and young Jews who spoke refined German and for whom a few doors were opening in polite German society. Many believed that an age of Jewish enlightenment and Christian acceptance was dawning. They dubbed this age the *Haskalah* (Enlightenment) and themselves *Maskilim* (enlighteners), spreading knowledge and sophistication among their own people.

For a few brief years, the German-Jewish Maskilim believed they could feast simultaneously at two tables—their religious-literary Hebrew heritage and modern secular German culture. Hebrew could thus regain its rightful place as the Jewish classical language, the aesthetic and social equal of Latin; Christian academics—but, alas, not contemporary Jews—had already recognized as much with their sophisticated Hebrew grammars and lexicons. Most exhilarating, no doubt, were Johann Gottfried Herder's paeans to Hebrew. The father of romantic nationalism had written in his "Discourse on the Origin of Language" (1772, pt. 1, chap. 3) that Hebrew vowel sounds "had such a vitality and organic fine-tuning and its breath was so spiritual and ethereal, that they could not be captured as letters." Herder went on to compose "On the Spirit of Hebrew Poetry" (1782–1783). Entertaining hopes that Hebrew could be modernized to do what Standard German did, some Maskilim experimented with Hebrew journalism and poetry. They believed that, given the vocabulary, Hebrew could express everything as well as a European language, and could thus be revived both as a classical *and* as a modern tongue.

Thus, in Königsberg, at the easternmost reaches of the German world, a Society of Friends of the Hebrew Language proclaimed in 1783 the birth of a Hebrew periodical entitled *Ha-Me'asef* (The collector)—the first of its kind. Its goal: "to spread our holy language among our people and to demonstrate its beauty to all nations." It garnered 213 subscriptions (substantial for those days) from as far afield as Strasbourg and Copenhagen.

But the dream was ephemeral. German Jews opted en masse to turn outward, abandoning tradition and assimilating linguistically. By 1811, *Ha-Me'asef* had closed its doors, eclipsed as the leading maskilic periodical by the German-language *Sulamit* that had been launched in 1806. At its founding, *Ha-Me'asef* was read by a wide audience of yeshiva-trained Jews eager to expand their intellectual horizons—horizons that had been narrowed by their ignorance of other languages. By the time it closed, this cohort had evaporated and been replaced by a new generation more at home in German than in Hebrew. Mendelssohn's Torah translation bore some responsibility here, having ironically been used by Jews not to understand the Torah but to learn modern German.

By the early nineteenth century, Hebrew in Germany, although still used in the synagogue, was no longer systematically taught to children. The local form of Yiddish, too, would soon be forgotten. For the first time in a millennium, a Jewish community was on the way to becoming functionally monolingual—a transformation that was as much a part of becoming modern as better-known phenomena like secularism, urbanization, mass politics, communication, and literacy. As modernity advanced across the Jewish world in the nineteenth and early twentieth centuries, more and more Jews abandoned their Jewish vernaculars (Yiddish, Judeo-Arabic, Ladino). Simultaneously, functional literacy in Hebrew retreated into pockets of erudition. Only in those few regions where Orthodoxy still held firm would Hebrew live to regrow flesh and sinews. The ḥasidic heartland of eastern Europe was such a region. There, ironically, a very different kind of modernity sowed the seeds of Hebrew's eventual revival.

Ḥasidism and the New Hebrew Populism

The founder of Ḥasidism, Rabbi Israel Baal Shem Tov (1700–1760), did not commit his teachings to writing, thus setting the tone for a religious populism that spread, above all, by word of mouth. In subsequent decades, as Ḥasidism grew and evolved, it placed special emphasis on the relationship between charismatic rabbinic masters and their followers. Metaphysical discourses—delivered in Yiddish and often interlaced with lengthy parables—were the central interactions between master and Ḥasid. Eventually, such discourses were translated from spoken Yiddish into written Hebrew either by the masters themselves or, often, by their disciples. Out of this, in the nineteenth century, arose a ḥasidic literature.

The rise of this new literary form created a Hebrew style that was more immediate and more closely tied to spoken language (and to Yiddish) than the highly artificial rabbinic Hebrew that preceded it. Ḥasidic writers seemed to revel in infusing the Holy Tongue with Yiddish and with Yiddish-like turns of phrase, often playing fast and loose with the finer (and even the grosser) points of Hebrew grammar such as agreement for gender or for the definite article.

Ḥasidism did more than create its own style: it fundamentally altered the Jewish *philosophy* of language. Drawing on the mystical thought of Isaac Luria (1534–1572), it taught that just as divine sparks of holiness permeate mundane life, waiting for the pious to capture and rekindle them, so too the sparks of the Holy Tongue permeate everyday language. Thus Yiddish or even Russian, when used by the pious, could express holiness. Rabbi Yehudah Aryeh Leib of Gur (1847–1905) explained it thus: "Every utterance from the wise is sacred, and so the Creator clothed the Torah in narratives, clarifying them in every language and empowering each language through the purity of the Revelation at Sinai" (*Sefat Emet, Devarim* 5639 = 1878).

This ḥasidic "communication ethos," as Naftali Loewenthal has called it,[1] elevated the status of Yiddish even while simultaneously, in its own way, revitalizing Hebrew. As Ḥasidism became a mass movement in the early nineteenth century, its leaders began to cultivate literature for the masses. Their medium of choice was the simple story. By the 1860s, anecdotes about the ḥasidic masters had been published by the hundreds—both in Hebrew (for the better educated) and in Yiddish (for the less tutored). The literary genius Rabbi Naḥman of Bratslav (1772–1811) went one step further, publishing his own famous collection of tales in a bilingual Hebrew-Yiddish edition. Ḥasidic tales captured Ḥasidism as authentically, in Yoav Elstein's words, as all the discourses.[2]

In the West, as Maskilim began to develop their own Hebrew style known as *melitzah*—characterized by flowery turns of phrase and "cleansed" of medieval accretions and grammatical improprieties—they often contrasted their mode of writing with what they saw as the sloppy and ungrammatical Hebrew of the Ḥasidim. Yet as much as the *melitzah* of the Maskilim has been regarded by cultural historians as a precursor of modern Israeli Hebrew prose, it was Ḥasidim who were reconnecting Hebrew with spoken language—and long before Zionists did. Indeed, at least a few ḥasidic leaders spoke Hebrew on the Sabbath in imitation of earlier generations of mystics. Thus the Russian Zionist politician and essayist Nahum Sokolov recalled an event in 1866:

> The first spoken Hebrew I heard in my childhood, which left an indelible impression on me, was the speaking of the hasidic rabbi Shmuel Abba of Zikhlin, who on the Sabbath would speak only in the Holy Tongue. . . . I was then seven, and he tested me in talmudic problems, not particularly difficult ones, but the Hebrew talk with talmudic intonation quite carried me away.[3]

West and East: A Spiritual Chasm Opens

A spiritual and cultural chasm between western and eastern Jews opened in the first half of the nineteenth century. The former inhabited western and central Europe and America. The latter, by far the majority, lived in the Jewish heartlands of eastern Europe and in the Muslim world.

For western Jews, the social and political future looked bright, at least at times, holding out the prospect of more civil rights, access to public schooling, and the opportunity to master Gentile languages. With this came a general desire to shed their traditional Jewish way of life for one more attuned to modern Christian societies. Only small pockets of the old piety survived here. As a result, knowledge of Hebrew declined rapidly. Whereas, traditionally, the ability to read and understand the Pentateuch and the prayer book was held up as a universal male ideal (if not necessarily a reality), the new ideal demanded only the ability to read the letters and pronounce the words of the prayers. As synagogue attendance declined, many Jews were not able to do even that. In other words, a situation emerged not unlike that in most non-Orthodox American Jewish circles today.

FIGURE 22. Children being taught the Alef-Bet in a traditional ḥeder.

The Jews of eastern Europe and the Muslim world, however, continued for the most part to live their lives in separate traditional communities up to the late nineteenth century or even beyond. There
were some signs of change, but they were slow and limited. Only in
the last third of the nineteenth century did this Jewish way of life
really start to crumble, with mass migration to the big cities and to
the West and the lure of secular nationalism and radical politics. Two
world wars, the Holocaust, and the Arab-Israeli conflict dealt the final
blow. Still, even on the eve of World War II, a third of Poland's Jewish
children and most Sephardi youth were learning Hebrew in a way not
very different from how their forefathers had learned it.

And how, exactly, did this system of education work? Unlike in
the medieval or classical eras, where we can only form conjectures
about Jewish education from scattered scraps of information, we
have a fairly good sense of how nineteenth-century eastern European Jewish children learned Hebrew. Starting at age four or five,

boys were sent to the *ḥeder*, a one-room school often inside the teacher's home. There might also be a few girls. There they learned the Hebrew alphabet and then progressed straight to reading the prayers and the Ḥumash (Five Books of Moses), along with Rashi's commentary. The division of students of different ages into grades was unknown.

Hebrew as a language was not formally taught: there was no instruction in grammar, no lists of vocabulary words or textbooks. Writing and composition were given no attention. Instead, the teacher read from the Hebrew text with a chanted word-by-word translation into Yiddish. The children repeated after him. It would have sounded like this (with the Yiddish replaced by English):

Bereyshis—in the beginning
boro elokim—God created
eys ha-shomayim—the heavens
ve-eys ho-oretz—and the earth.

Around age eleven or twelve, boys switched to an advanced *ḥeder* where they studied Talmud—again without any formal instruction in the Hebrew and Aramaic it was written in. A few young men with an aptitude for the legal and verbal intricacies of Talmud would go on to full-time Talmud studies. This might be at a local *beys medresh* (house of study), where they joined adults to pore over the Talmud semi-independently until they were rewarded, still in their teens, with a bride from a well-to-do family. Alternatively, they might spend some years in high-level study at a yeshiva. Here, too, there was no formal language teaching, and dictionaries and concordances were a rarity. In the Muslim world, traditional Jewish education was conducted on rather similar lines.

The skills required at every level were remarkable: the texts to be studied were in a foreign language (often mixed with Aramaic), unpunctuated (not even with question marks or periods), often unvo-calized, unformatted, with commentaries arrayed around the text but not keyed to it. The rabbis and educators presiding over this whole system made no apology for the absence of formal language teaching or printed aids like dictionaries and grammars. Indeed, they took pride in it. And of course it *is* possible to learn a language without referring much to grammar, as any modern language teacher will confirm.

The success of this system is hard to measure, but it seems to have been remarkably high when judged by its own objectives. Even intellectually unimpressive students would emerge able to follow along with the prayers and weekly Torah reading in synagogue and to read a Yiddish translation of the Torah at home. Many more students understood enough Hebrew to continue studying the Five Books of Moses, Rashi's commentary, and other foundational texts as adults. Indeed, in Lithuania and parts of the Sephardi world, *ḥev-rot* (study groups) were where most men spent their leisure hours.

Chasm within the Chasm: The Gap between Boys and Girls

Most daughters in the traditionalist pre–World War II Ashkenazi milieu were homeschooled. Female relatives taught them Jewish customs, and usually imparted just enough Hebrew literacy to en-able them to read basic Hebrew as well as Yiddish prayers and pious literature. (Yiddish was always written in Hebrew characters.) And that was all. Many attended synagogue only on holidays, often just responding *amen* to a *zogerin*, a woman who read the prayers out loud. Nevertheless, much as generations of Catholics revered the Latin Mass, many of these women felt a powerful emotional con-nection with Hebrew.

And there was an unintended, subversive consequence to the gender gap: reading the Hebrew alphabet enabled many girls to read Yiddish, and thus gave them access to impious influences. By the mid-nineteenth century, there were Yiddish newspapers and Yiddish cheap romances, and women were reading them voraciously in addition to the religiously edifying literature their mothers expected them to read.

But why the gap in the first place? Religious doctrines, sexual attitudes, and economics all played a part. As we have seen earlier, talmudic doctrine obliged all males to devote themselves, livelihood permitting, to the study of Torah; females were exempt.

Jewish society and the position of women were actually prime targets of Haskalah writing. Perhaps the most seminal feminist statement in Jewish history was *Kotzo shel Yud* (1878), a narrative satire by the (male) Russian-Hebrew poet Judah Leib Gordon (1830–1892). It began (in my translation):

Hebrew woman! Who can know your life?
Darkness ushered you in, darkness ushers you out.
Your pain and your joy, your woes and your desires
Are born within you and perish within you.
A whole world of bounties and pleasure
Is the happy lot of women of another race,
But the Hebrew woman's life is eternal bondage.

The Maskilim harbored further aspirations for Hebrew: they also labored to appropriate the European classics. Gordon penned one hundred poetic fables in quasi-biblical Hebrew for children, modeled largely on the work of La Fontaine and Aesop; Micah Lebensohn (1828–1852) translated Schiller's German version of Virgil's *Aeneid*. They experimented gamely, sometimes ineptly and melodramatically, with new Hebrew genres: short stories, travelogues, biographies, natural history. Above all, they craved linguistic beauty and eternity: striving to re-create the unadulterated beauty of biblical Hebrew before it had been sullied by rabbinic and diasporic "accretions" (a damning word).

Most famously, the Maskilim tried to rework biblical stories to suit modern romantic sensibilities. Abraham Mapu's *Ahavat Tsiyon* (Love of Zion, 1853), a tale of romance and intrigue set in ancient Judea—but composed in Kovno, Lithuania—was the first of four novels the author produced in pseudobiblical Hebrew. Mapu immersed himself in the biblical landscape and language as perhaps no one had done in two millennia; the result, in a Hebrew that might have been written by Isaiah himself, was as graphic as one might find in the novels of Thomas Hardy. Readers were electrified. Young men breathlessly declaimed passages from *Ahavat Tsiyon* before their mirrors:

And Maakhah beheld Amnon and his beauty overwhelmed her. And she addressed Tamar: "My lady, indulge not in daydreams lest they mislead you and your visions drive you insane." But Tamar gave no heed to Maakhah's words. Instead, she approached Amnon and thus she spoke: "O good youth, if your heart be as generous as your looks are kind, give me the garland of roses in your hand."

But what if you wanted to report the news or to write realist fiction? Everyday prose had the Haskalah in a linguistic bind. Authors were torn between a biblical Hebrew ideal, followed in their artistic work, and the arcane rabbinic or medieval Arabicized Hebrew employed in nonfiction prose. Something was wrong. Their readership remained small and for the most part soon "graduated" from Hebrew to Russian or German. One author, looking back to the maskilic literature he had read as a teenager in the 1870s, would report:

> Their ideas seemed to appear as though through a fog, blurred, lacking a clear outline. The most everyday needs were conveyed amid rhetoric. Sentences were a maximum of words and a minimum of content. Take color: Hebrew authors could see only the colors for which the Bible had names. Or food: when they were not having to eat dry bread, people were always partaking of "delicacies," but the reader was never informed what these were.

From Poetry to Pragmatism

In the modern era, every national language—English, German, and Russian included—has had to undergo a process of modernization, usually involving extensive and confused linguistic engineering. Sometimes, extreme measures were considered. Mori Arinori, a leading figure of the Meiji enlightenment in Japan (which shared much in common with the Haskalah), despaired of creating a modern language out of Japanese; instead, he proposed that English be adopted as Japan's national language.

In almost every case, modernization was not the result of a coordinated plan but the work of a motley collection of groups driven by multiple forces. Even more so was this the case with Hebrew, whose modernization began in the absence of a centralized system of education or a political authority. There were not even native speakers. But there were men and women passionately dedicated to bringing Hebrew's modernization into being. Four driving forces stand out: the spread of ḥasidic populism described earlier, the advent of newspapers, the new spirit of realism in the European arts, and a political force—the rise of political anti-Semitism and the Jewish political response, above all Zionism.

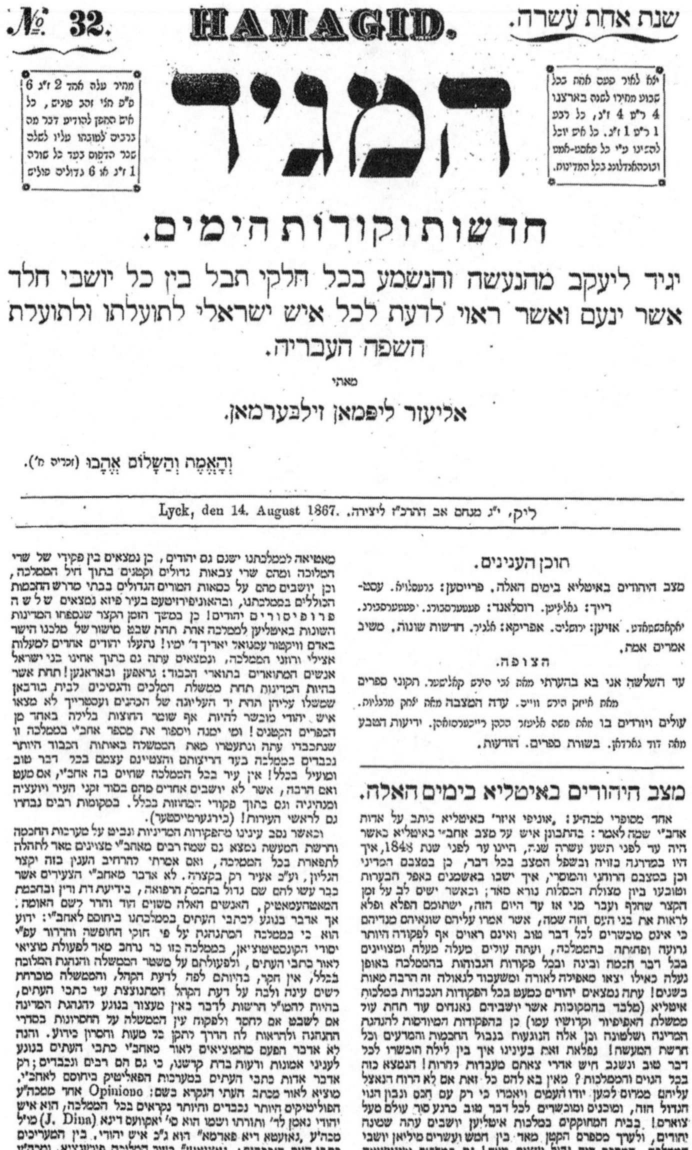

FIGURE 23. *HaMagid*, the first Hebrew newspaper.

First the newspapers: in the 1850s and 1860s, railroad lines and telegraph wires began to crisscross eastern Europe. With them came the latest news—and Jews wanted to know it. These were times of genuine hope for Jewish intellectuals who wanted to forge a new educated class informed about the world around them with all its fast-paced political and technological changes. They also wanted to launch public forums for the discussion of such key issues as educational reform, the possibility of emancipation, anti-Semitism, and more. They created real newspapers, very different from the older maskilic journals with their earnest poetry and ponderous essays.

If, in the mid-nineteenth century, only a minority of Russian Jews could read a Hebrew newspaper, this was a much larger number of people than those who could read Russian or German. There were now *Ha-Magid*, *Ha-Melitz*, *Ha-Tsefirah*, *Ha-Levanon*, weeklies and sometimes dailies with all the news that was fit to print for every shade of Jewish opinion and belief. As I write, I am looking at the May 9, 1860, issue of *Ha-Magid*. Page 1 is taken up by a lengthy obituary; pages 2 and 3 are split between foreign news and a report on the Jewish manuscripts at Leiden University; page 4 contains social and commercial updates, complete with currency and commodity rates.

Now newspapers required an extensive vocabulary for describing the modern world, a concise style, and precision. It was not only necessary to invent words denoting locomotive, telegraph, or parliament; the language would also need to express such conceptual distinctions as people, nation, and state. On what was the new style to be based? Not on the Bible or medieval Iberian poetry, but on the lucid, no-nonsense rabbinic style of Rashi and Maimonides—on which the new generation of readers and writers had still been raised. For vocabulary, they drew on the entire breadth of rabbinic literature, ancient and modern. Of course, the alignment of Hebrew vocabulary with other languages, as we saw in chapter 4, was not something new. It had been proceeding piecemeal for centuries.

By 1885, *Ha-Melitz* had a circulation of 2,500 but was probably being shared among 25,000 or even 50,000 people—still, to be sure, a much smaller circulation than that of Yiddish newspapers. In fact, even in the Zionist press, Russian soon outranked Hebrew. Nonetheless, for Hebrew, at that point in history, this was a minor miracle. And these papers did not have to be read (or heard) for their influence to be felt. Their mere presence demonstrated to the Jewish masses that Hebrew *could* be a modern language.

The European Hebrew Revival—and Its Double

In 1881, Tsar Alexander II, the "Tsar Liberator" to whom so many Russian Jews had looked for deliverance from persecution and poverty, was shot dead. Years of anti-Semitic repression followed. Some three million Jews migrated westward. Others clung to their old way of life. But many turned to political action and to a variety of causes: socialism, liberalism, anarchism, and also, increasingly, Jewish national-political revival, or *Tehiyah.*

The *Tehiyah* was a revolt against both assimilation and traditional religiosity. Its proponents rejected the Haskalah for its lack of commitment to Jewish nationhood and its belief in the potential benignity of Gentile governments. They wished to create a culture that was modern, European, and secular yet at the same time authentically Jewish. Among the movement's greatest luminaries were the Zionist theoretician Aḥad Ha'am (1856–1927), the poets Judah Leib Gordon and Ḥayim Naḥman Bialik (1873–1934), and the lexicographer Eliezer Ben-Yehudah (1858–1922).

Here, again, other European language movements showed the way. Many national languages in Europe were only then undergoing standardization: Romanian, Hungarian, Lithuanian, Finnish, and even Italian. Of course, these languages differed from Hebrew in that they had native speakers. But they nevertheless needed to undergo a process of modernization, led by cultural nationalists and involving the creation of uniform spelling, pronunciation, and grammar, historical dictionaries, anthologies of literature and folk epics, modernized vocabularies, newspapers, novels, and schools—the same things that Hebrew needed.

Education was a key part of the Hebrew revival. High on the agenda of the revivalists was revolutionizing the Jewish school curriculum to include the Bible, Jewish history, and Hebrew grammar (all to be taught in Hebrew), and educating the adult masses in history, geography, philosophy, and the sciences. Some, like the novelist Micah Joseph Berdichevsky (1865–1921) and the poet Saul Tchernichovsky (1875–1943), sought to enact a Jewish version of Nietzsche's ideology of psychic power, peeling back Judaism to uncover a pagan, pre-Mosaic, "Canaanite" tradition. Here in my translation is the opening of Tchernichovsky's *Lenokhah pesel apolo* (Before the statue of Apollo, 1899):

> I come to thee, god long forgotten,
> God of ancient times and other days,
> Regnant over effervescent human torrents,
> Their potent surges of might in the flow of youth.

Others sought to create nursery rhymes and folk songs like those of other cultures. Israeli toddlers still sing Bialik's *Nad Ned* (Seesaw) (1906):

> See saw, see saw.
> What's up? And what's down?
> Only me, you and me,

Both weighing in the balance,

Between the earth and sky.

(My translation)

Bialik appealed to scholars to scour the archives for the accumu-
lated literature and thought of three thousand years of Jewish creativity so that writers, publishers, and educators could bring it
proudly into libraries, schools, and lecture halls. Everyone believed
in the importance of translating other nations' literatures into
Hebrew.

The first successes with modern, precision Hebrew had already
been chalked up in newspapers and translated textbooks. The essay
now made its appearance. And in 1886 there came a great moment
for Hebrew realist fiction in the person of the most unlikely of figures: Shalom Yaakov Abramovitsh (1836–1917), better known by his
pen name, Mendele Mokher Sforim, the "grandfather" of modern
Yiddish literature. Or maybe he was not so unlikely a figure after all.
Mendele had begun his literary career in the 1860s as a Maskil, writing short stories in Hebrew with the goal of educating and enlight-
ening the masses. He made the then-shocking decision to switch to
Yiddish when he realized that it was the only language in which he
could actually reach those masses. Soon he developed a devotion to
Yiddish itself, and his artistic sensibilities assumed priority over his
didactic mission. He opened the door for generations of Yiddish
writers, and inspired a Yiddish literary and cultural revival that became the *Tehiyah*'s greatest competitor.

But, unlike later writers, Mendele did not believe Hebrew and
Yiddish were necessarily in competition. In 1886, he returned to
Hebrew with a short story, written in an innovative style that he
described as "speaking clearly and precisely, like people of the times
we live in." In fact, this style was much closer to matter-of-fact rab-

binic prose than to the language of earlier Hebrew literary forays. Mendele had taken the language of nonfiction, shorn it of archaisms, and garnished it with a down-home Jewish touch: a stream of quotations, half-serious, half in jest, from the sacred texts. The new style "resonated," as one biographer put it, with "the inner melody of the nation's soul."

> Kisalon [Dummytown] is a thoroughly Jewish town down to the last detail. It doesn't give a fig for architecture and follows not in its ways. Its houses don't rear cockily to heaven; they're humble, some even bent over with their roofs pressed to the ground. Outside they are plain and unvarnished, for charm is false and beauty vanity and not worth a dime. The glory of a Jew's dwelling is entirely within. There are his bed, his table, his washbasin, his bed-pans, all his home goods. (Mendele, *Beseter Ra'am.* My translation)

Thus Mendele had rebranded both Hebrew and Yiddish. He had simultaneously created two Jewish realist literary idioms, both attuned to the modern world in all its banal detail and both attuned to the popular soul. This was a key stage on the way to what would become, in Israel Bartal's formulation, an exceedingly complex triglossia,[4] involving Hebrew, Yiddish, and a Gentile vernacular.

But was there still really an audience for Hebrew? These were surely the worst of times. Eastern Europe was hemorrhaging Jews and Judaism. For every small-town yeshiva student thrilled by a Hebrew essay on Kant or a Hebrew rendering of *King Lear*, there were many more teaching themselves to read German, Russian, or Polish. Yiddish, meanwhile, was following a trajectory parallel to Hebrew. By the 1890s, it had gone from a "jargon" (as it was frequently called) to a recognized *language*, with a standardized grammar and spelling conventions and an openness to the latest foreign words that made it the envy of Hebrew writers. It was, quite simply, the easiest way for both women and men to read the news and absorb a bit of education. For many, it had still more attractions: socialist propagandists were successfully promoting it as the authentic folksy idiom in which to reach the Jewish proletariat.

But the *Teḥiyah* was itself finding a friendly political movement in Zionism. Aḥad Haʾam and Bialik believed that the Diaspora had left Jews with a no-win choice between assimilation and anti-Semitism. The land of Israel would need to be the center of any real revival. Aḥad Haʾam lamented, "The nation of the Book is slave to the Book, a people whose soul has departed and been absorbed entirely into the written word."

Of course, not all Zionists were Hebraists: Theodor Herzl, the first leader of the Zionist movement, assumed German would be the language of his envisioned Jewish state. Similarly, not all Hebraists were Zionists: Gordon was never fully on board with political Zionism, nor was Mendele.

Meanwhile, many feared that the *Teḥiyah*, to paraphrase the English historian G. M. Trevelyan, was a turning point at which modern Hebrew failed to turn. Mendele's own son, Michael, was one of many who became revolutionaries and ended up in Siberia. The erstwhile leader of Russian Zionism, Moses Lilienblum—himself a gifted Hebrew writer—declared that Hebrew's time was up.

These Bones Shall Live: Ben-Yehuda's Vision and the Little Children

Will our language and literature last much longer if we do not revive it, if we do not make it a spoken language? And how can that work other than by making Hebrew the instructional medium of our schools? Not in Europe, nor in any of the lands of our exile, where we are an insignificant minority and no amount of

FIGURE 24. Eliezer Ben-Yehuda (1858–1922) and his second wife Ḥemda (1873–1951), Zionists and Hebrew visionaries.

teaching effort is going to succeed, but in our land, the land of Israel.

With these words, printed in 1880 in the newspaper *Ha-Magid*, a revival of *spoken* Hebrew was first publicly mooted. The author was an unknown, twenty-two-year-old, fiercely secular Russian Jew using the pseudonym Eliezer Ben-Yehuda.

In 1881 Ben-Yehuda sailed for Palestine, one of the first Zionists. The pious Jewish communities deeply rooted there, Sephardim with an admixture of Ashkenazim, had a spiritual bond to the land

and dreamed of a messianic ingathering and restoration of past glories, Hebrew included. Ben-Yehuda's vision of a reborn nation and a reborn Hebrew was, on the face of it, secular and foreign in inspiration. One night, shortly after graduating from high school—as he lyrically recounts in his memoirs—he was reading the news about the Russian-backed Bulgarian uprising against Ottoman rule, and feeling proud to be a (Jewish) Russian, when

> the heavens opened and I saw a brilliant flash of light. My thoughts flew from the Shipka pass in the Balkans to the banks of the Jordan river, and I heard a mighty voice within me calling: "The rebirth of the Jews and their language on ancestral soil!"

Ben-Yehuda's logic was inexorable: If modern-minded Jews resettled the Holy Land and spoke Hebrew, Hebrew literature might be saved, and in turn the Jewish people might be saved. Neither could survive a Gentile environment in a modern world.

The idea of using Hebrew for spoken conversation was not in itself far-fetched. Ben-Yehuda had once managed a halting Hebrew exchange, about politics, with a Sephardi friend. Sent to Algiers to convalesce from tuberculosis, he had also indulged his exotic yearnings by conversing with Sephardi sages who, he claimed, spoke a fluent Oriental Hebrew. But to turn Hebrew into the everyday idiom of an entire nation was pure fantasy. Theodor Herzl's First Zionist Congress was fifteen years in the future. The Jewish populace that Ben-Yehuda and his fellows found in the Holy Land was largely impoverished and overwhelmingly traditional. The idealistic settlers knew nothing of farming and managed to survive only through the help of European Jewish philanthropists, who had no interest in establishing Hebrew-language schools.

Ben-Yehuda, however, was uncompromising and undeterred. Once he had reached his conclusion, he followed through, whatever the obstacles or risks—to himself or others. Two women had an equal share in his venture and its risks: Dvora and Beila Jonas, two thoroughly modern young sisters each of whom became in turn Mrs. Ben-Yehuda (Beila, also known as Ḥemda, after the death of Dvora). Arriving in the land of Israel, Eliezer and Dvora vowed to speak only Hebrew in their home—an agreement that initially bound her to silence since she knew none. They then agreed to raise their first child, Bentzion, born in 1882, solely in Hebrew, and somehow found a wet nurse willing to speak Hebrew to the baby. Dire warnings by fellow Zionists that the child might grow up retarded seemed confirmed when he turned three without yet uttering a word—until one day (as told to this author in 1990 by his last surviving daughter, Dola) Ben-Yehuda caught his wife singing a Russian lullaby and flew into a rage, when suddenly the frightened child blurted out *Abba, Abba!* (Daddy, Daddy!).

Were these the first native Hebrew words in two thousand years? Perhaps. But regardless of its veracity, the story reflects the very real anxieties that surrounded this unprecedented linguistic venture. What clearly distressed the Ben-Yehuda children much more, in any case, was being barred from other children's parties lest they come back speaking Yiddish. Bentzion nonetheless grew up speaking Hebrew as his native tongue. And "the first Hebrew child," as he was known, became, literally, a poster child for Zionism and the Hebrew revival. We will return to him presently.

Running a home in Hebrew remained a fringe proposition for some time, but Ben-Yehuda enjoyed greater success with another groundbreaking idea: Hebrew as a language of instruction. Here he drew on the so-called direct method for teaching language by immersion, which became all the rage among British educators in the 1880s. Ben-Yehuda was the first to attempt it with Hebrew; soon thereafter, other teachers in fledgling Zionist villages like Petaḥ

Tikvah and Reḥovot followed his lead. Although far from having all the Hebrew words they needed, they stoically pressed on.

In 1889, the first all-Hebrew elementary school opened its doors, and history, math, and basic science were taught in the holy tongue. Villagers and Sephardi townspeople were guardedly enthusiastic, some old-time, intensely traditionalistic Ashkenazim much less so. By 1898, twenty elementary schools were operating fully or partly in Hebrew, attracting twenty-five hundred pupils, or almost one in ten children. In that same year came the first Hebrew kindergarten. Children were beginning to speak Hebrew with their friends in the schoolyard and, critically, with younger siblings in the backyard. Hebrew was going native—a mother tongue without mothers.

For its Ashkenazi opponents, modern Hebrew was a sign of impiety. Using the holy tongue for everyday speech smacked of desecration, and its association with a modern political movement (even one that, at the time, had many religiously observant members) defiled it. Indeed, all modern education was a distraction from Torah. But among the settlers of the First Aliyah (Zionist immigration wave) of the 1880s, the idea began to catch on.

Hebrew's appeal was not strictly ideological. Deep schisms, religious and linguistic, between Ashkenazim and Sephardim plagued the country's Jews. The "Speak Hebrew" movement pointed to a way out. In the years leading up to World War I, pious Sephardim and Mizraḥim (Middle Eastern Jews), who were in the majority, showed growing zest for speaking Hebrew in place of Arabic or Ladino. Pious Ashkenazim, meanwhile, persisted in speaking Yiddish, which they began to invest with an almost-sacred status as a moat against "enlightenment," fired by the language ideology of Rabbi Moses Sofer (1762–1839), champion of traditionalism. However, for other Ashkenazim in those days, the ancient language of the Bible had suddenly become a symbol of modernity that could also serve to bridge the ethnic divide separating Jews from different countries.

And then, from the seeds sown by the first twenty-five hundred children in Hebrew elementary schools, a generation of native-born teenagers sprang up, proud of their *sabra* (local-born) identity and ready to fashion Hebrew into their own private and eventually public idiom.

Zionism Speaks Hebrew: The Second Aliyah

In 1897, the First Zionist Congress in Basel, Switzerland, briefly catapulted Zionism onto the international stage. But the revival of Hebrew was not even on the official agenda (which was, of course, written in German, the prestige language of the organizing body). It didn't help matters that the movement itself was initially led by Herzl and Max Nordau, men ill at ease with Judaism and Jewish culture. "Who among us knows enough Hebrew to use it to buy a railway ticket?" wrote Herzl in his 1896 Zionist manifesto *The Jewish State*.[5] Even a leading Hebrew writer like Mendele ascribed little value to the extraordinary things happening to Hebrew in Palestine. The authors of the *Tehiyah* struck western European Zionists— and many eastern European Zionists as well—as a mere curiosity. Not until 1907 did a Zionist congress proclaim Hebrew as "the language of Zionism."

By this time, however, the second wave of Zionist immigration was under way and facts on the ground were changing. Starting in 1904, thousands of young Russian Jews began arriving, eager to till the soil and build their own version of a Zionist utopia, which most imagined as secular and socialist. Fortunately, many, even most, had the solid literacy of a traditional full-time Torah education. Many had also been practicing their spoken Hebrew in anticipation of immigration. Inspired by Ben-Yehuda, Hebrew-speaking clubs had been springing up across the tsar's empire. In a display of national pride, their members declaimed Tchernichovsky's poems of Hellenic and Canaanite beauty—and Bialik's poems of wrath. His *Al haSheḥitah* (On the slaughter, 1903) concluded on the only note most Jews could sound to tsarist pogroms:

> A curse on him who says "Avenge!"
> A vengeance such as this, vengeance for an infant's blood,
> The devil has never devised.
> But may the blood pierce the deep,
> Pierce the deeps of darkness,
> Corrode in the murk, and sap
> All the putrid foundations of the earth.
>
>   (My translation)

Others, under the sway of socialism, had previously been drawn to the proletarian authenticity of Yiddish; setting foot in the land of Israel, however, seems to have stirred something in their hearts and tongues. Now Hebrew was romantic and revolutionary, and infinitely more sophisticated than Yiddish. Rachel Katznelson recalled the mind-set of the Kinneret commune, the epicenter of Zionist pioneering in the Galilee in the early 1920s:

> Although Yiddish was a living tongue, the tongue of the people and democracy, Hebrew was the language to express the current of thought that was revolutionary for us; in Yiddish literature thinking was limited, inert for the most part and reactionary to us, a faint echo of the revelations available in Hebrew.[6]

The Hebrew these men and women spoke was, of course, not their native tongue, and it must have felt quite stilted and precarious. But somehow it blended with and added a rich adult layer to the native Hebrew of the young children, thereby also lending it adult prestige.

A Designer Language?

How did they find the words? Not by committee, nor by scholarship, but by trial and error. Linguists would give a great deal to know more about how it worked. This was, after all, the first and perhaps the only known case of the total revival of a spoken language—but, maddeningly, it never occurred to anyone to observe how it was all happening. We will never know how teachers were teaching it, how children were speaking it, or how the young adult immigrants transformed the literary Hebrew they knew from Russia into an everyday tongue.

Most teachers had no qualifications and were unsupervised, determining their own curriculum as they saw fit. The decision about which Hebrew words and which pronunciation to use was up to individual schools, even individual teachers. "In every school I now find a word-minting factory," groaned a visiting author.[7] Little use was made of existing textbooks, which were usually devoted entirely to abstruse rules of biblical inflections.

Teaching may be a conservative profession, but in the circumstances of those days, a language had to be revived, a generation educated, and a new society built, all in a hurry. The entire process was thus one of glorious improvisation and individualism, though, as with other, European-language revivals, there was also an infatuation with the "folk," even if no real Hebrew-speaking folk existed. The greatest testament to the freewheeling spirit of this revival was the first Hebrew Teachers Union convention in 1903 in Zikhron Yaakov, where language issues were simply referred to the Hebraist scholars in Jerusalem and then forgotten. In other words, the finer points of usage were deemed irrelevant.

One question that obsessed the scholars was, in some ways, an old one: should the new Hebrew be biblical or rabbinic? Ben-Yehuda's son, for example, became a stickler for obsolete biblical suffixes, like his famous coinage *amerikata* (to America), which sounds ridiculous to any Hebrew speaker today. But to most people, even the teachers, it hardly mattered. The revival was not about one or another style of Hebrew; it was simply about Hebrew. The Israeli tongue that rapidly emerged was hence a mix of the biblical and rabbinic styles, with actual speakers of the language often imitating lowbrow Hebrew writing—thank goodness for those ḥasidic tales—with admixtures of their native Yiddish, Russian, or Arabic. Much of the time, rules and conventions took shape for no obvious reason.

If the scholars preferred reviving ancient words over coining new ones, the public loved new words generated from old roots. Even internationalisms like *posta* (post office), *adressa*, *telegrama*, and *veranda* were abandoned for *doar, ktovet, mivrak,* and *mirpeset.* At the same time, the Hebraists' penchant for applying old patterns to existing roots hit a chord: the ancient color words *adom, tsahov,* and *yarok* (red, yellow, green) were now joined by *afor, varod,* and *kaḥol* (gray, pink, dark blue); obscure biblical ailments like *yabelet* (wart) and *daleket* (inflammation) were joined by *ademet* (evoking reddishness) for rubella and *kalevet* (evoking dogginess) for rabies.

Some Hebrew words became legends or scandals. Tomatoes, for instance, were first called *bandorim* (from the Arabic), but in 1886 Yeḥiel Mikhel Pines, a Hebraist and mentor of Ben-Yehuda, translating a German farming text and faced with the German word *Liebesäpfel* (literally, love apples), coined the word *agvaniyot*, from *agavim* (lust). Why a rabbinically trained scholar would create such a risqué word is a mystery, but for twenty years it was boycotted as "vulgar" by the public and even by Ben-Yehuda himself, who may have been miffed that he hadn't thought of it first. But then the rebellious pioneers of the Second Aliyah mischievously adopted it—and the most pious of people use it today.

Perhaps most emblematic of the new Hebrew—what Itamar Even-Zohar has described as the simultaneous opposition and inertia of this "invented" new world[8]—was its new pronunciation. The Russian Zionists loved the local old-time Sephardi Jewish brogues (of which there were actually several). These, with their Middle Eastern gutturals, trilled r's, fully sounded vowels, and word-end stresses (*torAH* rather than *TOYreh*), provided aesthetic relief from the despised Yiddish overtones of Ashkenazi pronunciation. They were also thought of as more correct, at least by most scholars. A pronunciation soon emerged that Ashkenazim called Sephardi but which, to Sephardi ears, had an Ashkenazi ring. This turned out to be a stable compromise.

"The people need a hero, so we've given them one"

Although the living language naturally took on a life of its own, Ben-Yehuda did his best to provide a guiding hand. In a string of newspapers he produced to enlighten the local Jews, he systematically and stealthily embedded many neologisms: *bubah* (doll), *magevet* (towel), *milon* (dictionary)—to name some of those that stuck—as well as long-lost words he found in books and manuscripts.

Gradually, however, Ben-Yehuda retreated into a private world of words. He was at heart a solitary scholar. One thought consumed him: he did not feel he knew the precise meanings of many words that Hebrew authors had airily used. And so, single-handedly, he embarked on the research to assemble what no one had dared to think possible: a massive historical dictionary of Hebrew usage—what he described as "a temple to the Hebrew language." To the ordinary Hebrew speaker or author, it would be of little practical use, especially since it would take fifty years to complete, but that wasn't the point of the exercise.

The first volume appeared in 1909 and another four before Ben-Yehuda's death in 1922. The sixteenth and final volume was not released until 1959. To this day, for all its eccentricities, the *Ben-Yehuda Thesaurus* is *the* historical dictionary of Hebrew, equivalent to the *Oxford English Dictionary*. And it is to Ben-Yehuda's second wife and sole assistant, Ḥemda, that equal credit must go for the fact that his dictionary exists at all; for many years, Ḥemda was the financial and managerial brains of the project.

Was Ben-Yehuda, then, the "Father of Modern Hebrew"? Many encyclopedias say so. He and his family were certainly the pioneers who proved that Hebrew could be the working language of home and school. He was a great as well as a meticulous scholar. But the creation of modern *written* Hebrew was the work of others. As a word-maker, too, he had little direct effect: his 150 accepted coinages are a small fraction of the new vocabulary introduced during the *Teḥiyah* that remain in common use today. (His son's coinages were far more successful.) Asked in 1908 what Ben-Yehuda had done to earn his exalted folk status, the Zionist politician Menachem Ussishkin was candid: "The people need a hero, so we've given them one."[9]

Three Empires Intervene

The fate of languages does not rest with their speakers alone. When Ben-Yehuda began publishing his lexicon, the success of the Hebrew revival was by no means guaranteed. In 1914, most Jews in the land of Israel, many Zionists included, were skeptical about the future of the new Hebrew, and the majority were still not sending their children to Hebrew-speaking schools. German remained the official language of the international Zionist movement as well as a language spoken by many Jews in many countries. Some Zionists were learning Turkish, feeling that they had to be part of the state in which they lived. Yiddish, French, and Arabic also competed for linguistic attention.

But a decision taken in Berlin in October 1913 would have major, unintended consequences for the prestige of Hebrew. The first technical university in the Middle East, the Technikum (the future Technion), was about to open in Haifa, under anti-Zionist German-Jewish management. With the German Foreign Office in expansionary linguistic mood (and convinced that Zionism was a radical Russian plot), the German deputy consul in Palestine demanded that "Zionism must be denied any influence on the Technikum. A firm commitment is therefore required that the college and its feeder school will run in German."[10]

The Technikum's board of governors, meeting in Berlin, duly decided that science and technology would be taught in German. (Many saw this as the most pragmatic course; after all, Hebrew didn't have anything close to the necessary technical vocabulary.) But a Hebrew-language Technikum was more than a symbol: it promised jobs and untold influence for Hebrew speakers throughout the Levant. Two months of demonstrations and boycotts of German-funded schools ensued, climaxing in injuries and Turkish cavalry intervention. Ben-Yehuda threatened that "the Technion will open only at the cost of Jewish blood, and scores of young people will end up in jail."[11] In the end, no blood was spilled, but the pro-Hebrew movement proudly dubbed it the "Language Struggle." World War I, however, put the whole matter on hold.

Soon, such relatively minor disputes were overtaken by three epic developments, within the space of a single year. In February

1917 the tsar fell. What Kenneth Moss has called a "Jewish renaissance" in Russia followed.[12] All the pent-up energies of Hebrew and Yiddish cultural nationalism were unleashed. A Zionist school network, *Tarbut* (culture), was launched, and there was excited talk of state recognition of language rights. Hebrew and Yiddish political blocs took shape. The potential benefits for Hebrew in the Holy Land seemed incalculable.

Second, in October 1917 the Bolsheviks seized power. Overnight, both Judaism and Zionism were deemed subversive. All synagogues were padlocked and rabbis arrested. The state, at first, was not overtly hostile to Hebrew per se; in 1919 the People's Commissariat of Education ruled blandly that "Hebrew is not the spoken language of the Jewish masses and shall therefore not be considered a national minority language. Pedagogically, it is a foreign language."[13] But in the eyes of the *Yevsektsii*, the Communist Party's Jewish sections, which ran their own meticulous inquisition, the mere appearance of Hebrew in a school or paper or public library was a counterrevolutionary crime. Among the three million Jews in the USSR—then the heartland of Hebrew culture, religious and secular—resistance quickly crumbled. A few fled and then the gates shut. By 1928, the linguacide was complete.

It would be fifty years until the Jews of Silence, as Elie Wiesel would call them,[14] began to find their voice: private bar mitzvahs, smuggled books—and secret lessons in Hebrew, a precious link with the past and to the unreachable State of Israel. Natan (then, Anatoly) Sharansky describes his early days as a refusenik in 1973:

> I still remember the very first sentence we learned from our teacher: *Anaḥnu yehudim, aval anaḥnu lo m'dabrim ivrit* (We are Jews, but we do not speak Hebrew).[15]

Even as late as 1982, refusenik leader Yosef Begun would be sentenced to seven years' hard labor for parasitism—that is, teaching Hebrew. While it brought doom to the Jews of Russia, the year 1917 brought new hope to the Jews in their ancestral land. British forces entered Jerusalem, and His Majesty's government issued the Balfour Declaration endorsing a "national homeland for the Jewish people." Five years later, Britain was legally awarded control of Palestine by the League of Nations.

The British proceeded to do in Mandatory Palestine what they routinely did in their colonies: promote literacy and stability by providing recognition of and institutional support for the local languages. In the British House of Lords, on December 1, 1920, Lord Crawford declared that

in the application of [the Balfour] Declaration the revival of Hebrew is legitimately considered to play an important part. I am advised that the Hebrew language recognized officially is classical Hebrew, with such modifications as modern conditions require, and that the percentage of the Jewish population in Palestine speaking this particular style of Hebrew is probably between 60 and 70. (Hansard)

That percentage was a rank exaggeration derived from a highly charged census—but nonetheless one of Britain's first promulgations had recognized Hebrew (along with English and Arabic) as an official language. For Zionism, this was a dream come true: a school system entirely in Hebrew, to be funded and guaranteed by the British government, and an entire regime—complete with courts, regulations, radio broadcasting, and currency—that made it necessary for Jews to know Hebrew or English.

The Jewish population in Palestine jumped from 80,000 to 175,000 during the 1920s, and by 1946, swollen by Holocaust survivors, it would hit 600,000. But almost all new immigrants were speakers of Yiddish, Polish, or German. Would Hebrew not be inundated? Before we return to the situation in the Holy Land, let us first have a look at where the vast majority of Jews (over thirteen million) were to be found between the world wars: Europe, the Arab world, and the United States.

The Old Country's Last Hebrew Gasp

The new, freer eastern European states created after 1918 promised civil and linguistic rights to all ethnic groups. Many Jews held fast to a traditional way of life. Just as many, however, rooted in the Jewish world but modernizing, in Ezra Mendelson's words,[16] strove for a new, more secular Jewish culture—be it in Polish or in a modernized, upgraded vernacular Yiddish, or in a modern Hebrew embodying hopes for a Jewish state.

Sadly, little remained of the Hebrew literary life of pre-1914 eastern Europe. The publishers soon closed, the journals dried up. Agnon, Hazaz, Greenberg, and other great authors headed west or to Zion. Most who stayed turned to Yiddish or a Gentile language. And yet, remarkably, one in four Jewish children in interwar eastern Europe were enrolled in Zionist elementary schools, with most subjects taught in Hebrew by teachers trained in methods and terminologies, and often emerged able to speak it—an achievement unparalleled in the Diaspora. Some made Aliyah, among them the fifteen-year-old Natan Alterman (1910–1970), raised in a Warsaw family that lived and breathed Hebrew, schooled in Bessarabia, but soon to shine as the star poet of the nascent Jewish state. Many, like Menahem Begin, went on to join the Betar youth movement, in

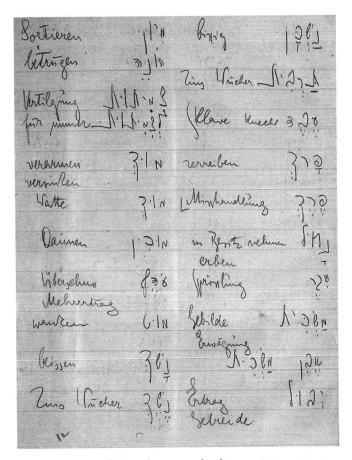

FIGURE 25. Franz Kafka's Hebrew notebook, ca. 1920: a step toward metamorphosis.

which Hebrew was accorded reverence. But there was no Jewish region or jurisdiction to underpin the language, and pressures to be more Polish or Hungarian or Latvian grew apace. Whether, thirty years on, modern Hebrew would have mattered any more than it would in America is a moot point; most of those young European Jews were liquidated in the Holocaust.

Sephardi Jewry: Grasping the Old, Seizing the New

The grand old Sephardi Jewries of North Africa, the Near East, Yemen, and Persia are sometimes portrayed as having been "frozen in time" until the expulsions and migrations after 1948. Not exactly. In the late nineteenth century, under European sway, the first sparks of Haskalah and *Teḥiyah* already began to be felt. But unlike in Europe, these were a stimulus not to literary revolt or acculturation but rather to reinvigorating traditional values and embracing Zionism and the Hebrew revival. By the 1930s, a Zionist-Hebrew culture was flowering in Morocco. After the mass exodus of the 1950s, Arabic-speaking Jews were able to adopt Hebrew with ease.

American Hebrew Dreams

America, Britain, and other Western countries gave Jews civil and cultural rights—but with a difference. There was little room for separate ethnic-linguistic identities; instead, there was a "melting pot," and the Jewish masses gratefully jumped in. The old intensive Jewish education melted away. Children were raised in the vernacular and enrolled in state schools. At most they learned some prayers and their bar mitzvah portion. Yiddish faded more slowly.

But social forces are complex, even unpredictable. Among the 7–8 million Jews now settled in the West, a Hebrew intelligentsia, numbering maybe 20,000–30,000 souls, emerged for whom writing, reading, and teaching the new-old tongue were of paramount importance. Some chose Germany or the United Kingdom. Most settled in the United States—and there, a Hebrew culture blossomed overnight, wedding Americanism with Hebrew nationalism. In fiction and verse, realism and symbol, it explored the country's vistas and peoples, its beauties and blemishes. The Negro and American

Indian experiences elicited special fascination and rare empathy. Binyamin Silkiner's epic *Mul Ohel Timurah* (Before Timurah's tent, 1910) echoed to Longfellow's *Hiawatha* as much as to Bialik:

> There lived braves, ancient as thunder, nursed by the storm,
> Of the Rock-Tribe, and with their mighty Katsika, the brave
> Would ride out to affright their tribal foes.
>
> (Adapted from a translation by Stephen Katz)[17]

Ephraim Lisitzky's collection *Be-Ohalei Kush* (In Negro tents), published in 1953 on the eve of the civil rights era, came as a climax to forty years of Hebrew writing about African Americans. These simple lines embody the tie between the Negro spiritual and the Bible:

> Helter-skelter to the raft
> Hurry, man! / Helter-skelter to the raft
> Taking you across
> To God's shores—
> Hurry, man . . . Up and over the river's mighty waters
> Burning, churning
> It's the river of sin,
> We shall turn our boat.
>
> (My translation)

Ambivalences fueled both the poetry and the prose: fear of Christian America, alienation from the city, a deep Zionism—and gathering intimations of rootlessness. Israel Efros's epic *Vigvamim Shotkim* (Silent wigwams, 1933) encodes the decline of American-Hebrew culture—in Alan Mintz's words, the "failure of a noble dream."[18] The last and greatest poet was Gavriel Preil (1911–1993). Raised in Lithuania, he wrote of Brooklyn Heights, New Hampshire, Jefferson, Lincoln, in a straight, "modern" style, unleashed from erudite allusions, which came to embody American Hebrew writing. From *Mitziyurei Maine* (Maine sketches, 1972):

> True, you are not my tortured country, . . .
> But your white sheltered villages, their even-tempered earth
> and sky
> Have names testifying-proclaiming the heritage of sacred
> Canaan.
> (Translation by Ezra Spicehandler)[19]

But as for where he belonged:

> There is no escaping my time.
> It is Lithuania, it is America, it is Israel.
> I am a unique copy of these lands
> And one way or another they've absorbed my weathers.

When asked "What is a good poem?" Natan Zach, high priest of Israeli verse, answered, "A poem by Gavriel Preil."[20] American Hebrew literature was the extraordinary finale to Diaspora Hebrew culture. But few remember its representative figures; even fewer read them.

In their time, however, they were not alone. Thousands of Jewish immigrants thirsted for Hebrew. In the 1920s, the polished cultural monthly *Hatoren* had thirteen thousand subscribers; its successor *Bitzaron* continued to publish until 1992. The weekly *Hadoar* peaked at fifteen thousand subscribers in the early 1940s. Hebrew-based teachers' colleges in New York, Boston, Philadelphia, and Baltimore awarded degrees; thousands attended Hebrew-based after-school Talmud Torahs and all-Hebrew summer camps such as the legendary Camp Massad, whose campers included Alan Dershowitz, Ralph Lauren, Hillel Halkin, and Rabbi Shlomo Riskin. But the 1950s marked a precipitous watershed. The immigrant generation was

FIGURE 26. Camping in Hebrew: Camp Massad staff picture, USA, 1941.

aging, Hebrew literacy was out of step with the latest developments in language teaching, and now that a State of Israel was established on its own soil, it just seemed odd to nurture a Diaspora Hebrew.

"Valiant but misguided," Arnold Band has called the American Hebrew dream.[21] Misguided in hindsight, I would add, and no less valiant for that. But the periodicals have indeed gone, as have almost all Hebrew-only camps and the rest. Israelis living in the Diaspora speak English to other Jews.

Hebrew Nation: Israeli Identity in the Making

A new kind of Jewish society took shape in the land of Israel during the years of British rule (1918–1948). Some of its members were simply refugees. Many others were Zionists, intent on creating a new society that would do away with old stereotypes of the Jew. Through their efforts, a new collective identity emerged, which they pointedly described as *ivri*—Hebrew.

FIGURE 27. The first Israeli stamps, *Doar Ivri* (Hebrew Mail), (May 16, 1948); designed before the state had adopted the name 'Israel.'

The essential thing about the term *ivri* was what it excluded. Being an *ivri* was different from being a *yehudi* or a *Yisrael*—the two traditional words for "Jew" or "Jewish." (The choice of *Yisrael* [Israel] as the name of the Jewish state still lay in the future; up until 1948, it simply meant "the Jewish people.") *Ivri* had been used sporadically in rabbinic writings for the Hebrew language. In the Bible, Abraham, Joseph, and Jonah were occasionally called *ivri*, which seems to have been an ethnic label—so adoption of the term was meant to evoke biblical Israel rather than Diaspora Jewry.

Loaded with symbolism, *ivri* would now denote *speaking* the new Hebrew (*ivrit*); *being* a Hebrew; and acting in a Hebrew way—an entire cultural, social, and philosophical post-diasporic identity. Tel Aviv was heralded as the first Hebrew city; the Hebrew University, founded in 1925, was deliberately not named the Jewish University. The avant-garde Yiddish poet Uri Zvi Greenberg, the voice of blood-and-fire Hebraism after his arrival in the country in 1923, spoke of an "exodus from the jungle of a paralytic [diasporic] Hebrew to the regal highway of sovereign Hebrew, nourished by the new Hebrew who eats bread and drinks water . . . in perfect simplicity." Some went even further: Judaism itself, for them, was associated only with Diaspora Jews (*yehudim*) and Jewishness; the new, modern Hebrew had to connect to secular, universal values or (for the poet Tchernichovsky and his disciples) ancient pagan ones. But arguably "*the* historic moment in modern Hebrew poetry," for the literary historian Dan Miron,[22] was the appearance in 1924 of the translations from Dante and Poe by the charismatic Russian-Zionist politician-litterateur Zeev Jabotinsky—in an Israeli rhythm and graphic modernistic style totally shorn of classical allusions. A similar sea change was then under way among Hebrew poets in America.

There were clearly limits, however, to how much modernity the public would stomach. Thus abandoning the Hebrew alphabet for the Latin seemed eminently sensible to Jabotinsky. Turkey, after all, had recently discarded the Arabic alphabet (likewise associated with religion) for the Roman as part of its transition from sultanate to modern secular nation-state. An admirer of western European culture, Jabotinsky envisioned the arrival of millions of Jews with no Jewish schooling—not far from what in fact transpired—and saw the Hebrew alphabet as an unwarranted nuisance. But the public thought otherwise.

Cartoonists had long portrayed Hebrew as a lady and Yiddish as a maid. In another dualistic characterization, even before the Hebrew revival, Hebrew was considered masculine and Yiddish (known as the *mame-loshn*, or mother tongue) feminine—a natural consequence of the gender divide in education and literacy. With the advent of the new Hebrew, Yiddish (literally, Jewish) was variously portrayed ideologically as intimate, motherly, effeminate, weak, or ambivalent, as opposed to Hebrew, which was masculine,

אונטן — שטאַרקע טענות מיט אַ שוואַכן שטאַנדפּונקט...

FIGURE 28. "Those Hebraists scream about Soviet suppression of Hebrew yet they trample on Yiddish!" A Yiddish cartoon, New York, 1926.

strong, decisive, overbearing. Hebrew in Greenberg's vision was "rocky, hammer-like." He wrote in a 1937 collection:

A great new Hebrew language is being carved out here
From the rock of the messiah.[23]

But even Greenberg, like many milder men, lamented the loss of his Yiddish mother tongue.

Of course, many Yiddish writers and champions of the Diaspora proletariat saw things differently: "Yiddish, the national tongue of the Diaspora!" "Yiddish in every school in Tel Aviv!" But by this time, in any case, the direction of Hebrew was slipping out of the hands of poets and theoreticians and into the grasp of mass institutions and the masses: "sociolinguistic normalization" of sorts, to use Joshua Fishman's phrase.[24] The development of the language was proceeding rapidly. Soon there was no longer one Hebrew daily newspaper but eight, as well as twenty publishing houses and scores of professional journals. Hebrew writers relocated from Europe en

FIGURE 29. "Hebrews, ask for the phone number in Hebrew!" Brigade for the Defence of Hebrew, Jerusalem, ca. 1930.

masse, and by 1930 the indisputable literary capital of the Hebrew world was Tel Aviv.

This was perhaps Hebrew's finest hour, even as the aesthetic dreams of the *Teḥiyah* were being betrayed. Between 1918 and 1948, many thousands of words were coined or resignified, and at least four thousand of them became permanent fixtures of the language, from *ketsitsah* (meatball) to *meshek* (economy) to *maḥberet* (notebook). The words coming out of the laboratories and classrooms at the Technion and Hebrew University were infusing Hebrew with scientific-technical capabilities that would serve it well when statehood came. An official Language Committee (*Va'ad ha-Lashon*) ploddingly tried to codify these coinages in some sixty-five lexicons for algebra, archaeology, beekeeping, banking, and so forth.

Pressure to use Hebrew in public came from many sides and created mixed feelings. Foreign films and performances were often disrupted. Non-Hebrew signs in storefronts invited polite letters of protest and the occasional brick. Tel Aviv's city hall returned letters written in languages other than Hebrew. The students and workers of the self-styled "Language Defense Squad" ran a rousing and occasionally noxious campaign, issuing warnings to leading personalities, including Tel Aviv mayor Meir Dizengoff, not to use English on their letterhead. One flyer urged the public to ensure that bus drivers speak only Hebrew:

HEBREW PERSON: When you board the bus, speak only Hebrew to the driver! Do not answer if he speaks any other language! Should you hear others talking in a foreign language, point out their wrongdoing.

Bialik himself, the national poet laureate, was forced to post apologies in the press for speaking Russian in public. There was no need, though, to pressure the youth. The schools and, above all, the youth movements, produced a generation of enthusiastic Hebrew speakers who were eminently comfortable in the language.

To be sure, many immigrants, for their part, were less than eager to trade their Jewish identity for a new Hebrew one. Before World War II, Tel Aviv and Haifa buzzed with Polish-speaking merchants and German professionals who were there seeking safety, not new identities. If they had to acquire the dominant host language, which, like immigrants anywhere, most of them eventually did, it was because there was growing social and economic pressure to know it and because their children came home speaking it. But among themselves they still spoke and especially read and wrote a Babel of Yiddish, German, Polish, and Hebrew.

In 1936, one-third of Palestine's 300,000 Jews could not communicate in Hebrew, prompting an urgent memo to David Ben-Gurion, the Zionist leader, warning that speakers of Hebrew might soon become "a tiny minority." It is a cruel irony that this threat was nullified by the 1939 British ban on Jewish immigration and then, forever, by the Holocaust.

Socially, politically, and economically, the Jews under British occupation had plenty to worry about in the form of mounting Arab and British hostility and the horrific reports coming out of Europe.

But the threats served to unite the Jewish population around the Hebrew language. So did the children born in this new land: by 1948, 93 percent of children under age fifteen were using Hebrew as their sole language. Their very names embodied the new values of Zionism: biblical names evoking the ancient Hebrew race, such as Avner (King Saul's chief general), Nimrod (a primeval conqueror, literally, let us rebel), or Michal (a wife of David); Zionist values like Oded (motivate), Uzi (my might), or Renanah (joy); the new land-scape, as in Nir (field) and Ḥoresh (wood); and, increasingly, its flora and fauna, as in Rakefet (cyclamen), Smadar (vine blossom), and Ofer (young deer).

And so the revival (or "revitalization," as Spolsky and Shohamy would call it)[25] of Hebrew appeared to be complete: the language itself and all it could do, the wish to use it and hand it on, the schools and institutions, the demographics. But a lot could still go wrong. The task had little in common with reversing language shift; rather, Zionism had set itself, in Joshua Fishman's words, "an unprece-dented goal."[26]

Max Weinreich, the great Yiddishist and linguist, is said to have defined a language as "a dialect with an army and navy." The last two goods, and the legitimacy they granted, were all that Hebrew now lacked.

9
The Hebrew State

A million arrive. Modern Hebrew survives.

The State of Israel was proclaimed on May 15, 1948. Some two thousand years earlier, when a sovereign Jewish state last stood on the same soil, only a minority of its Jews spoke Hebrew as a first language. In 1948, the picture was rather different. Of the 650,000 Jews in the new state, about half were already native speakers of Hebrew and an additional 25 percent spoke it as their main language.

But, in the course of just one decade, a million destitute Jewish refugees would arrive from Europe and Arab lands, well outnumbering the existing Jewish population. Few were functionally literate in Hebrew and even fewer could speak it, but the new state was determined that all should. Hebrew language and culture were to be the beating heart of this newborn society of Jews.

No country had ever attempted such a grand linguistic transformation, let alone an impoverished country fighting a protracted war of survival against a ring of foes. But in Prime Minister David Ben-Gurion, the State of Israel and the Hebrew language had an extraordinary leader. A wily politician and tenacious idealist with a Napoleonic gift for organizing men to achieve the seemingly impossible, he had insisted on proclaiming a Jewish state when international opinion had urged him to delay; he had thrown precious forces into battle for the holy city of Jerusalem when his generals thought doing so was militarily suicidal; and he clung to the ideal of making Hebrew *the* Jewish language of the new state.

Ben-Gurion held several cards in his hand: an efficient Hebrew-language school system with highly motivated teachers deeply dedicated to the new language, backed up by Hebrew-speaking youth movements; two to three years of compulsory service in the Israeli armed forces for men and many women; and the continued suppression of any public role for Yiddish (Hebrew's only plausible rival) and total denial to it of educational or cultural resources. Finally, to buy the new nation's cooperation and gratitude, Ben-Gurion employed a well-organized political patronage system that offered the immigrant masses party-sponsored employment, housing, health care, and free and compulsory education.

As in so many new nations emerging from colonial occupation in the shadow of World War II, the Israeli state was desperate to project a strong and unified identity. The Israelis (as they were now known) had come from vastly different cultural and social backgrounds. A shared religious heritage apart, what they perhaps had most in common was a Jewish penchant for fractiousness. They had to be bonded into loyal citizens of a new nation, and Hebrew was a key ingredient in the process. There were also more practical considerations at play. Immigrants from Iran and Morocco, France and Romania, needed a common language in which to communicate. Most would prefer to discard their native language for Hebrew rather than master some other diasporic tongue.

Privately, nonetheless, many lamented the public humiliation of Yiddish. This was especially true of Holocaust survivors, for whom Yiddish was all they had left of their former world. Yet, as the sociolinguist Joshua Fishman put it, "Yiddish was [also] a reminder of things that many Israelis would rather forget"[1]—namely, eastern Europe, powerlessness, and, for some, the straitjacket of religion. By

1961, just 5 percent of Israeli Jews claimed Yiddish as their main language. Not that Yiddish vanished overnight; rather, as almost everywhere else, it would die quietly as its speakers aged—cherished only by some Ḥaredim ("ultra-Orthodox" Jews).

One highly charged issue centered on names. Under the unambiguous slogan "No more foreign names in our midst," the president of the National Council (the central body of the provisional government during the first months of statehood) declared in June 1948: "The citizens of a Hebrew state cannot continue to appear in personal and public life with foreign names, which account for 90 percent of the surnames among us. A radical change is required." Officials, health workers, teachers, and youth leaders set about hebraizing the names of young arrivals, often without asking for their approval. One teacher recalls how she changed a Fairuz (a Persian name) to a Yitzḥak and dealt similarly with young Jean, Sa'id, and Salimah. The biggest concession was to seek a semantic or phonetic approximation of the youngster's former name.

Older Israelis similarly came under pressure, if perhaps more subtle, to hebraize both their given and their family names. Immigrants might still go on using their Diaspora name with close friends and family, though how much this happened is uncertain. Research and memoirs suggest that most young people, and their parents, quickly appreciated having names, especially first names, like their Israeli peers. Many Ashkenazim were in fact eager to exchange the shtetl whiff and the unwieldiness of a Rabinowitz or Leibovici for a streamlined Rabin or Lev. One of the aesthetic pleasures of using Hebrew in place of European languages like Yiddish or Russian was its no-frills, clean-cut feel.

The only official requirement to hebraize surnames applied to senior army officers and official representatives overseas, with the latter category even including Miss Israel beauty queens. This was one of Prime Minister Ben-Gurion's pet projects in his zeal to construct and project an Israeli identity. He had changed his own name from Gruen in 1917, and among his associates, Kozolovski became Sapir, Shkolnik became Eshkol, Shertok Sharett, and Persky Peres ("bearded vulture"). The last three would serve as prime ministers. In fact, every Israeli prime minister has borne a Hebrew given name, with one exception: Golda Meir, who changed her surname from Meyerson upon becoming foreign minister in 1956, but refused to change her given name.

The Zionist militias had long required members to adopt a Hebrew alias. The new Israel Defense Forces (IDF) promptly created a Name Committee, and all military letters concluded with the message "Soldier, hebraize your name!" Within fourteen months, twenty thousand citizens obliged. Of the nineteen IDF chiefs of staff prior to 2011, only one, Ḥaim Laskov, did not change his name, having been granted an exception as an orphan.

Learning Hebrew

In the first, epic decade of statehood, an entire younger generation of immigrants emerged from Israel's schools, its youth movements, and the IDF with a fully functional Hebrew, equipped to conduct their daily lives in it and to read biblical prose and the daily newspaper with ease.

Many adult immigrants, however, particularly those who had received neither traditional nor Zionist educations, did not find the challenge at all easy. For them, the Ministry of Absorption developed its "secret weapon," the *ulpan*, or Hebrew immersion course. Pictures of pretty *ulpan* teachers imparting the Hebrew alphabet to beaming immigrants became a staple of Zionist public relations, suggesting that mastering Hebrew was no problem. In reality, however, most adult immigrants would never learn to read a Hebrew newspaper or write Hebrew well enough to find a good job. Nevertheless, they would somehow learn enough to speak it with the boss, the neighbors, and their children—or end up working with or living near people who shared a language they knew better.

In the twentieth century, print, writing, and speech were not the only indicators of a language's status. There was also radio. The British-run pre-1948 Palestine Broadcasting Service had allotted several hours a day to Hebrew radio; highlights included readings from the Hebrew Bible, a fitness show, and heavily censored news reports. Even more thrilling, no doubt, were the clandestine stations run by the underground militias: the Haganah, Etzel, and Lehi. With independence came Kol Yisrael (Voice of Israel), the official Hebrew broadcasting service of the Jewish state. By 1952 there were three stations. And perhaps the greatest mark that Hebrew had arrived on the world scene came in October 1949, when the BBC World Service launched its own daily Hebrew broadcasts to Israel.

It is hard to appreciate how new and exciting radio of any sort, let alone a Jewish station, still was in the early 1950s to a population hailing largely from eastern Europe and the Middle East. Kol Yisrael was perhaps the most powerful embodiment of the state, its national consensus, and its national language. Even if many immigrants (particularly women) could barely read a Hebrew sentence, radio provided Hebrew listening—folk songs, documentaries, hourly news bulletins, and regular news in simplified Hebrew—that helped bind the nation together.

But radio also inflicted deep linguistic wounds: Yiddish, Judeo-Arabic, and Ladino were classified as foreign. The only crumb thrown their way was a twenty-minute slot in the early evening dedicated to "Programs for Immigrants," where they were lumped together with French, Romanian, Turkish, Hungarian, and Persian. In those years you could hear far more Yiddish on the New York radio dial than in Israel. Not until the turn of the twenty-first century could one tune in to a brief Yiddish news roundup on Israeli TV. For Israel's Arab citizens, the law provided an Arabic school system, Arabic radio, and the right to use Arabic in court. (To this day, most Arab Israelis speak Arabic among themselves, though as adults they often have a firm grasp of Hebrew as a second language.) Arabic and English were recognized as official languages alongside Hebrew, but no such rights were granted to other languages, Jewish or non-Jewish. And Hebrew reigned supreme, anchored in a plethora of legal regulations and policies.

Straight-Speaking Nation

As much as Hebrew was rapidly becoming the language of the mundane and everyday, the first generation of Israelis were often acutely aware that they were engaged in an exciting experiment, eagerly watched by parents from another planet called Diaspora. Speaking Hebrew was often a self-conscious activity. Like children everywhere—and especially children of immigrants—Israeli children wanted to distinguish themselves from their old-fashioned, somewhat embarrassing, parents.

A certain mode of speech was expected: blunt (no prevaricating, no *sir* or *madam* or other empty expressions of etiquette), simple (no fancy words), and minimalist—talking straight, as Tamar Katriel has put it.[2] They called this mode of speech "talking *dugri*" (from the Turkish/Arabic for "direct"), in contrast to the stereotype of the loquacious, jabbering Diaspora Jew, perpetually compelled to live by his verbal wits. This new way of speaking was suited to a tough, hardened nation of farmers and soldiers. Henceforth, what would matter (they believed) was not what Jews said but what Jews did.

Native-born Israelis also began to make their own lexical contributions. They took a delight in colloquialisms and slang, much of which has become part of the language. There were the Arabic emotives like *zift* (rotten) and *mabsut* (glad). These were more than just loanwords; they were ways of indicating that you were one of the natives, as it were. Similarly, the arcane abbreviations concocted by the army served to distinguish the in-group young enough to be new conscripts or respected veterans from the out-group of recent adult immigrants. Of course, plenty of words from Yiddish, Russian, and English made their way into the language as well, like *shpakhtl* (scraper), *ḥaltura* (moonlighting), *breks* (automotive brakes).

There was also a constant tension between the organically evolving spoken language and the vocabulary of language planners, enforced by teachers and intellectuals. Why, they lamented, borrow *hishpritz* (to spray) from Yiddish when the Bible has a perfectly good word, *hitiz*? Why take the word *nora* (awesome) that Jacob had uttered at the foot of the angelic ladder and degrade it to mean "terribly" (as in, "I was terribly hungry")? New words for new things were one thing, but this was a desecration of the Hebraic heritage.

And so every young Israeli in those early days was expected to "connect" with lengthy sections of Bible, Midrash, medieval and modern poetry, and elegant fin de siècle essays and fiction. Not all of this was as remote from life as might appear. True, this was a predominantly secular society, but these texts mattered. Zionism was still strong, and the Bible served as a credential for the Jewish state and a guidebook to the land. The popular songs that young people sang were often drawn from the prophets and studded with biblical motifs and turns of phrase. Rock music wouldn't arrive until the late 1960s.

When they wrote, young Israelis were taught to use the spare, precise Hebrew that had recently evolved in the Israeli press. No one wanted the florid literary style of the nineteenth century, which by now seemed as remote and unwieldy as Victorian journalism appears to an English reader today. Even their handwriting was a simple cursive, mostly unjoined, shorn of their grandparents' ornate penmanship—which they could barely decipher. The wider public picked up on the down-to-earth trend. Highflown or flowery Hebrew (even in writing) was mocked as *Ivrit shel Shabbat* (Sabbath Hebrew) or as *Ivrit Tsiyonit* (Zionist Hebrew)—an echo of the public's impatience with the verbose political rhetoric that had dominated life for a half century.

Poets vs. Peasants (and Some Canaanites)

The various social and cultural pressures of this era in Israel created a grand linguistic standoff, which has eased only recently. In the one corner was colloquial Hebrew, evolving organically and haphazardly and for its native speakers a source of pride. In the other were the combined forces of the Ministry of Education, the broadcasting authorities, the literary establishment, and the publishing industry, determined to hold the line against bad grammar and bad language. Their writ extended wide: to children's schoolbooks, storybooks, and magazines; to scripted broadcasts and commercials; to textbooks for new immigrants; to fiction and nonfiction of almost any sort. In publishing houses, shadowy figures known as *mesagnenim* (style monitors) left the manuscripts of accomplished authors covered with red ink. The book you are reading now, if written in Hebrew, would have been copiously corrected to meet the inscrutable standards of the "Hebrew police."

The effects were often ludicrous. Israeli toothpaste commercials ran in quasi-biblical Hebrew. If the score was 27–26, breathless basketball commentators had to remember to say *esrim va-sheva, esrim va-shesh* with the classically correct *va* for "and" rather than, as in the dreaded colloquial, *esrim ve-sheva, esrim ve-shesh*. The Hebrew on Kol Yisrael was famously described by a critic as sounding as if "broadcast in a can of disinfectant." Children in storybooks spoke in a classical Hebrew that would never have been heard in ancient Israel. Even the authoritative Even-Shoshan dictionary ignored such everyday usage as *dey* for "rather" and *ambatya* for "bathroom" because they were too colloquial.

Israeli authors were the most egregiously out of step. Like many Western literatures in the twentieth century, Hebrew letters had made the jump from florid to plain. But incorporating the colloquial was painfully slow in coming, even for children's literature. (By contrast, as early as the 1920s, British children's publishers allowed child characters to speak colloquially.) Most Israeli authors, right up to the 1990s, hewed quite tightly to the basic Haskalah style developed in fin de siècle eastern Europe: a blend of biblical and rabbinic Hebrew, adjusted to European patterns.

What, then, bothered them about native Israeli speech? What charms could an old diasporic Hebrew possibly hold? The answer seems to lie in a compulsive aversion to the folksy style of popular ḥasidic folk literature in Hebrew and popular Yiddish fiction. Scratch the surface of Israeli speech, they feared (not entirely wrongly), and you'll find Yiddish. Or worse yet, the language of stuffy talmudic discourses. The only resort, then, was the urbane idiom of the old Haskalah.

But who could admit to this? The new Israeli literati had to cover their traces by inventing a linguistic ideology. In their imagination, they saw themselves breathing life into ancient, pure Hebrew. The poet Yonatan Ratosh experimented with an archaic style redolent of Ugaritic myth. One poem, provocatively titled *Et Nishmat* (playing on the hallowed Jewish prayer for the departed) committed the dead to *elohey ruḥot yam, qerev afiq tehomotayim*, "the god of the winds of the sea, midst the channel of the twin abysses." Ratosh

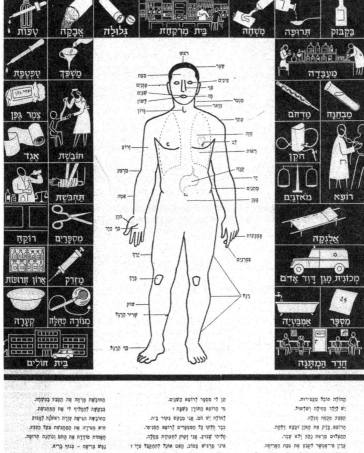

FIGURE 30. "Speak Hebrew at the clinic and you shall be healed" (Israeli Ministry of Education, 1950s).

became high priest of a group of self-proclaimed "Canaanite" writers and artists, disciples of Tchernichovsky, who promoted an imagined pre-Jewish "Hebrew" identity grounded in the archaeological imagery of the ancient Levant.[3]

Others were content just to go "Israelite." The novelist Amos Oz, known for his European style, ventured: "Hebrew cherishes total concision because its origins as a written language are in verse incised on stone."[4] In an interview in 1990, this flag-bearer of the Israeli cosmopolitan Far Left reaffirmed his conservative linguistic outlook:

Hebrew, like any language, has an integrity that I would not like to lose in the euphoria of renewal. For example, ancient Hebrew tradition often places the verb initially. . . . Sentence structure is a profound expression of a cultural ethos, a scale of values par excellence, one I favor and would not like to lose.[5]

Others, like the poet Yehuda Amichai (1924–2000), constructed a bleak aesthetic out of the very confrontation of ancient and modern:

To speak now in this tired tongue, tongue torn from biblical
   sleep:
Blinded, it wanders from mouth to mouth.
To say, in a tongue that described wonders and God,
mekhonit, petzatzah, elohim (car, bomb, God).
   (My translation)[6]

But few Israeli poets have exploded today's norms of grammar and syntax—or experimented with the things that make Hebrew so un-European.

New immigrants, meanwhile, were placed in immersion schools staffed by a cadre of teachers indoctrinated in the belief that they were still reviving the language. The curriculum was quite divorced from the realities of spoken Hebrew, an oddity that, astonishingly, the Ministry of Education did not seek to reform until the 1970s. As a result, the phrase to "speak like a new immigrant" meant not to speak haltingly but to speak in a stilted, overly formal manner.

The Academy of the Hebrew Language

The Academy of the Hebrew Language nestles modestly amid the physics and life-sciences buildings at the Hebrew University of Jerusalem. It has much to be modest about. For all the erudition of its distinguished members, the academy has done little for the development or promotion of the Hebrew language. But then again, it is unlikely that many of its members would ever have claimed otherwise.

For years, under the British Mandate, the scholars of the semi-official Language Committee had labored heroically to issue word lists. But in February 1948, with statehood in his sights, Ben-Gurion appealed to the committee

> to compile all linguistic material and terms relating to the life of the state, its constitution, institutions, officials, . . . courts of law, police force and army, their headquarters, offices, units, and ranks, . . . ambassadors, consuls, attachés, and their assistants; the secret service, the information and propaganda service, and the like.[7]

The committee sought background advice and sprang into action. By the summer, with war raging, a draft dictionary of military Hebrew was also under way. It would ultimately number thousands of terms. By 1952, several scientific terminologies had been promulgated, and welcomed with approval and joy. There already was a scientific terminology for the Technion and for high schools, but now it was all official.

The Academy of the Hebrew Language was established by law only in 1953. Many countries have a supreme language body of a kind, some with sweeping powers, some just toothless, some focused on spelling, some on keeping English at bay. In Israel, the law seemed quite clear. The academy had a bold remit: "to steer the future of Hebrew, by means of wide-ranging research into its past," and its rulings were to be adhered to "by educational and scientific institutes, the government, its departments and agencies, and the local authorities . . . in matters of grammar, spelling, terminology, and transliteration."[8]

But that is not how things turned out. The academy morphed into a research institute. Its prime mission of developing and promoting the reborn national tongue withered, while its gargantuan computerized *Historical Dictionary of the Hebrew Language* (a world-class project, to be sure) consumed its energies. Surveying four decades of the academy's work, one of its leading lights, Professor Aharon Dotan, painted a gloomy picture:[9] guidance for spelling, punctuation, words, syntax, and pronunciation was sorely lacking. It had taken decades to decide on a spelling system for indicating vowels. (Publishers, teachers, the public, and even the academy's website have widely ignored the spelling system, and it is still being reworked.) Word development for daily needs or the realms of culture and society had dwindled. "Sometimes, we seem to be no more than a terminology lab for the Technion."

In everyday life, academy-approved words have had only a modest impact, and car mechanics, photographers, and practitioners of every other trade seem to have gone on using words they'd always used (*visherim*, "wipers"; *klatsh*, "clutch"; *egzoz*, "exhaust"). The academy has not investigated why. Nor has it ever surveyed Israeli language, colloquial or formal—fearful, perhaps, of seeming to close off old norms when the language may not yet have settled down. It is not surprising that most Israelis think the Akademya, as they call it, exists only to concoct new words that no one wants to use anyway. They have a good laugh about it. And more than anything, they laugh at its pedantic daily one-minute radio spot. Worse, as Dotan observes, "The Akademya has left a wide-open field where pedants peddle their own crazy rules."

However, the Akademya has never claimed a monopoly on coining words. It prefers to vet and validate. It loves to consider the coinages of poets or, even better, a pearl retrieved from the medieval past. The principle stated a century ago by Yeḥiel Mikhel Pines still stands: "The best new words aren't even new."

The institution's very name, Akademya, embodies another dilemma. Were foreign words helpful guests or menacing aliens? This question, which persistently riled Hebrew circles during the Haskalah and the *Teḥiyah*, returned again to haunt the academy. The word *akademya* has no deep roots in Hebrew; it comes from the Greek *akademia*, the school founded by Plato, but has since acquired international currency. Internationalisms were perfectly acceptable to the leaders of the Hebrew academy-to-be. "Do we, who aspire to be a bridge between the peoples of Europe and Asia, need to forswear every international word or phrase?" they asked, rhetorically.[10] The government, however, preoccupied with political symbolism, insisted that the academy find itself a Hebrew name. "Do the Chinese or Persians use the word *academy*?" huffed Ben-Gurion.[11]

The proviso that the academy find a Hebrew name was written into the law that founded it. The search failed. In 2012, some fifty-nine years on, the academy voted formally to endorse its Greek

FIGURE 31. New stuff just keeps popping up: dispenser for *kakit* (dog poop bag).

name. As its president, Moshe Bar-Asher, observed, "*Akademya* has now become as deeply-rooted as the word Sanhedrin itself."[12] Since *Sanhedrin*, the name for the Jewish supreme court of the talmudic era, was a Greek word, Bar-Asher was thereby appealing to what is perhaps the strongest argument for admitting foreignisms to Hebrew: they were nothing new.

But where to draw the line? Israel's language guardians have generally been accepting of internationalisms with a Greco-Latin derivation: *kognitivi*, *migraina*, *aplikatzya*, *individuali*, and so forth. This kind of word has a good profile: as Greco-Latin derivation once enjoyed a rabbinic imprimatur, today it has academic cachet; it also positions Hebrew as part of an international language scene (and not, heaven forfend, a vassal of English). Often, as with *kognitivi*, there is an acknowledged gap in the Hebrew semantic field. Nonetheless, the Akademya is always on the lookout for creative Hebrew alternatives, and there have been many popular successes, including such high-tech coinages as *maḥshev* (computer), *nayad* (mobile), and *sharat* (server). But a sharp line has been drawn against mass imports of any sort, especially from such serious competitors as German, Yiddish, and, today, English. The academy will have no truck with such common words as *lobist* (lobbyist) or *klip* (clip). None of this could be called intervention. Nor does the academy have much of a voice in the Ministry of Education. But where TV and radio are concerned, language watchdogs prowl, out of sight. Once upon a time, broadcasters pledged allegiance to a thousand-rule style book and radio announcers were picked for the propriety of their pronunciation. Today, they don't even get language training. Nonetheless, a hardy band of broadcast monitors still checks news bulletins, commercials, and other scripts for proper Hebrew, making considerable changes while advising on the pronunciation of unusual words; it also does spot-checks and critiques of non-news programming. No station, public or private, escapes surveillance.

In the public arena, rather than wage war for linguistic propriety or honor or just to display a presence, the Akademya has until recently kept its silence. Only rarely, when some political decision directly threatens the language, will it raise a cry. But the Internet is changing this. Almost everything the Akademya has ever produced is now available on its website, from the *Historical Dictionary* to an app for translating foreign terms. Facebook and Twitter, clips and games, are the Akademya's answer to English.

Critics of the Akademya like to point to Britain or America, which get along without a supreme language body. The comparison is misguided: Israel was until recently an emerging nation with a language whose very viability was in question. In any case, British and American media are themselves in thrall to style guides, editors, big dictionaries, language columnists, and shadowy bodies like the BBC Pronunciation Unit. An American might once have written to a newspaper with a language query; each week, thousands of Israelis visit hebrew-academy.huji.ac.il. In January 2016 alone, fourteen hundred questions were received by e-mail and answered.

The 1980s: Israeli Language Policy
Goes into Reverse

Sometime in the late 1970s, a tectonic shift occurred in Israeli politics and society. The long-standing social, cultural, and political domination of the secular, Labor-Zionist Ashkenazi establishment came under attack. Leading voices lamented the dissolution of traditional (especially Sephardi) religion and culture in the Israeli cultural melting pot. Established dogma about Israeli-Arab relations, synagogue and state, the agricultural commune, doctrines of defense, and more crumbled at the edges. Some of these changes came from the political shake-up following the near calamity of the 1973 Yom Kippur War and the electoral victory of Menachem Begin in 1977. But this was also a time when major social and cultural changes in the West were starting to make themselves felt in Israeli society. New multiculturalist dogmas, spreading from academia into the education system—the "silent revolution," as Israel Bartal dubbed it—rapidly eroded the national consensus about the Jewish historical heritage.[13]

Attitudes toward Hebrew changed, too. In 1979, in Israel's leading educational journal, the superintendent of teacher training in Hebrew made a groundbreaking prediction: the norms of formal Hebrew as taught in schools would have to be adapted to the "new, easier standards of speech." At a scholarly retreat in 1980 for discussion of the theme "Is Hebrew Declining?" almost every participant was in favor of relaxing the rules.

At the same time, the humanities in Israel (as elsewhere in the West) were beginning their own slow, steady decline. The study of Hebrew language and literature came under postmodern and post-Zionist assault. In state-run schools, the space given to Hebrew language and literature in the curriculum began to shrink. Hebrew, and perhaps Zionism itself, was suffering a crisis of confidence.

The late 1980s and the 1990s provided two new challenges that helped restore some of the lost confidence. From Ethiopia, some sixty thousand immigrants arrived; from the disintegrating Soviet Union, one million. The Ethiopian Jews were absorbed and hebraized by Israel's traditional paternalistic methods. But the Soviet and post-Soviet immigration produced an unprecedented response: no top-down absorption, and no hebraization. Instead, the Russian immigrants were allowed, indeed encouraged, to find their own way (with some help from government, business, and other Soviet/Russian Jews). If they and their children wished to study Hebrew, good; if not, they could set up Russian schools. If they wanted to create large Russian-speaking neighborhoods, that was fine.

Businesses and politicians responded as one might expect. Many big-city neighborhoods got plastered with Russian signs and posters. Russian newspapers outnumbered Hebrew ones. The director of the Israel Broadcasting Authority, flouting all precedent for immigrant-language broadcasting, launched a twelve-hour-a-day Russian-language radio station; it would, he explained, introduce listeners to life in Israel while making them feel they hadn't ever left home.

How has the Russian reversal turned out for Hebrew? One million Russian migrants accounted for an astronomical 20 percent of the Israeli Jewish population. But by 2005 there was evidence that they were slowly being integrated quite nicely, if not completely, into Israeli culture. The young, meanwhile, were already more involved in things Israeli than in things Russian. Even though many were educated in Russian-language Israeli schools, the Israel Defense Forces remained the highly effective language school they had been in the first days of statehood.

In other words, the successful hebraization of the Russians (and in their own way the Ethiopians) suggests that the institutional suppression of Yiddish and other Jewish Diaspora languages in the 1950s had been not just heartless but unnecessary.

Hebrew in the Age of Global Commerce

Globalization, combined with American economic and cultural power, has made English the international language par excellence—now aided and abetted by the Internet. And even for Israelis who don't identify with Anglo culture, URLs in roman characters are just part of life:

www.facebook.com ... www.badatz.biz ... www.hevra.org.il ...
www.shtraymel.co.il ...

At almost any Israeli shopping mall, English storefront signs and brand labels leap out at you. In many cities, there are actually language laws (technically, script laws) that require Hebrew lettering to occupy as much space as foreign letters, but little attempt is made to enforce the rules. Mayors want to attract business, not to alienate it.

The language of advertising, indeed, reveals interesting things about Israeli attitudes toward Hebrew and what marketers in turn believe about those attitudes. A survey of twenty-three malls in 2012 confirmed what everyone knew about the dominance of English in the Israeli shopping experience. Almost two-thirds of storefront signs were devoid of Hebrew lettering. At the Ramat Aviv mall in Tel Aviv, the figure was 79 percent. Many of these signs were foreign trademarks, and few followed the example of Burger Ranch by transcribing the English name into Hebrew letters. The opposite occurred in many cases, as with the chain that has a Hebrew name (meaning "seasons") but insists on displaying it in English characters as ONOT.[14]

When it comes to individual products, international brand names are again rarely hebraized; thus the popular breakfast cereal is simply called "Honey Nut Cheerios." Similarly, higher-end Israeli brands will often use English names: a popular Israeli-made snack is called "Energy." One marketer, interviewed in the newspaper *Yediot Aharonot*, bluntly asked, "Who's going to buy a brand with Hebrew lettering?"[15]

English also connotes quality in many product sectors—although sometimes, again, the opposite is true. Domestic beer and chocolate are generally branded in Hebrew, and the yogurt maker Danone switched the labeling of its Activia line of products from English to Hebrew after a survey found that people felt more "intimate" with the latter. It is a mark of how things have reversed themselves in fifty years that it is now considered hip and retro to give a Tel Aviv nightclub a Hebrew name.

A Lot's in a Name

Personal names, like brand names, are not normally treated as a core component of language. They often seem to be a matter of choice, random affairs. Many dictionaries ignore them. Yet naming practices often speak loudly and have an impact on social realities.

For the first few decades of Israel's history, as we saw in the previous chapter, children were given Hebrew names, sometimes traditional but often new names celebrating the land, its past glories, and its beauty. Starting in the 1970s, however, out went biblical names and in came a generation of newly minted names crafted to sound intimate, unpretentious, and/or occasionally strong: Lihi (she is mine), Liora (I have light), Ram (high), Tal (dew), Mor (myrrh), Moran (a variation on Mor). Many of these are monosyllabic and unisex. Like American Jews who found English equivalents for the traditional names of deceased relatives they wished to honor (e.g., Florence after Frida or Morris after Moshe), Israelis found Israeli equivalents of traditional Hebrew names: Sarah became Sarit, Moshe Mishael, and Aharon Ron.

Many of these names are no longer Hebrew words per se but derivatives of Hebrew words. Nonetheless, since their meaning is usually obvious, they reflect a persistent enthusiasm for Hebrew itself. But of course there is also a trend of westernization, tempered by a desire to borrow only such names as fit easily into the Hebrew language. Thus Guy, Tom, and Shelly have become popular, but you don't meet many Israelis named Andrew, Steven, or Alison. Another trend is to find Western names with Hebrew meanings, such as Shirli (song to me) and Keren (ray). In short, even the adoption of Western names speaks to the vitality of Hebrew. Still, the top twenty baby names for 2015 were mostly Israeli-biblical (such as Noa, Tamar, Itai, Ariel) and even a touch old-worldly (Sarah, Yosef, David).

Meanwhile, with surnames, the trend toward hebraization has decidedly slowed. In 1995, the director of the Interior Ministry reported that more people were reverting to a former non-Hebrew surname than the reverse. The novelist Yitzhak Orpaz (originally Averbuch), after losing a brother in the Yom Kippur War, famously changed his name to Orpaz-Averbuch in tribute to his parents' roots. The speaker in a poem by the Moroccan-born Erez Bitton confesses he would like to cry, "I am not called Zohar [a common Sephardi-Israeli name], I am Zaish, I am Zaish!"[16]

In 1995, a Foreign Ministry spokesperson announced that the hebraization requirement for diplomats had been shelved; the legal department had advised that it violated ministers' dignity and liberty. In 2009 Avigdor Liberman became minister of foreign affairs. In 2015, Gadi Eizenkot became IDF chief of staff. Neither hebraized his last name.

Shalom, America, and *Hepi berthdey tu yu*

The close of 2012 was marked in Haifa by the glitter of Christmas trees and New Year celebrations. Haifa, traditionally a secular city, is also home to a sizable Christian Arab population. But Haifa's first locally born mayor chose the occasion to announce a ban on English terms like "pilot project," "globalization," and "fine tuning" in municipal paperwork. What stirred him, he said, was the English sign "Hair Stylist" over his favorite barbershop.

There are more ubiquitous barbarisms that the mayor might have mentioned. The greeting *Shalom* was once iconic; tourists thrilled to the fact that it means "peace" as well as, curiously, both "hello" and "good-bye." Today, however, *shalom* is heard much less than *hi* and *bye* or *lehitraot bye* (see-you, bye). For "gotta go," you are likely to hear the Yiddish-Arabic-English hybrid *nu yala bye*. Still, what could be more Israeli than this decidedly un-Hebraic fusion?

At the same time, the introduction of foreign words continues apace: *fayter*, *killer*, and so forth. Sometimes nouns bring English suffixes with them, such as *selebs* (celebrities). But Hebrew also continues to impose a no-exceptions Hebraic system on any foreign verbal imports, metabolizing them into a consonantal root that it then proceeds to inflect. In this way, Hebrew borrowed the noun "telephone" directly from English but coined the corresponding verb *le-talfen* (to phone). However, the sheer quantity of English words and, above all, the rapid cultural Americanization that they signal, do worry some Israelis. If children no longer learn the old-fashioned Hebrew kindergarten songs and instead sing *Hepi berthdey tu yu*, are they losing part of their Israeliness?

Language is often likened to a living organism. It can comfortably absorb a certain number of external cells and even thrive. But there is a social tipping point (often recognized too late) where the entire organism threatens to be overwhelmed. At that point, language conflict can sometimes arise.

When it comes to formal, and especially written, language, Israelis take these things more seriously. Some of Israel's best-known authors, like Etgar Keret, have taken to writing fiction in a colloquial Hebrew. But other writers and intellectuals are more conservative: unperturbed by the changes in spoken Hebrew, they worry when an educated Israeli sits down to write a formal report or letter or delivers a formal talk and uses Anglicisms. The award-winning translator Esther Caspi confessed, "I have no problem rendering street English into street Hebrew; what Hebrew lacks is a polished style of the kind used by an educated English-speaker."[17]

In 1994, the minister of education, Amnon Rubinstein, pressed some wrong buttons. As part of a globalization-driven shake-up of the school system, he announced that Bible, Hebrew language, and Hebrew literature would no longer be core subjects required for high-school matriculation. He also proposed that parts of Israel's primary and middle-school curriculum be taught not in Hebrew but in English.

In the latter proposal, Rubinstein was actually referring to electives—music, sports, crafts, and so on—and his stated goal was to give less academically inclined teens a chance to acquire English in a less formal way. But reactions were white-hot. The writer Amos Keynan denounced the demotion of Bible and Hebrew as a prescription for a mediocre society, proclaiming that "a people who has lost its key to the past will lose its future."[18] Why, asked several leading writers, was the government more interested in promoting pseudo-English on street corners than in teaching young Israelis to read and write the nuanced, polished Hebrew of their grandparents? The novelist Shulamit Hareven predicted a dystopian future of linguistic miscegenation, where a teacher would tell students:

> *Yeladim, I told you to jump, lamah lo jamptem?* ["Children, I told you to *jump*. Why didn't you *jump?*" The actual Hebrew word for "to jump" is *likpots*.][19]

Under a *Haaretz* newspaper headline "War of the Languages Again," the director of the Academy of the Hebrew Language warned that the national language was at risk. What other developed country, he asked, teaches all of its noncore subjects in a foreign language? And how ironic that music, sports, and crafts had been the first school subjects to be taught in Hebrew a century earlier. It was, finally, the intervention of the ordinarily reclusive academy that tipped the balance. The introduction of an English-medium curriculum was hurriedly shelved.

With all of its nuances, the ongoing debate about Hebrew seems to lead back to a debate about cultural philosophy. For some, cultural heritage and distinctiveness are paramount; for others, they are just a commodity in a fast-changing world. The mixed feelings about English felt by many Israeli intellectuals are not unlike those felt almost everywhere where English is not already the first language. English is a valuable tool but one that can get out of hand, triggering a zero-sum game. And at the same time, English is a lightning rod for a nation's anxieties about how distinctive it wishes to be.

Hebrew Gets a Graphic Interface

The twentieth century, with the rise of the typewriter, the computer, and the text message, saw what might be the greatest changes in the appearance of written Hebrew since the introduction of the

אבגדהוזחטי
כדלממנןסע
פףצץקרשת

אבגדהוזחטיכלמנסעפצקרשת
אבגדהוזחטיכלמנסעפצקרשת

FIGURE 32. Frank-Ruehl (top) versus Fat Haim (bottom).

square script in the sixth century BCE, and certainly since the invention of the printing press.

The story of modern Hebrew typography begins in 1910, when typesetters in Germany created a Hebrew font that rapidly came to symbolize the emerging utilitarian, secular style. Named Frank-Ruehl, it gave the Hebrew alphabet a clean and modern look. From the 1920s up to the present, Frank-Ruehl has been the standard for running text in printed Israeli books, magazines, and newspapers. It's the first font that children learn to read, and it remains popular with adults. Even the new daily *Yisrael Hayom* has stuck with Frank-Ruehl. When the mass-circulation *Maariv* switched to something more up-to-date in 1987, there was such an outcry that the paper eventually switched back.

As for headlines and brand names, there was Haim, even more modern, designed to imitate European styles as closely as possible. It was the first ever geometric Hebrew font, based on straight lines and angles and consistent thicknesses, shedding traditional curls and serifs and the combination of thick and thin lines. Haim's Bauhaus style has been adapted perfectly for screaming tabloid headlines.

Although these fonts continue to dominate in print, the digital age has seen a wave of typographic creativity that might earlier have been channeled into literature or the scribal arts. Israeli font designers have generated a riot of Hebrew shapes for brand names, album designs, book covers, and everything else that leaps out at you. It was Microsoft that wrought the greatest change in Hebrew graphics. Its engineers took a delicate font designed by Zvi Narkis and shaped it into what is now the standard for Israeli computer screens, the utilitarian no-frills Arial. What will become of the printed book or newspaper and of Frank-Ruehl and fat Haim, no one can say. For many young Israelis, Arial is virtually the only font they read.

"Golda, teach us Yiddish!": The Sephardi Language Stigma

Israeli society has been overshadowed by a deep and often painful ethnic-cultural divide between Ashkenazim and Sephardim (or Mizrahim, a term accentuating Middle Eastern ethnicity and social divisions). Israeli Hebrew bears the marks of this divide—and of the attempts by Sephardim to surmount it or accept it with pride.

As described in the preceding chapter, starting in the 1890s, Ashkenazi Zionist immigrants had begun to exchange their old Yiddish-sounding pronunciations for what they imagined to be a Sephardi pronunciation. In reality, the Sephardi phonetics with its throaty consonants was no draw; they were content with replacing a handful of vowels and consonants with others they already had, and—perhaps the most satisfying—placing the stress on the last instead of the last-but-one syllable, thus *shaLOM* instead of *SHOlem*. The result certainly "felt" Sephardi.

By 1948, the Ashkenazim in Israel far outnumbered the local Sephardim and Mizrahim and overshadowed their traditional Hebrew pronunciations. Most Ashkenazim regarded those at best as quaint but at worst as uncomfortably Arabic-sounding and unsophisticated: Sephardi spoken Hebrew maintained something of the traditional pronunciation, with the letter *resh* rolling off the tip of the tongue (as in Spanish or Italian) rather than sounding like the guttural *r* of most Hebrew speakers (borrowed directly from Yiddish and German); Sephardim also pronounced the letters *ayin* and *ḥet* with guttural sounds strange to European Jewish ears.

Things changed with the arrival, between 1948 and 1972, of some 600,000 Mizraḥi immigrants, largely from Morocco, Iraq, and Egypt but also from Yemen, Persia, and elsewhere. This was roughly half of the entire immigration of the period, and by 1970 there was demographic parity between Ashkenazim and non-Ashkenazim, a situation that would persist until the massive influx from the Soviet Union in the 1990s.

Most Mizraḥim were settled in rundown "development towns" and in the slums of the big cities; here, for a generation, the guttural *ayin* and *ḥet* remained common. There were differences in the traditional Hebrew pronunciations (and culture) among the various Sephardi and Mizraḥi ethnic groups, but to most Ashkenazim they were one huddled mass, their rich history and culture unappreciated and ignored. Thus all of those pronunciations became markers of poverty and lack of education. It hardly helped that the older elite were still given to talking and joking in Yiddish. When Sephardi radicals began agitating in the 1970s, they famously jeered (alluding to Prime Minister Meir's first name): "Golda, lamdi otanu [teach us] Yiddish!"

However, there was little ethnic segregation but instead an unequal melting pot of school, work, and army service, in which younger Mizraḥim, particularly women, felt they had to shed their *resh* and guttural *ḥet* and *ayin*, in a bid to fit in. A sad irony: the Mizrahi traditions for Hebrew consonants were unanimously adjudged by scholars to be historically more correct. Israel Radio even used to give preference to announcers with a Mizrahi accent. It was not until the 1980s that Sephardi identity would start pushing back, in another aural form: Mizrahi music and its Middle Eastern sounds—the voice quality, the melodies, scales, oudhs and percussions—and, as we will soon see, the free recourse to traditional religious poetry. A large share of what's played on Galgalatz, Israel's top radio station, is now Mizrahi.

Is Modern Hebrew Still the Holy Tongue?

A widespread myth holds that Haredim (ultra-Orthodox Jews) refuse to speak Hebrew because to do so would be to profane the holy tongue. In fact, the vast majority of Israel's Haredim (most of them Ashkenazi, and projected to number one million by 2020) use Israeli Hebrew as their primary language. There is some resistance, but it is found mainly in fringe groups who reject anything symbolic of Zionism and secularism.

However, this shared language masks a cultural and social divide between haredi and secular Jews in Israel, deeper in many ways than the Ashkenazi-Sephardi divide. It, too, involves language. Haredi Jews intensively nurture another Hebrew, infused with the knowledge of the Hebrew text of the Bible, Talmud, and other religious sources. Out of reverence for it, they refer to this Hebrew not as Ivrit but by its traditional name of *leshon kodesh* (or, in its Ashkenazi form, *loshn koydesh*).

Ashkenazi Haredim maintain an additional distinction. When they pray, recite blessings, or read the Bible, Talmud, and other sacred texts, they *pronounce* the Hebrew in the old Ashkenazi fashion. As for Yiddish, the mother tongue of many of their grandparents and elder rabbis, it is becoming a thing of the past, although it is

FIGURE 33. A kosher McDonald's (Ramat Gan, Israel).

still the language of instruction in some elite yeshivot as well as the language of the ḥasidic sermon. In other words, Yiddish is becoming a secondary sacred tongue—much like Aramaic.

But the Israeli Jewish mainstream—over five million—spans a religious-to-secular spectrum. For many ("Orthodox" or just "Traditional"), male and female alike, studying the ancient texts and reciting prayers is part of upbringing and daily life, combined with modern education and leisure pursuits. Indeed, the religious population in Israel and the Diaspora has created its own mass musical culture, parallel to secular culture but based on religious texts, graced by the technological and stylistic trappings of secular folk and pop culture and iconic singers like Shelomo Carlebach, Avraham Fried, and Ehud Banai. And now the performance of medieval and modern Sephardi/Mizraḥi religious *piyyut*—hitherto on the margins of Israeli culture—is mainstream, celebrating the Jewish-Arab musical symbiosis of such fabled poet-cantors as Rabbi David Buzaglo while resonating to contemporary Israeli fusion music.

By contrast, many secular Israelis (who make up some 45 percent of Israel's Jews) have all but lost contact with the traditional sources and the Hebrew and Aramaic in which they are couched.

Most public schools today impart just a smattering of biblical and rabbinic texts (two periods a week), thus fostering not only ignorance of the Jewish religion but also an inability to understand much nineteenth- and twentieth-century secular Hebrew literature. An abiding memory of the funeral in 1995 of the assassinated prime minister Yitzḥak Rabin was of his son stumbling over the ancient Kaddish prayer.

And in the Diaspora: *plus ça change . . .*

In 1948, the ratio of Jews in the Diaspora to Jews in Israel was over 20:1. In 2014 that ratio was around 1:1 and is likely to tip still further. The Jewish birthrate in the Diaspora has been plunging, and the outmarriage rate soaring.

This does not necessarily add up to an Israeli cultural or linguistic domination. Instead, a linguistic and cultural rift that began to open up before World War II has become a chasm and shows no signs of narrowing, except by dint of immigration to Israel.

By force or by choice, Diaspora Jews have overwhelmingly jettisoned their Jewish languages. By the 1970s, few Israeli and Diaspora Jews had a functioning Jewish language in common, spoken or written. The European-born, Hebrew-literate intelligentsia that used to write innovative Hebrew literature in New York and London had become a thing of the past.

This was altogether a new era in which most Western societies had little appreciation for multilingualism. Jewish identity now found its new level in Jewish practice, Zionism, family, foods, humor, and anxiety over anti-Semitism. Knowledge of a token handful of Hebrew words was now sufficient. Although Zionism became a powerful force, it rarely involved intensive education in Hebrew. Its linguistic impact lay elsewhere: in the 1950s, American synagogues began adopting the Israeli pronunciation, which is now standard outside of ultra-Orthodox communities—a token identification with Israel.

If language never stops changing, neither do the social wheels that drive it. Linguistically, the two American Jewish groups most at odds, Reform Jews and Ḥaredim, have recently been drifting in convergent directions. The Reform movement was long committed to transparency of worship; only a token smattering of Hebrew remained in its liturgy. Since the 1970s and '80s, however, Hebrew has been slowly returning to Reform worship, embodied in its *Mishkan T'filah* prayer book (2006), along with other once-rejected rituals. One leading rabbi has quipped that to pray in Hebrew would shield his congregation from sentiments voiced in traditional prayers that they wouldn't agree with anyway.[20] The trend has only intensified in recent years.

Also in the 1970–80s, Orthodox Judaism worldwide began a resurgence, attracting increasingly high numbers of college-educated devotees. To meet their thirst for Jewish knowledge, a slew of Hebrew classics began appearing in English, French, and Spanish, replete with commentaries and formatting that mirrored the traditional Jewish book. These in turn also attracted a large readership of Torah-educated men and women. American-born Ḥaredim, less adept at Hebrew than many of their fathers' generation, were also less satisfied with the narrow selection of reading materials available to the common folk.

And then a small, very Orthodox Brooklyn publishing house hit upon a formula that married Hebrew and English with traditional erudition, religious stringency, and slick fonts and formatting. It adopted the brand name ArtScroll. This quite untraditional name embodied a new Orthodox Hebrew aesthetic, which tacitly made a virtue out of what was ostensibly the unfortunate need to translate

FIGURE 34. Advertisement for the ArtScroll Talmud, 2015.

the Hebrew. The crown of the "ArtScroll Revolution," as Jeremy Stolow has dubbed it,[21] is the handsome seventy-three-volume bilingual, annotated "Schottenstein" edition of the Babylonian Talmud, completed in 2004.

In one way, there is no language revolution here at all: Jewish study groups have always been conducted in the vernacular, with the Hebrew text being given impromptu interpretation and translation. But setting large parts of the page in English is an acknowledgment that the Hebrew and Aramaic text is itself a challenge too far, and that any aids to understanding it are legitimate. In effect, with the help of ArtScroll, podcasts, and other modern wonders, Hebrew erudition is being opened up to anyone who wants to learn. No longer are the Hebrew and Aramaic of the Talmud a language for the elite.

The English that the Orthodox and Ḥaredim speak also contains much less Hebrew than did their grandparents' Yiddish: perhaps two hundred to three hundred Hebraisms in all, most of them reflecting Jewish values and practices—*tznius* (modesty), *goen* (genius), *menahel* (headmaster), *droshe* (sermon)—or argument-markers like *mistome* (probably) and *mamesh* (really). Often, though, an English word is used where a Hebraism might be expected, for example, *school*, *love*, *help*.

This Orthodox English is arguably distinct enough to be considered the kind of "new Yiddish" that the novelist Cynthia Ozick foresaw in 1970 in a celebrated essay,[22] and is thus a kind of linguistic self-segregation in its own right. And, as in Israel, the Ashkenazi pronunciation serves as a boundary marker between Ḥaredim and everyone else, and not just in prayer and study but also in the popular Hebrew religious music referred to earlier: on one side, ḥasidic stars like Avraham Fried and, on the other side, "modern" songsters like Debbie Friedman. The markers and the very boundaries keep changing, but the need to differentiate continues. Language is rather like a game of chess: the pieces keep moving and the battle lines keep shifting, but the roots and goals of conflict are largely unchanged.

Some—both traditionalists and twentieth-century thinkers like Franz Rosenzweig and Gershom Scholem—have insisted that Hebrew in the religious Diaspora never died but that, to the contrary, what threatens the language is the loss of Jewish heritage in both Israel and the Diaspora alike. Others insist that the revival of spoken Hebrew saved the language (and the Jewish spirit) from the "fossilization" it had long endured. In any event, the chasm we observed between the Diaspora and Israel can be viewed from many angles. The ongoing pressure to Anglicize and globalize, while liable to make serious inroads into Israeli education and into the ability of

Hebrew to compete at the highest technical levels, is also making English more accessible. Or, while an Orthodox Diaspora Jew and an Orthodox Israeli may not share a language to converse in, they do share an intimacy with the Hebrew religious heritage unavailable to their secular peers.

The Hebrew state is in many ways a triumphant stage in the story of Hebrew. But it is not the final word on the state of Hebrew.

Epilogue

An Israeli teenager today can open a three-thousand-year-old chapter of biblical prose and understand it almost unaided. Indeed, many Jewish teens, both in Israel and in the Diaspora, sit and peruse ancient Hebrew texts every day for hours on end, in depth. By contrast, no English speaker today could open a one-thousand-year-old "English" text and make sense of it unaided; it's another tongue. The same has happened to every European national language.

Hebrew's fortune, one sometimes hears, is precisely that it was no one's mother tongue for two millennia—left in semihibernation until charmed awake in its pristine beauty in the name of Enlightenment and the Return to Zion. But that would be to fall for the fallacy that languages are just linguistic organisms. Rather, they are first and foremost social organisms, and how they are *used* has a profound effect on their structure and evolution. A written language may be silent, or heard and recited; it can be "trapped" in a body of texts mouthed or memorized, rigidly understood or creatively interpreted—or its users may produce new texts, new words, and new structures in undreamed-of ways, enriched/subverted by outside influences. The language community may be an elite or a mass, driven variously by religion, nationalism, ethnic belonging, economics, or sundry other beliefs and goals. Many classical languages have played, and continue to play, a vital role in the lives of nations.

But is there, one wonders, a parallel anywhere on earth to the intimate and unbroken engagement of Jews with their ancient literature, in its original tongue?

The story of Hebrew in Jewish life demonstrates what, given the incentives (and the constraints), a nation is capable of doing to preserve its linguistic and cultural heritage. It adds a new dimension to models of "ethnolinguistic vitality," developed to understand the fate of languages.[1] Crucial to the story is the extraordinary social and political history of the Jews and their treatment by non-Jews, climaxing in the events of the past hundred years. A major factor in this social-political process has been the Hebrew language itself.

With respect to that language, a broad Jewish narrative has emerged: first, a consciousness of Hebrew as the language and spirit of Holy Writ, surviving dispersion, assimilation, and persecution to figure centrally in the renewal of Jewish destiny; second, a consciousness of Hebrew as a *practical* language that historically sustained an economically and intellectually self-regulating Jewish communal life against heavy odds, often on a par with Latin, literary Arabic, and other high-level tongues that have underpinned the cultures of advanced societies.

And there is another, higher level at which the "serious" melts into "play." Amid all the linguistic norms born of perpetual study of revered writ, we have also seen a love of verbal novelty and sheer play—not just for producing prose and poetry but even for interpreting the sacred texts themselves. Indeed, play is embedded in the sacred texts: in the Bible's verbal halls of mirrors, in the disparities between biblical Hebrew and the Hebrew of the Rabbis, in the elegance (and enigmas) of the triconsonantal Hebrew root and the words built upon it, in the nuances of meanings and the shapes of letters, the mysteries of biblical and midrashic word echoes, the familiarity or superiority of a Jew's regional pronunciation or Torah chant.

This zest for change amid constancy is perhaps a reflection of Judaism itself. The Talmud wondered how well Moses the Lawgiver, coming back to his people, might have understood a legal seminar taught by Rabbi Akiva fifteen hundred years later. And yet Akiva maintained that he was guided strictly by Moses's own principles, which he used to generate new law fitting the exigencies of his time. The Talmud's generative doctrine of law holds equally true for language: Moses might be all at sea with today's Hebrew sounds and scripts—and current Jewish ways of life—but, suitably sedated, he would find relatively clear sailing with an Israeli novel or a fine-print contract. At root, it is the same tongue.

It was widely expected in the mid-twentieth century that, with the rebirth of the Jewish state, Hebrew language would at last become an all-purpose, "normal" language of a normal country. And indeed it has. Perhaps the most striking confirmation of this are Israel's Arab citizens, over 1.7 million (20 percent) in 2016: many of them use spoken Hebrew as an adult second language, acquired at school and at work—and Israelis take this largely for granted. But, as we have seen, there is much more going on: both in Israel and in the Diaspora, Hebrew flows on in deep channels and in profoundly different Jewish cultures—religious and secular, Torah-centered and self-consciously cosmopolitan—or just as a token boundary marker between Jew and Gentile.

These categories themselves divide and overlap. Orthodox Israelis, for example, consider Hebrew the sacred language of Torah—but they also use it, nonchalantly, for all things mundane. Self-declared secular Israelis, meanwhile, will also have learned some biblical Hebrew in school and often cherish it for the connection it provides with their roots. And many people just fit somewhere in between.

Ironically, however, much of the narrative presented in this book is largely unknown by the parties involved. For the Orthodox, the secular Hebrew literature of the medieval and early modern Diaspora, though a product of religious minds, is a closed book. Most secular Jews, for their part, imagine Diaspora Hebrew to be entirely a language of religion divorced from the practicalities of life or from the world of literature and ideas. Unfortunately, the generation of Israelis who knew better, and who once studied the Hebrew literature of the Middle Ages and Enlightenment in school, is now aging fast.

The narrative that Christians told or enacted for Hebrew seems to be different and much simpler: a quest, at times, for Christian truth in Hebrew sacred literature. This was primarily an interpretive enterprise but could sometimes also be a creative one: a thirst to unlock the language's esoteric powers or to use it, as did the Puritans, for political ends. In either case, however, entirely absent was the quintessentially Jewish sense of shared national loyalties and ethnicity.

Christian Hebraism seems for now to have run its course. Outside the Catholic priesthood, and even there sparingly, few contemporary Christians are stirred by the language. Still, one cannot help wondering whether the existence of the Jewish state and its epic tribulations—with the challenges it presents to Christian doctrine, not to mention the strong appeal it holds for many sectors of the Christian community—may not yet stimulate a new turn to Hebrew.

In 2016, Israel's Jewish population stood at 6.3 million. In the Diaspora, there were perhaps an equal number of Jews. What will Hebrew be, two generations or three from now? The answer, in its barest terms, must hinge on where Israel and the Diaspora are headed.

On their present cultural and social path, most Jews in Israel will effortlessly be speaking and reading a Hebrew ever more disconnected from its Jewish and early Zionist roots, and ever more crowded with English—but still proudly regarded as Hebrew and, in its grammar and vocabulary, very recognizably so. In the Diaspora, bar mitzvahs and High Holy Days will still present a cherished "ordeal by language," though for a shrinking number of Jews. Meanwhile, the Orthodox, in ever larger numbers, will be perusing the Torah and the Talmud as they have always done—and in Israel speaking everyday Hebrew with scarcely a second thought. Are Israel and the Diaspora, like so many of the technologically advanced societies presciently portrayed by Roy Harris, "a society whose linguistic capacities and facilities have fast outgrown its comprehension of them"?[2] Very likely.

Yet history has sprung some big surprises on this ancient linguistic brand, and one can be confident that history is far from done with it.

Acknowledgments

A book like this, which seeks to bring together the many facets of Hebrew—spiritual, cultural, social, political, just verbal—seems not to have been attempted since William Chomsky's groundbreaking work of 1957, *Hebrew: The Eternal Language*. In writing *The Story of Hebrew*, I have drawn on a plethora of sources and studies, specific and theoretical. Space precludes a full listing of these and of where I have differed on facts or interpretation. But I owe a special debt to the work of Joshua Fishman, father of the sociology of language, Michael Halliday, Dell Hymes, John Edwards, Howard Giles, Kathryn Woolard, Joseph Dan, Rina Drory, Raphael Loewe, Judith Olszowy-Schlanger, Gareth Lloyd Jones, Jerome Friedman, Allison Coudert, Naftali Loewenthal, Shalom Goldman, Yaakov Shavit, Israel Bartal, Shaul Stampfer, Alan Mintz, Dovid Katz, George Mandel, Itamar Even-Zohar, Tamar Katriel—and, above all, Chaim Rabin and Roy Harris, my first mentors in language and society.

I wish to express my gratitude to the Tikvah Fund, its chairman, Roger Hertog, and its executive director, Eric Cohen, for their generous support of this project; to its senior director, Neal Kozodoy, for nurturing my initial dream to its fruition, and to Andrew Koss, his colleague at *Mosaic*, for helping to shape an early draft; to Dartmouth College for granting me sabbatical leave to complete this book and for funding the preparation of the index; to Fred Appel and the Princeton University Press for transforming a manuscript into flesh and sinew. To all of them, in the words of the prophet Zechariah, *teshuʾot ḥen ḥen*, "gratias, gratias."

Notes

Chapter 1. "Let There Be Hebrew!"

1. Shemaryahu Talmon, "Did There Exist a Biblical National Epic?" in his *Literary Studies in the Hebrew Bible: Form and Content* (Jerusalem: Magnes Press, 1993), 91–111.
2. Adele Berlin, *The Dynamics of Biblical Parallelism* (Bloomington: Indiana University Press, 1992), 17.
3. James Kugel, *The Idea of Biblical Poetry* (New Haven, CT: Yale University Press, 1981), 8.

Chapter 2. Jerusalem, Athens, and Rome

1. Meir Bar-Ilan, review of Catherine Hezser, *Jewish Literacy in Roman Palestine*, *Hebrew Studies* 44 (2003): 217–222.
2. Yosef Yahalom, *Poetry and Society in Jewish Galilee of Late Antiquity* (Hakibbutz Hameuchad, 1999), 15 (Hebrew).
3. Aharon Mirsky, *Hapiyut* (Jerusalem: Magnes Press, 1990), 84 (Hebrew).

Chapter 3. Saving the Bible and Its Hebrew

1. Yaakov Elman, "Orality and the Redaction of the Babylonian Talmud," *Oral Tradition* 14, no. 1 (1999): 52–99.
2. Mary Carruthers, *The Book of Memory: A Study of Memory in Medieval Culture* (Cambridge: Cambridge University Press, 1990), 8.

Chapter 4. The Sephardic Classical Age

1. Menachem Kellner, "Maimonides on the Normality of Hebrew," in *Judaism and Modernity: The Religious Philosophy of David Hartman*, ed. Jonathan Malino (Jerusalem: Shalom Hartman Institute, 2001), 435–471.
2. Josef Stern. "Meaning and Language," in *The Cambridge History of Jewish Philosophy*, ed. Steven Nadler and Tamar Rudavsky (Cambridge: Cambridge University Press, 2009), 1:249.

3. Maud Kozodoy, *The Secret Faith of Maestre Honoratus: Profayt Duran and Jewish Identity in Late Medieval Iberia* (Philadelphia: University of Pennsylvania Press, 2015), 163.

4. Moshe Idel, *Golem: Jewish Magical and Mystical Traditions on the Artificial Anthropoid* (Albany: State University of New York Press, 1990), xxvii.

5. Gershom Scholem, *On the Kabbalah and Its Symbolism*, trans. Ralph Manheim (New York: Schocken Books, 1965), 43.

6. Yosef Tobi, *Proximity and Distance: Medieval Hebrew and Arabic Poetry* (Leiden: Brill, 2004), 355.

7. Isadore Twersky, *Introduction to the Code of Maimonides* (New Haven, CT: Yale University Press, 1980), 350.

8. Ezra Fleischer, *Hebrew Liturgical Poetry in the Middle Ages* (Jerusalem: Magnes Press, 2007), 414 (Hebrew).

9. Raymond Scheindlin, *Wine, Women & Death: Medieval Hebrew Poems on the Good Life* (Oxford: Oxford University Press, 1986), 89.

10. Eli Yassif, *The Hebrew Folktale: History, Genre, Meaning* (Bloomington: Indiana University Press, 1999), 248.

11. Ross Brann, *The Compunctious Poet: Cultural Ambiguity and Hebrew Poetry in Muslim Spain* (Baltimore: Johns Hopkins University Press, 1991), 21.

Chapter 5. Medieval Ashkenaz and Italy

1. *Die Hebräischen Übersetzungen des Mittelalters und die Juden als Dolmetscher* (Berlin, 1893). Partly translated and updated as *The Hebrew Translations of the Middle Ages and the Jews as Transmitters*, vol. 1, ed. Charles H. Manekin, Y. Tzvi Langermann, and Hans Hinrich Biesterfeldt (Dordrecht: Springer Verlag, 2013).

2. Translation by Gerrit Bos, in his "Medical Terminology in the Hebrew Tradition: Shem Tov ben Isaac, *Sefer ha-Shimmush*, Book 30," *Journal of Semitic Studies* 55, no. 1 (2010): 53–101.

3. Translation by Maud Kozodoy, in her "Medieval Hebrew Medical Poetry: Uses and Contexts," *Aleph: Historical Studies in Science and Judaism* 11, no. 2 (2011): 213–288.

4. Petrus Mosellanus, *Oratio de variarum linguarum cognitione paranda* (Leipzig, 1518), 49. Accessed on August 4, 2016, at https://books.google.com. Cited in Harry Friedenwald, "Note on the Importance of the Hebrew Language in Mediaeval Medicine," *Jewish Quarterly Review*, n.s., 10, no. 1 (July 1919): 19–24.

5. In *Diwan of Immanuel ben David Frances*, ed. Shimon Bernstein (Tel Aviv: Dvir, 1932), 65.

6. Dan Pagis, *Change and Tradition: Hebrew Poetry in Spain and Italy* (Jerusalem: Keter, 1976), 247 (Hebrew).

7. Yoav Elstein, Avidov Lipsker, and Rella Kuschelevsky, eds., *Encyclopedia of the Jewish Story*, 3 vols. (Ramat-Gan: Bar Ilan University Press, 2004–2013).

8. Rella Kuschelevsky, *Penalty and Temptation: Hebrew Tales in Ashkenaz—Ms. Parma 2295* (Jerusalem: Magnes Press, 2010).

9. David B. Ruderman, *Jewish Thought and Scientific Discovery in Early Modern Europe* (Detroit: Wayne State University Press, 2001), 229.

10. Ephraim Kanarfogel, *Jewish Education and Society in the High Middle Ages* (Detroit: Wayne State University Press, 1992), 19.

Chapter 6. Hebrew in the Christian Imagination, I

1. James Barr, "St Jerome's Appreciation of Hebrew," *Bulletin of the John Rylands Library* 49 (1966): 281–302; reprinted in *Bible and Interpretation: The Collected Essays of James Barr*, ed. James Barr and John Barton (Oxford: Oxford University Press, 2014), 3:484–499.

2. Michael Graves, *Jerome's Hebrew Philology: A Study Based on His Commentary on Jeremiah* (Leiden: Brill, 2007).

3. Jerome Friedman, *The Most Ancient Testimony: Sixteenth-Century Christian-Hebraica in the Age of Renaissance Nostalgia* (Athens: Ohio University Press, 1983), 120.

4. Beryl Smalley, *The Study of the Bible in the Middle Ages*, 2d ed. (Oxford: Blackwell, 1952), 311.

5. Translated in Beryl Smalley, *The Study of the Bible in the Middle Ages* (Oxford: Clarendon Press, 1941), 156–157.

6. Judith Olszowy-Schlanger, ed., *Dictionnaire hébreu-latin-français de la Bible hébraïque de l'abbaye de Ramsey* (Turnhout: Brepols, 2008).

Chapter 7. Hebrew in the Christian Imagination, II

1. Moshe Idel, introduction to *De Arte Cabalistica*, ed. Martin and Sarah Goodman, Bison Book Edition (Lincoln: University of Nebraska Press, 1993), xi–xvi.

2. Allison P. Coudert, *The Impact of the Kabbalah in the Seventeenth Century* (Leiden: Brill, 1999), xiii.

3. Frank E. Manuel, "Israel and the Enlightenment," *Daedalus* 111, no. 1 (Winter 1982): 33–52, at 35.

4. Don C. Allen, "Some Theories of the Growth and Origin of Language in Milton's Age," *Philological Quarterly* 28 (1949): 5–16, at 7.

5. Theodor Dunkelgrün, "The Humanist Discovery of Hebrew Epistolography," in *Jewish Books and Their Readers: Aspects of the Intellectual Life of Christians and Jews in Early Modern Europe*, ed. Scott Mandelbrote and Joanna Weinberg (Leiden: Brill, 2016), 211–259.

6. Cited in Eric Zimmer, *Fiery Embers of the Scholars:The Trials and Tribulations of German Rabbis in the Sixteenth and Seventeeth Centuries* (Jerusalem: Mosad Bialik, 1999).

7. Cited in Ira Robinson, "Two Letters of Abraham ben Eliezer Halevi," in *Studies in Medieval Jewish History and Literature*, ed. Isadore Twersky (Cambridge, MA: Harvard University Press, 1984), 2:403–422.

8. Jerome Friedman, *The Most Ancient Testimony: Sixteenth-Century Christian-Hebraica in the Age of Renaissance Nostalgia* (Athens: Ohio University Press, 1983), 26.

9. Amnon Raz-Krakotzkin, "Censorship, Editing, and the Reshaping of Jewish Identity: The Catholic Church and Hebrew Literature in the Sixteenth Century," in *Hebraica Veritas? Christian Hebraists and the Study of Judaism in Early Modern Europe*, ed. Allison P. Coudert and Jeffrey S. Shoulson (Philadelphia: University of Pennsylvania Press, 2004), 131.

10. *Conversations with Luther*, trans. and ed. Preserved Smith and Herbert Percival Gallinger (Boston: The Pilgrim Press, 1915), 181–182.

11. Cited in Salo Baron, *A Social and Religious History of the Jews*, vol. 13 (New York: Columbia University Press, 1937), 233.

12. Translation by Jacob Mombert, *William Tyndale's Five Books of Moses* (New York and London, 1884), li–lii.

13. *A True Chronologie of the Times of the Persian Monarchie* (1597), 171.

14. Cited in Erwin Rosenthal, "Edward Lively: Cambridge Hebraist," in *Judaism, Philosophy, Culture: Selected Studies by E.I.J. Rosenthal* (Richmond, Surrey, UK: Curzon, 2001), 147–164, at 161.

15. Eric Nelson, *The Hebrew Republic: Jewish Sources and the Transformation of European Political Thought* (Cambridge, MA: Harvard University Press, 2010).

16. "Governor Bradford's First Dialogue" (1648), 136–137.

Chapter 8. Can These Bones Live?

1. Naftali Loewenthal, *Communicating the Infinite: The Emergence of the Habad School* (Chicago: University of Chicago Press, 1990), 140.

2. Yoav Elstein, *Ma'aseh Hoshev: Studies in Hasidic Tales* (Tel Aviv: Eked, 1983), 41 (in Hebrew).

3. "Ishim" (1948), 199.

4. Israel Bartal, "From Traditional Bilingualism to Modern Monolingualism," in *Hebrew in Ashkenaz: A Language in Exile*, ed. Lewis Glinert (Oxford: Oxford University Press, 1993), 141–150.

5. *Der Judenstaat* (English) (Mineola, NY: Dover Publications, 1988), 145.

6. *The Plough Woman: Memoirs of the Pioneer Women of Palestine*, trans. Maurice Samuel (New York: Herzl Press, 1975).

7. Ahad Ha'am, "Emet me-Eretz Yisrael" (1893).

8. Itamar Even-Zohar, "The Emergence of a Native Hebrew Culture in Palestine: 1882–1948," *Studies in Zionism* 4 (1981): 167–184.

9. Aharon Bar-Adon, "S. Y. Agnon and the Revival of Modern Hebrew," *Texas Studies in Literature and Language* 14, no. 1 (Spring 1972).

10. *Leqet Te'udot*, Academy of the Hebrew Language (1970), 104–115.

11. Ibid.

12. Kenneth Moss, *Jewish Renaissance in the Russian Revolution* (Cambridge, MA: Harvard University Press, 2009).

13. Avraham Greenbaum, "The Status of Hebrew in Soviet Russia from the Revolution to the Gorbachev Thaw," in *Hebrew in Ashkenaz: A Language in Exile*, ed. Lewis Glinert (Oxford: Oxford University Press, 1993), 242–248.

14. Elie Wiesel, *The Jews of Silence: A Personal Report on Soviet Jewry* (New York: Holt, Rinehart & Winston, 1966).

15. Anatoly Sharansky, *Fear No Evil* (New York: Random House, 1988), 48.

16. Ezra Mendelson, *The Jews of East Central Europe between the World Wars* (Bloomington: Indiana University Press, 1983), 257.

17. Stephen Katz, *Red, Black and Jew: New Frontiers in Hebrew Literature* (Austin: University of Texas Press, 2009).

18. Alan Mintz, "Hebrew Literature in America," in *The Cambridge Companion to Jewish American Literature*, ed. Hana Wirth-Nesher and Michael P. Kramer (New York: Cambridge University Press, 2003), 92–109, at 104.

19. Ezra Spicehandler, "*Ameriqa'iyyut* in American Hebrew Literature," in *Hebrew in America*, ed. Alan Mintz (Detroit: Wayne State University Press, 1993), 68–104.

20. Hana Shapira, "ha-Outsider ba-Shira Ha-Ivrit," *Makor Rishon*, September 9, 2011.

21. Arnold Band, "Regelson, Pagis, Wallach: Three Poems on the Hebrew Language," in *Solving Riddles and Untying Knots*, ed. Adele Berlin, Seymour Gitin, and Michael Sokoloff (Winona Lake, IN: Eisenbrauns, 1995), 505–522.

22. Dan Miron, *Hagavish Hamemaked* [Studies in Zeev Jabotinsky: Raconteur and poet] (Tel Aviv: Mosad Bialik, 2011) (Hebrew).

23. *Sefer HaKitrug VeHaEmunah* (Jerusalem and Tel Aviv: Sadan, 1937).

24. Joshua Fishman, 1975. "The Sociolinguistic 'Normalization' of the Jewish People"(1975), in *Linguistic and Literary Studies in Honor of Archibald A. Hill*, vol. 4, ed. Mohammad Ali Jazayery, Edgar C. Polomé, and Werner Winter (The Hague: Mouton, 1978), 223–232.

25. Bernard Spolsky and Elana Shohamy, "Hebrew after a Century of RLS Efforts," in *Can Threatened Languages Be Saved? Reversing Language Shift, Revis-*

ited: A 21st Century Perspective, ed. Joshua A. Fishman (Clevedon, UK: Multilingual Matters, 2001), 350–363.

26. Joshua A. Fishman, *Reversing Language Shift: Theoretical and Empirical Foundations of Assistance to Threatened Languages* (Clevedon, UK: Multilingual Matters, 1991).

Chapter 9. The Hebrew State

1. Joshua A. Fishman and David E. Fishman, "Yiddish in Israel: A Case-Study of Efforts to Revise a Monocentric Language Policy," *International Journal of the Sociology of Language* 1 (1974): 126–146.

2. Tamar Katriel, *Talking Straight: Dugri Speech in Israeli Sabra Culture* (New York: Cambridge University Press, 1986).

3. Yaakov Shavit, "Hebrews and Phoenicians: An Ancient Historical Image and Its Usage," *Studies in Zionism* 5, no. 2 (1984): 157–180.

4. "Hirhurim al ha-safa ha-ivrit," in Amos Oz, *Be-Or ha-Tekhelet ha-Aza* (Tel Aviv: Sifriyat Poalim, 1979).

5. Cited in Yitzhak Laor, *Dvarim she-ha-Shtika (lo) yafa lahem* (Tel Aviv: Babel, 2002), 35.

6. "Now in the Storm," in *Poems 1963-1968* (Tel Aviv: Schocken, 1968).

7. Letter to the Vaad HaLashon, February 5, 1948. Accessed on August 8, 2016, at http://mevakrim.hebrew-academy.org.il/wp-content/uploads/sites/2/2014/08/dbg19481.jpg.

8. The Supreme Institute of the Hebrew Language Act, 1953. In Scott B. Saulson, *Institutionalized Language Planning: Documents and Analysis of Revival of Hebrew* (The Hague: Walter de Gruyter, 1979), 77–91. http://hebrew-academy.huji.ac.il/English/AboutTheAcademy/Foundation/Pages/default.aspx.

9. Aharon Dotan, "The Academy, Language, and Life," in *The Development and Renewal of the Hebrew Language* (Jerusalem: Academy of the Hebrew Language, 1996), 191–211 (Hebrew).

10. Joseph Klausner letter to David Ben-Gurion, November 23, 1952. Accessed on August 7, 2016, at https://docs.google.com/file/d/0BxpR2lHZaDkHVzBFZFM1VFBybVk/edit.

11. David Ben-Gurion letter to N. H. Tur-Sinai, November 5, 1950. Accessed on August 7, 2016, at https://docs.google.com/file/d/0BxpR2lHZaDkHSDQ2eHowX1NKRkk/edit.

12. "What Word Sparked a Row at the Country's Highest Level?" (in Hebrew), Maariv online (NRG), August 2012. Accessed on August 7, 2016, at http://www.nrg.co.il/online/1/ART2/400/633.html.

13. Israel Bartal, " 'The Silent Revolution': Myth, Science and What Lies in Between," *Katedra*, September 1996, 177–180.

14. http://www.omnot.co.il/.
15. Ynet, September 4, 2009. Accessed on August 7, 2016, at http://www.ynet .co.il/articles/0,7340,L-3772140,00.html.
16. *Timbisert: Tzipor Maroka'it* (Tel Aviv: Hakibbutz Hameuchad, 2009).
17. Yisrael Landers, "Ledaber ivrit," *Devar Hashavua*, October 21, 1988.
18. Amos Keynan, "Shalom kita alef," *Yediot Ahronot*, August 12, 1994.
19. Shulamit Hareven, "Lama lo jamptem?" *Haaretz*, August 18, 1994.
20. Richard N. Levy, "The Reform Synagogue: Plight and Possibility," *Judaism* 18 (1969): 159–176, at 160.
21. Jeremy Stolow, *Orthodox by Design: Judaism, Print Politics, and the ArtScroll Revolution* (Berkeley: University of California Press, 2010).
22. Cynthia Ozick, "Toward a New Yiddish" (1970), reprinted in Cynthia Ozick, *Art and Ardor* (New York: Alfred A. Knopf, 1983), 151–177.

Epilogue

1. Howard Giles and Patricia Johnson, "Ethnolinguistic Identity Theory: A Social Psychological Approach to Language Maintenance," *International Journal of the Sociology of Language* 68 (1987): 69–99.
2. Roy Harris, *The Language Machine* (Ithaca, NY: Cornell University Press, 1987), 172.

Further Reading

Chapter 1

Alter, Robert. *The Art of Biblical Narrative*. New York: Basic Books, 1981.

Holtz, Barry W. *Back to the Sources: Reading the Classic Jewish Texts*. New York: Touchstone, 1984.

Chapter 2

Abramson, Glenda, and Tudor Parfitt, eds. *Jewish Education and Learning*. Chur, Switzerland: Harwood Academic Publishers, 1994.

Fishman, Joshua A., ed. *Can Threatened Languages Be Saved? Reversing Language Shift, Revisited: A 21st Century Perspective*. Clevedon, UK: Multilingual Matters, 2001.

Hengel, Martin. *Judaism and Hellenism*. Philadelphia: Fortress Press, 1974.

Horbury, William, ed. *Hebrew Study from Ezra to Ben-Yehuda*. Edinburgh: T&T Clark, 1999.

Safrai, Shmuel, and Menahem Stern, eds. *The Jewish People in the First Century: Historical Geography, Political History, Social, Cultural, and Religious Life and Institutions*. Assen: Van Gorcum, 1974.

Chapter 3

Schäfer, Peter, and Joseph Dan, eds. *Gershom Scholem's Major Trends in Jewish Mysticism 50 Years After*. Tübingen: JCB Mohr, 1993.

Chapter 4

Zwiep, Irene. *Mother of Reason and Revelation: A Short History of Medieval Jewish Linguistic Thought*. Amsterdam: Gieben, 1997.

Chapter 5

Kanarfogel, Ephraim. *Jewish Education and Society in the High Middle Ages*. Detroit: Wayne State University Press, 1992.

Zborowski, Mark, and Elizabeth Herzog. *Life Is with People: The Culture of the Shtetl.* New York: Schocken, 1952.

Chapter 6

Cohen, Jeremy. *The Friars and the Jews.* Ithaca, NY: Cornell University Press, 1982.

Goodwin, Deborah L. *Take Hold of the Robe of a Jew: Herbert of Bosham's 13th-Century Christian Hebraism.* Leiden: Brill, 2006.

Lapide, Pinchas E. *Hebrew in the Church: The Foundations of Jewish-Christian Dialogue.* Grand Rapids, MI: Eerdmans, 1984.

McKane, William. *Selected Christian Hebraists.* Cambridge: Cambridge University Press, 1989.

Chapter 7

Burnett, Stephen G. *From Christian Hebraism to Jewish Studies: Johannes Buxtorf (1564-1629) and Hebrew Learning in the Seventeenth Century.* Leiden: Brill, 1996.

Coudert, Allison, trans., and Taylor Corse, introd. *The Alphabet of Nature: By F. M. Van Helmont.* Leiden: Brill, 2007.

Coudert, Allison, and Jeffrey Shoulson, eds. *Hebraica Veritas? Christian Hebraists and the Study of Judaism in Early Modern Europe.* Philadelphia: University of Pennsylvania Press, 2004.

Dan, Joseph, ed. *The Christian Kabbalah: Jewish Mystical Books and Their Christian Interpreters.* Cambridge, MA: Harvard College Library, 1997.

Goldman, Shalom, ed. *Hebrew and the Bible in America: The First Two Centuries.* Hanover, NH: University Press of New England, 1993.

Lloyd Jones, Gareth. *The Discovery of Hebrew in Tudor England: A Third Language.* Manchester: Manchester University Press, 1983.

Moore, Helen, and Julian Reid, eds. *Manifold Greatness: The Making of the King James Bible.* Oxford: Bodleian Library, 2011.

Chapter 8

Aberbach, David. *Revolutionary Hebrew, Empire and Crisis: Four Peaks in Hebrew Literature and Jewish Survival.* New York: New York University Press, 1998.

Alter, Robert. *The Invention of Hebrew Prose: Modern Fiction and the Language of Realism.* Seattle: University of Washington Press, 1988.

Cohen, Richard L., Jonathan Frankel, and Stefani Hoffman, eds. *Insiders and Outsiders: Dilemmas of East European Jewry.* Oxford: Littman Library of Jewish Civilization, 2010.

Fellman, Jack. *The Revival of a Classical Tongue: Eliezer Ben-Yehuda and the Modern Hebrew Language.* The Hague: Mouton, 1973.

Gilboa, Yehoshua A. *A Language Silenced: The Suppression of Hebrew Literature and Culture in the Soviet Union*. Rutherford, NJ: Fairleigh Dickinson University Press, 1982.

Glinert, Lewis, ed. *Hebrew in Ashkenaz: A Language in Exile*. Oxford University Press, 1993.

Harshav, Benjamin. *Language in Time of Revolution*. Berkeley: University of California Press, 1993.

Katz, Dovid. *Words on Fire: The Unfinished Story of Yiddish*. New York: Basic Books, 2004.

Mintz, Alan, ed. *Hebrew in America*. Detroit: Wayne State University Press, 1992.

Saulson, Scott B. *Institutionalized Language Planning: Documents and Analysis of Revival of Hebrew*. The Hague: De Gruyter Mouton, 1979.

Shavit, Jacob. *The New Hebrew Nation: A Study in Israeli Heresy and Fantasy*. London: Frank Cass, 1987.

Stampfer, Shaul. *Families, Rabbis, and Education: Traditional Jewish Society in Nineteenth-Century Eastern Europe*. Oxford: Littman Library of Jewish Civilization, 2010.

Chapter 9

Baumel, Simeon. *Sacred Speakers: Language and Culture among the Haredim in Israel*. New York: Berghahn Books, 2006.

Ben-Rafael, Eliezer. *Language, Identity, and Social Division: The Case of Israel*. Oxford: Clarendon Press, 1994.

Fishman, Joshua, ed. *Readings in the Sociology of Jewish Languages*. Leiden: Brill, 1985.

Heilman, Samuel. *The People of the Book: Drama, Fellowship, and Religion*. Chicago: University of Chicago Press, 1983.

Shaked, Gershon. *The New Tradition: Essays on Modern Hebrew Literature*. Cincinnati, OH: Hebrew Union College Press, 2006.

Shapira, Anita. *Israel: A History*. Waltham, MA: Brandeis University Press, 2012.

Spolsky, Bernard, and Robert L. Cooper. *The Languages of Jerusalem*. New York: Oxford University Press, 1991.

Epilogue

Ehala, Martin. "Ethnolinguistic Vitality." In *The International Encyclopedia of Language and Social Interaction*, ed. Karen Tracy, Cornelia Ilie, and Todd Sandel, 1–7. Chichester, West Sussex, UK: John Wiley and Sons, 2015.

Index